Crimes against the State
Crimes against Persons

Crimes against the State
Crimes against Persons

Detective Fiction in Cuba and Mexico

Persephone Braham

University of Minnesota Press
Minneapolis • London

Parts of chapter 3 previously appeared in "Mrs. Watson in Havana," *Hopscotch* 2, no. 1 (2000): 52–59; copyright 2000 Duke University Press; all rights reserved; used with permission of Duke University Press. Parts of chapter 5 previously appeared in "Violence and Patriotism: The *novela negra* from Chester Himes to Paco Ignacio Taibo II," *Journal of American Culture* 20, no. 2 (1997): 159–69; copyright The Popular Press; used with permission of The Popular Press.

Published by the University of Minnesota Press
111 Third Avenue South, Suite 290
Minneapolis, MN 55401-2520
http://www.upress.umn.edu

Library of Congress Cataloging-in-Publication Data

Braham, Persephone.
    Crimes against the state, crimes against persons : detective fiction in Cuba and Mexico / Persephone Braham.
        p.   cm.
    Includes index.
    ISBN 0-8166-4134-X (HC : alk. paper) — ISBN 0-8166-4135-8 (PB : alk. paper)
    1. Detective and mystery stories, Cuban—History and criticism.
    2. Detective and mystery stories, Mexican—History and criticism.
    3. Cuban fiction—20th century—History and criticism.   4. Mexican fiction—20th century—History and criticism.   5. Politics and literature—Cuba.   6. Politics and literature—Mexico.   I. Title.
    PQ7382 .B73 2004
    863'.08720997291—dc22
                                                                    2003017865

Printed in the United States of America on acid-free paper

The University of Minnesota is an equal-opportunity educator and employer.

12 11 10 09 08 07 06 05 04   10 9 8 7 6 5 4 3 2 1

Contents

Acknowledgments

*T*o Marina Brownlee, my gratitude for her friendship and encouragement in this and other projects. To José Miguel Oviedo, for his criticism of this manuscript in its earliest stages, and for introducing me to the novels of Leonardo Padura Fuentes. To Leonardo Padura, Carlos Alonso, Justo Vasco, Ilán Stavans, Mauricio-José Schwarz, Gustavo Pérez Firmat, and Luis Adrián Betancourt, for sharing their time and insights so generously. To Bill for his careful objectivity, his synthetic criticism, and his untiring and perspicacious readings.

Introduction: Latin American Detective Literature in Context

*U*ntil the 1970s, the field of Latin American detective fiction was both limited and derivative. Through simulation or parody, authors engaged the marginal status and formulaic nature of detective narrative to dramatize Latin America's peripheral position with respect to modern Western culture. Detective writing in Spanish remains a marginalized endeavor, charting an uncertain path between the politicized arenas of literary production and the contested phenomena of popular culture. But the Latin American detective genre is also flourishing, on its own merits and as a source for other literary experimentation.

This book examines the trajectory of the detective novel in Mexico and Cuba from its obscure beginnings to its present success, and seeks to recognize the rationales by which it was adopted, as well as the aesthetic and ethical complexities of the process itself. What are the political and literary discourses governing the production of detective literature in Hispanic cultures, and in Mexico and Cuba in particular? What aesthetic, ideological, and practical obstacles do detective writers confront as they try to adapt the genre to reflect their own circumstances? Finally, can the exploration of this genre allow us to reflect on some of the broader literary and cultural questions pertinent to Cuban and Mexican realities?

The detective novel came late to Hispanic letters, and one of its defining characteristics has been a concern with foreign paradigms of modernity, and ultimately the failure of liberalism and its constituent elements in a Hispanic context. Leftist and socialist aspirations, also a part of the modern legacy, have proven equally difficult to realize. Because detective literature is a distinctly modern genre, it can serve as a fulcrum for exposing the fissures and divergences that characterize the performance of modernity in two very different settings: post–1968 Mexico, and Cuba in the heyday, then decline, of its modern Revolution.

Chapter 1 describes the origin and intellectual foundations of detective fiction in Cuba and Mexico. Jorge Luis Borges, the greatest proponent of detective literature in the Spanish language, wrote several influential essays on the Edwardian critic G. K. Chesterton that defined the terms of discussion about the detective genre in Spanish. Chesterton came to serve as a philosophical precursor for many detective writers in Latin America, particularly in his role as defender of detective literature's ethical dimensions. This chapter also discusses the function of parody as a tool of aesthetic or ethical legitimization under the cultural conditions of postcolonialism and globalization. In keeping with Latin American anxieties about artistic dependence, there is a prevailing belief that detective fiction in Spanish must always be a parody, or as Homi Bhabha would have it, a subversive colonial mimicry of metropolitan models.[1] Contradicting this accepted wisdom, contemporary Spanish American detective writers use the popular detective novel to deauthorize intellectuals who wield these models within Latin American contexts. While Cuban and Mexican detective writers borrow freely from Anglo-European traditions, they refigure the character of delinquency, the nature of victimization, and the process of detection itself.

Unlike traditional detective fiction in English, the majority of detective fiction in Spanish is *comprometido*, or socially committed. For both Mexican and Cuban authors, the very marginality of detective literature has allowed it to evolve into a tool of social criticism in a climate where the official press is unwilling or unable to perform this function. Spanish American detective novels comment specifically on an imperfectly realized modernity and a dread of having reached a condition of postmodernity in its most absolute sense: in form but not in substance, aesthetically but not ethically.

The title of this book, *Crimes against the State, Crimes against Persons*, alludes to the two categories of crime depicted in the detective literature of Cuba and Mexico after 1968. The Cuban socialist detective novel was created as prorevolutionary propaganda. If the socialist state was, effectively, the people, all crimes were by definition "crimes against the state." Chapter 2 describes the aesthetic and ideological conditions under which the socialist detective novel *(novela policial revolucionaria)* was constructed by a government seeking a new revolutionary aesthetics. Cuba's case pitted the hermeticism of modern (prerevolutionary) poetic language against the exigencies of liberal and anticolonial political endeavors, which required clarity and moral commitment of the intellectual voice. While the socialist detective novel was created to disseminate an idealized vision of the new revolutionary society, deteriorating conditions in Cuba eventually led to a reevaluation of the genre. In the 1990s under the "special period" in Cuba, chronic shortages and ideological exhaustion paradoxically created a space for dissidence. The detective novel gained a new function and complexity in the novels of Leonardo Padura Fuentes, which offer a unique chronicle of Cuban life under a decaying regime. Chapter 3 examines intolerance under socialism in the metaphor and performance of "masking," through which Cubans both hide and reveal their ideological disenchantment as a mode of survival.

In contrast with Cuba, the year 1968 marked a moment of severe disillusionment with the revolutionary legacy in Mexico, following the October 2 massacre of student protesters at the Plaza de las Tres Culturas in the Tlatelolco section of Mexico City. In the Mexican context, "crimes against persons" refers to the systematic persecution of citizens by government and law-enforcement authorities, a persecution that seeks its rationale in the drive for modernity. This violence is grounded in, condoned by, an oppressive discourse of "Mexicanness" (*mexicanidad*) represented in elite culture, official history, and the mass media. Mexican writers implicitly reject the cerebralism of the classic detective novel by creating protagonists whose scarred bodies become visible testaments to the abuses of power. Chapter 4 describes how early detective writers Antonio Helú, Rafael Bernal, and Jorge Ibargüengoitia used the "popular" detective novel to question Mexico's myths of authority and identity. The French sociologist Pierre Bourdieu regards the international student movement of 1968 as evidence of a struggle over cultural consumption, arguing that formalist movements establish borders between those with "high educational capital" and the rest of society. Writers were seeking to democratize the terms of this cultural capital. A contemporary of the *Onda* generation in Mexico, the best-selling writer and historian Paco Ignacio Taibo II also turned to the detective novel after the disillusionment of 1968 to interrogate ruling cultural and political representations. Chapter 5 traces Taibo's debts to the African American writer Chester Himes, whose nightmarish ghetto, Harlem, prefigures the chaos of Mexican society under neoliberalism. Taibo is a historian by training; his novels offer reflections on popular culture and an interrogation of official history. Responding to a generalized anomie, he and subsequent writers use the detective genre to demarcate an alternative space for representation and the articulation of ethicopolitical concerns. Ultimately, Cuban and Mexican detective narrative concerns the failure of revolutionary projects. In both cases, the revolutionary ideal was bound to a preoccupation with an elusive modernity that led, by reaction, to a mistrust of empirical and rationalist precepts and a deep pessimism about the prospect of economic and legal justice.

Because of its origins, Hispanic detective fiction is more truly globalized than most genres, as is evident in its many variants and nomenclatures.[2] Jorge Luis Borges observed insightfully that the detective story, like all other genres, thrives on "the continuous and delicate infraction of its laws."[3] There is no real consensus on what constitutes a detective novel, but most critics affirm that detective fiction is a product of mass culture, that it is formulaic, and that its nucleus is the reconstruction of events leading to a criminal act.[4]

Traditional detective fiction is genre fiction. The term—referred to in Spanish as *literatura de género, literatura de kiosco,* or best-sellers—commonly denotes formulaic popular fiction such as the detective novel, romance, and science fiction. Like all genres, detective fiction is not only definable by internal formal characteristics; it is also defined and modified by the texts and variations, or subgenres, that comprise it.[5] The so-called classical mystery story created by writers like Arthur Conan Doyle and Agatha Christie focused on the aesthetics of crime rather than on its social or psychological consequences. This type of detective novel usually opens with a mysterious crime, often in an enclosed, rather aristocratic setting such as a country house, a club, or a train. Through a series of conversations with the suspects and an evaluation of the available clues, a brilliant, typically amateur detective solves the mystery and dramatically presents his (generally he's a he) findings to an assembled group. The detective may have a Watson-type assistant, who accompanies the reader in deciphering clues. The classic mystery is often incorrectly described as a story of pure ratiocination in which character development and other novelistic elements are more or less subordinated to the puzzle. This is the form that inspired Jorge Luis Borges but that ultimately proved most recalcitrant to Hispanic adaptation.[6] The British-style mystery is rather confusingly referred to in Spanish as *"la novela inductiva,"* or more accurately as the *"novela enigma."* Early detective literature in Spanish generally followed this model. The terms *policiaco* or *policial* are also generic Spanish terms for the detective novel.

The hard-boiled stories created by Dashiell Hammett and Raymond Chandler during Prohibition in the 1920s were inspired by the rise of organized crime and police corruption. The genre achieved its greatest popularity after World War II, an event that shattered the illusion of order as the ruling principle of society. The Hammett-style hard-boiled detective is no longer a Nietzschean Superman but a vessel of human frailty. The hard-boiled genre is defined more by its mood and attitude than its plot structure: a definitively urban genre, it proclaims a dystopian view of the modern city in which chaos, alienation, and discord prevail. It portrays disaffection and alienation and focuses closely, often obsessively, on human character flaws; depicts in a more or less realistic fashion both its setting and the social or ideological problems of that setting; and often subordinates the puzzle element to moral or social criticism. The hard-boiled novel is an amalgamation of the heroic quest with the gritty, sometimes sensationalized violence depicted in early pulp magazines; its protagonist is the lonely private eye (a knightly hero), whose stoic cynicism is matched by his moral outrage. The Spanish term *novela negra*, used to describe the hard-boiled genre, is a French invention attributable to Marcel Duhamel's "Série Noire," initiated in 1945 and named in allusion to the American pulp series *Black Mask*. (The series also inspired the coinages *film noir* and *roman noir*.) The Spanish terminology reflects a specific perception of the American hard-boiled novel, filtered through the prestigious apparatus of postwar French intellectualism, according to which the North American hard-boiled narrative realistically portrays the injustices created by the capitalist system. The Argentine writer Ricardo Piglia has observed that the classic detective story eliminates social causes in order to better serve the mystery, while the *novela negra* privileges motivation, usually economic, over mystery. The criminals are the privileged and the powerful: institutions, rather than individuals.

The Spanish and Latin American *neopoliciaco* is loosely based on the hard-boiled genre: its detectives are vigilantes who expose themselves to the viciousness and corruption of society with a paradoxical mix of cynicism and idealism. Manuel Vázquez Montalbán's postsocialist detective, Pepe Carvalho, confronts municipal corruption in Barcelona; Paco Ignacio Taibo II's one-eyed protagonist, Héctor Belascoarán Shayne, defends the Mexican Revolution against the putrefaction of its institutions; and Leonardo Padura Fuentes's revolutionary policeman, Mario Conde, contemplates the stagnation of the Cuban socialist system after the collapse of the Soviet Union. The *neopoliciaco* is more overtly political and leftist than the American hard-boiled novel, and in keeping with its social concerns, portrays the personal life of the detective in a more detailed manner. Like the novels of Chester Himes, the *neopoliciaco* is primarily urban and atmospheric and represents an irrational, violent world. Taibo describes its main elements this way: "Characterization of the police as a force of chaos . . . presentation of the criminal event as a social accident, surrounded by the daily life of the big cities, emphasis on dialogue as the main method of narration; high quality of language especially in the creation of atmosphere; central characters marginalized by choice."[7]

Because of the impracticability of situating a private eye in a socialist society, the Cuban socialist detective novel is indebted to the police procedural. Like the French *roman policier*, it centers on the activities and private lives of the police rather than a lonely private eye or eccentric amateur. The early socialist detective novels were often written by policemen and based on real events and (at least nominally) modeled on testimonial or documentary literature such as Rodolfo Walsh's *Operación Masacre* (1957) or Miguel Barnet's *Biografía de un cimarrón* (1966). Since Cuban detective fiction was also defined in terms of a battle between ideologies, there was little thematic difference between the detective novel and the spy story (the *novela de contraespionaje*).

The detective story in general is a genre in perpetual flux. While strictly formulaic detective novels are still popular, Latin American detective writers naturally test generic boundaries as they try to write stories that reflect their reality, and many use detective formulas simply as a point of departure for other kinds of literary experimentation. This book is a selective investigation of authors who have taken up the genre seriously with regard to both form and content, consciously emulating or violating formal elements of the genre while fulfilling its essential function: the artful exposition of a criminal event. Paco Ignacio Taibo II and Leonardo Padura Fuentes have each created an idiosyncratic detective protagonist who appears in several texts. Other writers have chosen different models, such as true crime or psychological thrillers. However, generic boundaries, always suspect, have become increasingly irrelevant for many younger authors, and there is a growing consensus that existing labels and categories do not adequately reflect the structural heterodoxy of the newest detective literature.

Formula stories can be both an affirmation of existing social values and a way of setting new or controversial ideas against these values. Detective literature allows the reader to experience transgression of the rules of society in a controlled, pragmatically neutral interaction. If we accept Bakhtin's conceptualization of genre as a reflection of ideological and cultural currents in a given society, the examination of crime fiction genres in Mexico and Cuba can facilitate reflection on official organs of culture and their role in representing identity. Beyond their political intentions, detective writers like Paco Ignacio Taibo II, Manuel Vázquez Montalbán, and Leonardo Padura use the detective formula to chronicle daily life, offering portraits that include famous and everyday people, mundane events and human crises. Their richly detailed urban settings become protagonists in their own right. For Taibo this backdrop is Mexico City's *Distrito Federal,* the apocalyptic and compelling *Defe.* For Padura, Havana in the early 1990s reflects a society on the brink of economic and moral collapse.

If the detective novel was of little relevance to Latin Americans before 1968, Latin American writers have adopted the genre in the years since then precisely because it permits a critical scrutiny of their social institutions in the light of modern liberal principles and their late-twentieth-century manifestations in the ideological narratives of neoliberalism and globalization. Contemporary Hispanic detective fiction is an explicitly ideological literature with international connections. Its leftist politics were honed in the international student movements of 1968, Spain's post-Franco transition period, Argentina's Dirty War, and the Cuban Revolution.

While the traditional detective novel is a product of modern discourses, in the context of Hispanic letters it arose as an antidote to the solipsism of the modern literary avant-gardes. The *neopoliciaco* then began its ideological and epistemological transformation to a new form that attempts to describe the peculiarities of Latin American postmodernity. By audaciously engaging a distinctly foreign, metropolitan, modernizing genre, it comments on the positionality of Latin American cultural activity with respect to its metropolis and allows for a particularly fruitful investigation of the terms and conditions associated with it. By probing the doubly marginalized genre of Latin American detective fiction, we can begin to appreciate it as a response to Latin American modernity, modernism, and postmodernity.

1.
Origins and Ideologies
of the *Neopoliciaco*

By a curious confusion, many modern critics have passed
from the proposition that a masterpiece may be
unpopular to the other proposition that unless it is
unpopular it cannot be a masterpiece.
—*G. K. Chesterton, "On Detective Novels"*

*D*etective literature explores the relationship between authority
and justice. While classic detective stories present crime as the transgression of norms in an essentially just system, hard-boiled stories present the pursuit of justice itself as a transgression of norms in an essentially corrupt system. The nature of these transgressions reflects a series
of relationships between the individual and the corporate, the aesthetic
and the ethical, and the modern and the nonmodern.

The detective genre is a product of the conditions of nineteenth-
century modernity: the scientific and philosophical transformations of
the post-Enlightenment era; the emphasis on empiricism and ratiocination; and the burgeoning sciences of sociology, psychology, and forensic
medicine. As the tenets of economic liberalism promoted the growth of
industrial capital, newly professionalized police forces protected property and production in the great urban centers. Democratic and consti-
tutional reforms completed the liberal revolution, bringing the workings
of science and the law into the realm of public discourse. Edgar Allan
Poe synthesized these elements in the first detective story, "The Murders
in the Rue Morgue," in 1841.

The origins and assumptions of the detective genre a priori prevented
its easy adaptation to Latin American circumstances. Spain and its American colonies found themselves generally isolated from the modernizing
tide that swept through Western Europe and the United States from the
eighteenth century forward. Mired in wars and anticolonial unrest for

the greater part of the nineteenth century, Latin America underwent a complex process of nation building and modernization. Julio Ramos has described the resulting modernities experienced by Latin America as "divergent" both from each other and from a metropolitan norm; in particular, he describes the ethical crisis experienced by an emergent modern subject with respect to his role in the articulation of nationality: "it problematized the relation between aesthetic drive and ethicopolitical imperatives, since the radicalization of the aesthetic drive tended to collapse the economy of truth that formed the very basis of social communicability."[1]

Latin America's history of political and economic dependency problematized autonomous literary expression and at the same time led to misgivings about imitating foreign models.[2] The Hispanic concept of literary value was necessarily inflected with judgments about tradition and authenticity: Spanish *casticismo*, a peculiar, isolationist brand of cultural nationalism, was matched by the Latin American drive for *lo autóctono*, or home-grown self-expression. The production of a native detective literature is inconsistent with these concerns and serves as a metaphor for the position of Latin American cultural activity with respect to the Anglo-European academy and United States popular culture. As Thomas De Quincey foresaw, the classic mystery story poses death as an aesthetic phenomenon rather than a moral one: its modern, Western—even colonializing—underpinnings, coupled with its rigidly formalized, nonethical program, rendered it incompatible with Latin American realities.[3]

Detective literature thus began as an import in Spain and Latin America and had a wide audience from the nineteenth century forward, when stories by Edgar Allan Poe, Arthur Conan Doyle, and Gaston Leroux became paradigms for mystery and suspense narrative. The early twentieth century brought translated volumes by Dorothy Sayers, Agatha Christie, Carter Dickson, G. K. Chesterton, Ernest Bramah, Ellery Queen, E. C. Bentley, S. S. Van Dine, Rex Stout, Erle Stanley Gardner, and others.[4] The Argentine writer Jorge Luis Borges, who published numerous detective stories in translation (in his *Séptimo círculo* series) and wrote several of his own, was probably the single most influential advocate of detective fiction in Latin America. As the noted Mexican author Alfonso Reyes observed, Borges's collaborations with Adolfo Bioy Casares gave the detective narrative "citizenship" *(carta de naturalización)* in Spanish American literature.[5] In the 1940s and 1950s, French intellectuals like Roger Caillois, Jean-Paul Sartre, and André Gide helped popularize the hard-boiled genre among Spanish-speaking readers; the support of the Spanish and French left conferred a critical blessing on the genre and would ultimately inspire the socially committed *neopoliciaco*.[6]

According to Reyes's well-known essay "Sobre la novela policial" (1945), the detective story was the most popular kind of literature in Mexico during the 1930s and 1940s.[7] By the 1950s, Mexicans themselves began writing detective fiction in some numbers, including Pepe Martínez de la Vega (creator of the comical *pelado* detective Peter Pérez[8]), Antonio Helú, María Elvira Bermúdez, and the dramatist Rodolfo Usigli. Several "literary" writers like Carlos Fuentes, Vicente Leñero, José Emilio Pacheco, Rafael Bernal, and Jorge Ibargüengoitia also experimented with the crime genre in the 1960s and 1970s.[9] Paralleling Reyes, the prominent Cuban critic José Antonio Portuondo commented on the popularity of detective fiction in Cuba, asserting in a 1946 article that the detective novel was the "the most representative form of poetic expression in our era."[10] During that decade, Lino Novás Calvo published a few detective stories under the guise of reportage, but very few other Cubans attempted the genre until 1969, when Ignacio Cárdenas Acuña wrote *Enigma para un domingo*, which became the first socialist detective novel.

The real dawn of the detective genre in Cuba and Mexico was in the early 1970s, coinciding with the rise of the Spanish *novela negra* during the decline of the Franco regime.[11] Spain's most successful and original detective fiction is a post-Franco phenomenon that draws on the American hard-boiled tradition, especially Dashiell Hammett, Raymond Chandler, Ross Macdonald, and Chester Himes. The Spanish *novela negra* comments on the failures of the socialist program in the early years after Franco's death, as the hope for a new society was spoiled by economic chaos; an emerging drug culture and the corruption of democratic institutions contributed to a generalized cynicism amid the many political crises of the late 1970s and early 1980s. These stories succinctly expressed the predicament of an opening, rapidly modernizing society in the phrase "we lived better with Franco."[12]

Like all generic innovations, the *neopoliciaco* genre arose in times of upheaval, when epistemological and political conditions were undergoing major transformations and outcomes were uncertain. The death of Franco, the betrayal of Mexican student movements in 1968, and the controversy surrounding the Padilla affair in Cuba moved writers and intellectuals to rethink their ethical and aesthetic responsibilities and to question their position with respect to the academy, Western culture, and their readers. If the detective novel seemed at first an unsuitable means of expression, they soon began to adapt it to address these issues.

A product of economic politics and the cultural anxieties of underdevelopment, the Cuban socialist detective novel was specifically conceived as a tool of empowerment against the "Anglo-Saxon" detective novel, which the writer Luis Rogelio Nogueras described as "a genre born of the mire and blood of capitalism."[13] The Cuban genre sought to call attention to Cuba's postcolonial emergence into modernity after 1959. The massive modernizing project integral to the Cuban conversion to socialism required a forum of enunciation for which the realistic detective novel proved ideal. Cubans embraced the intellectual humbleness of the detective story as a corrective to avant-garde erudition and what socialist critics referred to generically as "formalism," or literature that favored formal experimentation over social content. The socialist detective novel was ultimately part of a comprehensive program, not only to restructure mass consciousness, but to reform Cuban literature in order to make it conform to—and support—the change in political circumstances. In the late 1980s and 1990s, Leonardo Padura changed the course of the Cuban detective genre. His detective novels and stories featuring the Havana policeman Mario Conde foreground postmodern anxieties about the legitimacy of totalizing narratives (even Marxist ones) and the rehabilitation of the aesthetic enterprise within the ethicopolitical sphere.

As opposed to the propagandistic socialist detective novel, the dark Mexican *neopoliciaco* contests official ideology. Reflecting the concerns of the *Onda* generation, who witnessed the student massacre in the Plaza de las Tres Culturas, the novels of Paco Ignacio Taibo II protest the oppressive politics of neoliberalism. Like Leonardo Padura Fuentes's Havana tales and Manuel Vázquez Montalbán's novels set in Barcelona, Taibo's stories, featuring the private detective Héctor Belascoarán Shayne, are distinctively urban. Taibo's promotion of the genre has inspired the newest generation of Mexican writers, including Juan Hernández Luna, Gabriel Trujillo Muñoz, and others. This group stretches the parameters of genre detective fiction, seeking innovative narrative techniques to depict the crisis of truth that afflicts Mexico at the turn of the millennium.

Despite the achievements of the past thirty years, however, Hispanic detective fiction bears the permanent stigma of being a foreign invention, reflecting a modernity incongruous with Hispanic realities, and supporting bourgeois Anglo-Saxon ideologies. Socialist intellectuals see national literatures as a direct expression of economic realities: for them the traditional detective novel is a product of modern capitalist industrialization, incapable of rendering justice to a Latin American economic system that was still predominantly feudal at the turn of the twentieth century. The Latin American's perspective on the detective novel is also necessarily colored by his own otherness as reflected in the orientalizing discourses of the colonial tradition. As one Cuban critic writes: "We are the exotic scenery for Agatha Christie's crimes, we are the slant-eyed servants, the passionate dancers that serve as bait to entrap ingenuous white men; we are the most despised detective of the crime genre: Charlie Chan. . . . The eyes of the ancient, astute Agatha . . . are, in reality, the eyes of empire."[14]

The classic detective novel also seems incongruous with the long tradition of dictatorship, corruption, and repression common to the vast majority of Spanish-speaking countries.[15] According to the Mexican journalist Carlos Monsiváis, many Latin Americans suffer too much mayhem in real life to be attracted by mystery stories: "Who cares who killed Roger Ackroyd . . . if no one knows (officially) who was responsible for the killings at Tlatelolco or who ordered the Falcons' assault on the 10th of June?"[16] If the general populace is persistently subjected to violence and deceit by authority, as Monsiváis suggests, the transgressive aspect of the traditional detective story becomes unrealistic and irrelevant.

As the Tlatelolco massacre demonstrated, violent action on the part of government against citizens often takes place within, and is justified by, the rhetoric of modernity: modernization, order, and progress. José Antonio Portuondo attributed the origins of deduction itself to the British Enlightenment philosophers Bacon and Mill; therefore, he reasoned, the literary form must be fundamentally linked to an *episteme* dominated by rationalism, capitalism, and democracy. In contrast, Spanish and Latin American reality is at least nominally governed by an antirationalist tradition in both the juridical and intellectual spheres.[17] Literary strategies from the *barroco/neobarroco* to magical realism and *lo real maravilloso* to Antonio Benítez Rojo's dynamic conceptualization of Caribbean poetics, all derive from and enhance this perception.

Carlos Alonso's conceptualization of "positionality" describes the dilemma of the Spanish American subject whose resistance to metropolitan discourse is couched in the language of the metropolis: his own status vis-à-vis external (modern, Western) and internal (national, autochthonous) cultural activity must be constantly reevaluated and renegotiated. The creation of an original detective genre in Spanish is both an assertion of this positionality and a critique of its attendant and underlying ideologies. Whether this demonstrates a subaltern or postcolonial internalization of metropolitan perspectives may be debated, but it is evident that contemporary Latin American detective fiction communicates an explicit defiance toward modern notions of rationalism, legalism, and even simple causality. In so doing, the detective novel has come to serve as a locus for the reenactment of the Latin American dilemma surrounding modernity, which from the moment of Independence, as Alonso asserts, "constituted both the bedrock of Spanish American cultural discourse and the potential source of its most radical disempowerment."[18]

G. K. Chesterton, Precursor of the Latin American Detective Novel

Although the Edwardian British critic Gilbert Keith Chesterton would seem an unlikely precursor to the Latin American detective story, his fundamental, antimodernist hypotheses about the detective novel influenced many of its most important Spanish American writers and critics, including Cuban critic José Antonio Portuondo, Mexican Alfonso Reyes, and most importantly Jorge Luis Borges. In the 1930s and 1940s Borges stimulated the public's interest in the detective novel with his translations, his own detective stories, and his numerous essays on Chesterton.[19]

The fact that Borges's concept of the detective story was inspired by Chesterton has been well documented. Borges shared Chesterton's facility with paradox, his humility before the enormity of the universe, and his ability to convey the vertigo of being, or "that eternal passion of astonishment (and gratitude)."[20] Thematic coincidences abound between the two, referring to parallel investigations into the nature of reality and the value of perception: the obsessions with the vertiginous, the infinite, heroic or fatal causality, history as literature, skepticism regarding logic, mirrors, the cabalistic investigation, dream/nightmare, and the unstable frontier between object and invention. Borges wrote of Chesterton's aesthetic appeal, "Each of Chesterton's stories comes to be in some way like a picture, then, like a stage piece, then like a parable. Then there are the backgrounds—the characters appear like actors entering a stage-set, and they are always very vivid, visually vivid. And then there is the solution, which is always ingenious."[21]

Through vivid visual forms, supernatural colors, distorted proportions and perspectives, the urban geography of Chesterton's stories gains a palpable character, and the city itself is transformed into a protagonist. Borges's vertiginous and reduplicative spaces in "Death and the Compass" recall Chesterton's suburban London, while "The Garden of Forking Paths," set in the English countryside, is an extension of the terrain of *The Man Who Was Thursday*. Chesterton's dizzying landscapes also prefigured the treatment of the city in the *neopoliciaco*: Taibo's apocalyptic rendering of Mexico's *Distrito Federal* and Padura's nostalgia for the balconies of Old Havana.

Chesterton argued in a 1901 essay, "A Defence of Detective Stories," that the detective story is a genre of and for modernity: "The first essential value of the detective story lies in this, that it is the earliest and only form of popular literature in which is expressed some sense of the poetry of modern life."[22] He used detective narrative to illustrate this "poetry," in reality the dangerous complexity of modern existence:

> Of [the] realization of the great city itself as something wild and obvious the detective story is certainly the 'Iliad'. . . . The lights of the city begin to glow like innumerable goblin eyes, since they are the guardians of some secret, however crude, which the writer knows and the reader does not. Every twist of the road is like a finger pointing to it; every fantastic skyline of chimneypots seems wildly and derisively signalling the meaning of the mystery.[23]

Chesterton's modern city was "wild"—mysterious and polysemic—but at the same time "obvious": reducible to a single reading. Borges suggested deceptively that each of Chesterton's detective stories "tries to explain, through pure reason, an inexplicable happening."[24] Chesterton, a converted Catholic, was in reality an antirationalist and an antimodernist, and he structured his stories according to a notion of faith that precluded or diminished the role of reason while foregrounding the potential for discernment kindled by Christian empathy. He mistrusted the modern paradigms of empiricism, reason, and order, which he was convinced would lead to lunacy:

> Destruction awaits not the man who swims in the sea, but the man who tries to plumb it . . . who tries to swim across the sea and make it finite. And in the same way the psychological danger lies in wait for the man who tries to measure all things, for it is that way that madness lies. . . . Consequently we may say truly that it is not the poets who go mad; it is the mathematicians, the logicians, the numberers of the stars and the counters of the grass.[25]

Chesterton's detective narratives also critiqued literary modernism and philosophical modernity, which he saw as complicit in the degradation of meaning. Just as he rejected the modern scientific method, Chesterton endeavored to prove through his stories that the rhetorical strategies of literary modernism—symbol, metaphor, allegory, parody, and all other significatory systems—are potentially subversive and therefore inherently nihilistic. At the same time, his stories exhibited what Foucault might call a premodern privileging of resemblance: the Father Brown mysteries are predicated on, and substantiated by, a strict, literal correspondence between signifier and signified; symbol and symbolized; history and allegory. Borges humorously described this technique of paradoxical literalism:

Few judge it necessary or agreeable to know *Les palais nomades*; many, *The Oracle of the Dog*. Clearly in the particular attraction of Chesterton's titles operates our consciousness that these names have not been invoked in vain. We know that in *Les palais nomades* there are no nomadic palaces; we know the *The Oracle of the Dog* will lack neither a dog nor an oracle, or a bona fide, oracular dog.[26]

There are abundant examples of this strategy throughout the Father Brown stories. In "The Hammer of God," an evil man is killed by a massive blow from above (a metaphorical hammer of God), which turns out to be from a hammer hurled from the tower of a church by a curate: in fact, the hammer of God. As one character mutters succinctly, "metaphors literally fail me."[27] Chesterton's objects and narratives (clues and solutions) are so transparent that ordinary phenomena become obscure and laden with meaning. Suspicion, intuition, and paranoia, as well as "scientific" interpretation, are nothing more than poetry inspired by the commonplace. Prosaic objects—lampposts, doorknobs—become indices of the whole network of human relations, common beliefs, and popular understanding. Ordinary figures are transformed into monsters, as in "The Invisible Man," where the banality of a postman converts him into an invisible assassin.

Chesterton used his detective stories to privilege the quotidian rather than to encourage learned or semiotic readings of the material environment. He poked fun at what he called the "Conanical" method and the quasi-cabalistic science of detection.[28] The successful detective must read his environment from a position of intellectual humility, reducing rather than multiplying or magnifying meaning. "The Absence of Mr. Glass" depicts an august sociologist who condescends to help Father Brown on a case; after semiotically "reading" the scene of the crime he produces a sophisticated scientific theory that overlooks all the facts (obvious to Father Brown):

> "Dr. Hood," [Father Brown] cried enthusiastically, "you are a great poet! You have called an uncreated being out of the void. How much more god-like that is than if you had only ferreted out the mere facts! Indeed, the mere facts are rather commonplace and comic by comparison."[29]

In this story a complex "locked-room" murder turns out to be exactly what it looks like: a magician practicing his illusions. Chesterton's signs are doggedly prosaic rather than poetic: no amount of interpretation can alter their meaning. Borges's story "Death and the Compass," in which the detective's forced cabalistic reading of a three-cornered mystery leads him to his own death, demonstrates more concretely these same dangers of hyperinterpretation.

For both Chesterton and Borges, then, detection and interpretation are equivalent hermeneutical activities. The crime is an excessive or thought-less exercise of signification that generates potentially equivocal readings: for Chesterton, cognitive and spiritual anomie. Borges calls this "game of vain repetitions" allegory: a masquerade unleashed by any system of equivalences between persons, objects, or ideas.[30] His understanding of allegory prefigures Jean Baudrillard's ideas on signification and simula-cra, in which the representation of a thing or phenomenon eventually competes with or replaces that which it represented; the representation no longer depends on the existence of any corresponding object in reality. Contrary to Chesterton, Borges embraces this state because it subverts the totalizing, symbolic, or mythical aspects of modern understanding. His mock division of the world into Aristotelians and Platonists describes this design:

> The latter intuit that ideas are realities; the former, that they are general-izations; for [the Aristotelians], language is only a system of arbitrary sym-bols; for [the Platonists], it is the map of the universe. The Platonist knows that the universe is in some way a cosmos, an order; that order, for the Aristotelian, could be an error or a fiction of our partial understanding.[31]

The Aristotelian, or modern, episteme is characterized by what Borges (using the medieval nomenclature) calls "nominalism," in which indi-vidual perception constitutes reality. In Platonism or "realism," on the other hand, universal, mutually comprehensible systems and truths form an external, objectively verifiable "reality."

Borges's philosophical probings often tested one-to-many and many-to-one correspondences as a way of exploring "Aristotelian" epistemology. In this realm, signs are eminently flexible and their interpretation is a contingent and personal (perhaps amoral) enterprise.[32] "Emma Zunz" is a play on signification in which the protagonist exacts vengeance on a man but disguises or replaces his true offense (which provides her motive) with a more "evident" one, that of her own rape. Although he is not the perpe-trator of this particular crime, the two perpetrators become one and the same through the sign of *honra*, the Spanish tradition that conflates family honor with female chastity. Both the subject and the object of the viola-tion are doubled in the story, and Borges implies that the metonymic act is as concrete as its referent, or perhaps supersedes it. The rape of Emma Zunz, like the murder of Stephen Albert through a fatal homonymy in

"The Garden of Forking Paths," derives meaning from its function as a flexible sign, not its essence as referent.

For post-Borgesian thinkers like Fredric Jameson, the postmodern flexibility of the sign represents a healthy iconoclasm with respect to the mythologies of modernity. By challenging the Word, diverse claimants degrade the frontiers between high culture and popular culture and reject modern classificatory systems as dependent on a false or authoritarian conception of the literary (or cultural) subject.[33] All kinds of signification can therefore be positive (although they are also dreadful, like procreation) because they have the potential to lead toward truth (knowledge) rather than away from it: "The proliferation of mirrors is all the more terrifying because each new image brings us closer to this face."[34] According to this scheme, devices such as parody are duplicative or mimetic reactions provoked by an oppressive authority and therefore ethically legitimate strategies of resistance or truth seeking. But for Chesterton, these activities entail a disorderly proliferation of meaning and are therefore essentially meaningless and nihilistic. In Chesterton's "Platonist" universe, names and symbols are equivalent, and names denote essences. Hence they are held sacred, and often occult: Chesterton assigns each symbol to a single entity within a system that excludes scientific, supernatural, or metaphysical abstractions. Myriad possible explanations for a given circumstance (clue or sign) are inevitably reduced to a single, ontologically true solution. The forcing of one-to-one correspondences between sign and referent exposes Chesterton's underlying fear of duplicitous duplication and constitutes his obstinate declaration of faith. This is the basis of his poetic vision and his disconcerting rendering of the detective story. For example, in *The Man Who Was Thursday* seven policemen pose as poets, who in turn pose as anarchists in a cell, who turn out to be businessmen posing as anarchists in order to infiltrate the cell. Their grotesque parodic masquerade ultimately erases any meaningful difference between anarchist and policeman, and the ensuing chaos threatens to destroy the world.[35]

Despite the common view that Chesterton was a humorist, his poetic vision is a terrifying one in which Arthur Conan Doyle's civilized London mutates into a bleak, garishly colored landscape.[36] Against this backdrop Chesterton's characters rush about like beetles, constantly hurling themselves toward a vanishing horizon. The looming hills and immense, bewildering spaces are recognizable signs of surrounding evil. The nature of the scenery is rigidly semiotic: a visual poetry of signs ruled by an absolute, one-to-one correspondence: "There is no stone in the street and no brick in the wall that is not actually a deliberate symbol—

a message from some man, as much as if it were a telegram or a postcard. The narrowest street possesses, in every crook and twist of its intention, the soul of the man who built it, perhaps long in his grave."[37] In this climate, suspicion is a healthy and effectively poetic exercise and is almost sure to be rewarded in the end by an epiphany that banishes allegory. Detective stories are the perfect expression of this suspicion, because they force one to stand back from the quotidian object and the nondescript citizen, compelling a reevaluation of the surface elements of human existence.[38]

Georg Lukács wrote that allegory is the modernist expression of "man's alienation from objective reality." He shared Chesterton's view of allegory as nihilistic, asserting that "allegory, in modernist literature, is clearly of the [ahistorical] kind. Transcendence implies here, more or less consciously, the negation of any meaning immanent in the work or life of man."[39] He extended Walter Benjamin's critique of allegory, concluding that through allegory "every person, every object, every relationship can stand for something else. This transferability constitutes a devastating, though just, judgement of the profane world—which is thereby branded as a world where such things are of small importance."[40] If modern interpretation devolves on the symbol, Chesterton pushed this principle to the forefront of his detective investigation, interrogating the sign as a locus of mediation between the subjective and the objective, the concrete and the ideal, the individual and the universal.

Chesterton's influence on Latin American literature was greatly magnified through Borges's lens. In Mexico and Cuba, it was Borges's reading of Chesterton, even more than Borges's own detective stories, that shaped the detective genre. Because Borges confined himself to the puzzle type of detective story, Paco Ignacio Taibo II and other writers consider his work on the genre in the 1930s and 1940s the "prehistory" of detective fiction.[41] Borges's detective stories influenced future Latin American detective writers in a stylistic, rather than a thematic sense, principally on a linguistic plane. Borges experimented with popular and street language in his "abductive" Isidro Parodi stories, and the *neopoliciaco* underscores popular language as a subversive and democratizing force that challenges the hegemony of national mythology and its literary manifestations.[42] Most importantly, Borges's detective stories are highly intertextual, incorporating and appropriating literary references from Plato to Anatole France, as well as popular literary and historical figures like José Martí. Like future detective fiction in Spanish, their intertextuality embraces the whole detective genre.[43]

Chesterton defined the central problems of the detective genre: what are the scope and function of reason and its modern expressions—order, jurisprudence, science, and progress—when applied to the eminently unreasonable phenomena of crime? What if rational order is not the norm but only a fleeting exception? Chesterton argued that the detective story reminds the complacent that "we live in an armed camp, making war with a chaotic world, and that the criminals, the children of chaos, are nothing but the traitors within our gates."[44] Chaos and illogic dominate contemporary Mexican detective fiction, whose writers portray the tragic irrationalism of crime and our equally tragic desire to comprehend it. Chesterton's stories anticipated the paranoid literality of the Cuban socialist detective novel, and his conception of the detective novel as a mirror of society gave writers an essential tool for creating a didactic popular genre that some, like Leonardo Padura, would transform into a chronicle of their time.

As Borges appreciated, Chesterton's sincerity and passion set the stage for many debates about the literary qualities of detective literature. Chesterton also looked forward to an eventual reconciliation of high and low art but ultimately omitted all mention of his Father Brown stories in his own autobiography. Latin American detective writers have consistently questioned the role of detective fiction both within literary production and within society in the Chestertonian manner. The *neopoliciaco* represents a reaction against the mythologizing aestheticism of the Latin American *boom* of the 1960s and 1970s. Coarse, realistic, and chaotic, it is marked by the same pessimistic idealism as the first hardboiled fiction. The hard-boiled detective novel of the 1920s and 1930s represented a sharpened perception of crime and institutional corruption and a general disenchantment with the effete British-style whodunit. It shifted the burden of detection from the mind and its rational processes to the body. In the tradition of Raymond Chandler's Philip Marlowe, the hard-boiled detective was a vigilante figure descended from the knights of Arthurian legend, whose romantic mission—the quest for truth and justice—contrasted tragically with the corruption of his society and its institutions. The disengagement of justice and authority corroded the hermeneutic enterprise, and the detective's body became a catalyst for discovery and a mnemonic archive of criminal events unrecorded by official history. The *neopoliciaco* is necessarily visceral and physically brutal: the systemic crises of society work themselves out through the body and psyche of the detective, marking him as damaged, contentious, and Other. Whereas, in Jameson's analysis, the mystery genre "features a hero, the detective, whose existence is a mere function of the mystery he is solving,"[45] the *neopoliciaco* depicts a detective process whose advancement depends largely on the actions taken by the detective, but this progress takes place on a physical rather than a hermeneutical plane. The detective heroes of Cuba and Mexico pursue an elusive truth behind official lies, ideological crimes, and institutionalized hypocrisy, interpreting the violence inscribed on their bodies in lieu of material evidence. These writers articulate the outrage of a generation at the betrayal of revolutionary aspirations, and its longing for a return to political innocence. Like Chesterton, they proclaim their populist ideology from the outer margins of literary discourse.

The Mexican critic Carlos Monsiváis asserts that the Mexican detective novel "isn't written": it doesn't contain "literary" writing, isn't "committed" in social and aesthetic terms.[46] Manuel Vázquez Montalbán, the Spanish creator of some twenty successful novels featuring the book-burning detective Pepe Carvalho—and one of the genre's harshest critics—complained that "the detective novel belongs to the kinds of cultural expression that continually have to be excusing themselves for being born."[47] The Cuban author Alejo Carpentier wrote in his "Apología de la novela policiaca" (1931) that "the detective novel is, of all the genres achievable through the printed letter, the most despised by serious minds."[48] The detective story's precursors—the Spanish *folletín*, the British "penny dreadful," and the North American pulps—evolved as reading for the masses, distinct from "high" literature. While the conceptualization of high and low culture is almost everywhere characterized by the elevation of the specialist and debasement of the layman, in the case of detective literature (and formula literature in general) the equation was inverted. Professionalism in literature is often associated with "hack" or commercial writers, prolific and therefore inferior output, and pandering to philistines.[49] The high/low dichotomy is not always valid, but it commonly inflects the discourse surrounding the detective novel.

In truth, genre fiction is rarely amenable to established literary-critical approaches. As a literary endeavor, the interpretation of a genre devoted to self-explication seems redundant.[50] Modern literary criticism associates the legibility of (implicitly "realistic") genre fiction with ethical and aesthetic conformity and generally favors the hermetic, inventive text. The fields of detective fiction and literary criticism are both modern phenomena, and the correlation between the critical status of the detective novel and the rise of modern criticism—detection and interpretation—is a fundamental component of the detective novel's low prestige.

The golden age of the mystery story in the 1920s and 1930s coincided with the maturation of criticism as a specialized discipline. The hermeticism of modernist and other avant-garde literatures supported the need for a body of qualified professionals—literary "detectives"—to decode obscure texts. The self-explicating detective genre not only resists the professional critics' decoding project but competes with it, since it functions both as the hermeneutic object and its own explication. The literary or "serious" novel is polysemous and conflictive, while the genre novel articulates a single, fixed viewpoint. In reality, the Latin American detective novel illustrates the fundamental interpretative dilemma that so engaged Borges and Chesterton: according to which framework— nominalist or realist—should the detective (literary or otherwise) interpret the signs presented by an essentially criminal text? Genre, in particular, would appear to prescribe a hermeneutic code at odds with an unknowable ontological object.

Despite a history of generic development and innovation, formula writing has been suspect in Hispanic letters ever since Cervantes poked fun at genre fiction in *Don Quijote*. Alfonso Reyes even hypothesized that the detective novel was despised *because* of its popularity.[51] Although a timid reevaluation of genre fiction began to materialize in the early 1970s in the context of mass-media studies, Hispanic critics see genre as a necessarily restrictive construct, and for most the term "genre fiction" itself has a pejorative connotation. They see the trajectory of the detective novel in terms of a dialectic in which a "literary" detective novel must contain the seeds of its own generic deconstruction, transforming itself into a "literature without adjectives" *(literatura sin adjetivos)*.[52] This mistrust of genre is a symptom of a still-prevalent modernist aesthetic that nurtures dichotomies such as high/low culture, universal versus regional themes, and aesthetic versus ethical concerns.

The exercise of an inherently prescriptive genre under pragmatically nonverifiable conditions has led to a consensus among Hispanic *neopoliciaco* writers that their detective stories are postmodern. Beyond the use of certain literary devices, most have not really demonstrated what they mean by postmodernism. Postmodernism is a slippery and contentious term in any context: in general historical and sociological terms, it describes a reaction to modernity conceived as a worldview rooted in rationalism, empiricism, industrial development, and political and economic liberalism (including both capitalist and Marxist philosophies).[53] Postmodernist devices in literature include parody, pastiche, references to popular culture, intertextuality, and a treatment of subjectivity as both desirable and suspect, depending on the position of the subject with respect to the modern episteme.

Postmodernist and poststructuralist theory attempt to discern the ideological undercurrents in literary discourse as a way of locating new voices and subverting the hegemonic subject and other totalizing paradigms.[54] This position values relativism, individualism, and the decentered subject. Because postmodernist criticism (in a very general sense) is interested in desacralizing or destabilizing the existing modernist tradition, it has tried to accommodate some of the more democratic and popular forms of cultural expression. However, Latin Americanists have argued that U.S. and European (especially French) postmodernist theory represents a common reaction to a modernity that itself is a self-affirming European construct.[55] Furthermore, the multiplicity of cultures within Latin America renders inoperable any single paradigm of postmodernity. Latin American postmodernist theorists therefore endeavor to merge the postmodern emphasis on diversity with a return to a socially responsible, humanist politics. Postmodern theory in Latin America is unified by its social agenda and concerns over globalization and neoliberalism. Economic modernity has very often been accompanied by extreme repression in Latin America; hence intellectuals seek to challenge hegemonic constructs of modern progress while developing ethical and aesthetic responses appropriate to Latin America's apparent epistemological impasse. In keeping with these concerns, postmodernism in the Latin American detective novel describes a critical stance toward a mythologizing ideological authority that corresponds to and supports a modernist aesthetic.

The Latin American detective novel challenges surprisingly persistent constructs of high and low culture; yet, inevitably, it has embraced these distinctions in the act of transgression. One result of this dilemma is a tendency to view all Latin American detective fiction as parody. Parody appropriates the formal elements of the detective genre, separating them from their ethical content. This critical espousal owes much to Bakhtin's assessment of parody as burlesque and transgressive, a definition that identified the subaltern mimic as transgressor of the hegemonic norm.[56] As parody addresses the disjunction of the aesthetic mode of expression and the ethicosocial reality, it became a fulcrum for separating the literary from the nonliterary; transgressiveness and marginalization became code words for quality for Latin Americanist literary critics preoccupied with both social and cultural legitimacy.[57]

This perspective paradoxically privileges an academic familiarity with the structures and devices of genre and further reinforces the high/low dichotomy that postmodernist criticism claims to confront. Genre fiction is by definition patterned on other texts within the genre and responsive or allusive to texts outside it. Every elaboration is a reelaboration of formulaic elements.[58] The Bakhtinian theory of parody can help us to understand the Hispanic detective novel at a specific moment in its history—the writings of Borges and Bioy Casares in the early 1940s—but it implicitly supports an elitist aesthetic even while appearing to undermine it.[59] Borges took up the detective story in its enigma form because it represented a set of structures and conventions whose mythic and psychological (or mimetic) dimensions were practically nil. As Michael Holquist suggests, he used it as a way of "disestablishing the mythic and psychological tendencies of the tradition" or modern canon.[60] It was the very "flatness" of the detective novel, its lack of symbolic layering, that intrigued Borges: signs were not symbols but indices of a hidden, yet concrete, reality.

The parody question is consistent with concerns about national expression and authenticity.[61] Spanish American writing has long suffered a postcolonial identity crisis arising from a critical discourse that marginalizes itself by a practice of internal orientalism. This is what Carlos Alonso means by "positionality," an expression of the "radical ambivalence to modernity" in which intellectuals simultaneously "devised ways in which to subvert the authority of the discourse of modernity even as they wielded it." But, like other metropolitan critical practices, parody does not always adequately describe Hispanic textual strategies. As Alonso observes, "Parody implies a process of distancing from an original model that does not accurately represent the relationship that obtains between the Spanish American work and its hegemonic models."[62] George Yúdice is also concerned that the emphasis on distancing through formal elements is an intrinsically metropolitan technique that is not necessarily appropriate to the Latin American condition: "To argue that classic aesthetic distancing (whose counterparts are the Russian Formalist Ostranienie and the Freudian Verfremdungseffekt) is the means by which the colonialized or subaltern 'otherness' makes itself present . . . is to misunderstand how two orders of sociality (aesthetics and politics) interact."[63] The uncritical embrace of parody as an ideologically legitimizing (because aesthetic) textual strategy oversimplifies the affiliation between the metropolitan model and the colonial "appropriation."

The *neopoliciaco* authors have proven that the self-conscious appropriation of structures and elements from the detective genre can lead to the creation of original detective stories rather than just literary parodies. Leonardo Padura Fuentes and Paco Ignacio Taibo II engage with postmodernism on both ideological and aesthetic terms: Padura as a way of confronting the apparently irreconcilable aspects of premodernity and postmodernity that define the Cuban predicament, and Taibo in an attempt to redefine the terms of nationalism through a subversion of the political and economic discourses of modernity that have ravaged Mexican society. The new genre transcends the mythologizing aesthetic represented by the *boom*. It is a novel informed by social, economic, physical, and symbolic trauma whose aesthetic sophistication is bolstered by postmodernist literary techniques. *Neopoliciaco* writers employ, in particular, a kind of intertextuality that crosses generic boundaries as well as discursive ones, incorporating popular culture, leftist ideology and literary theory, and critiques of national mythologies. These writers are a close-knit fraternity who have constructed an internally referential discourse of the *neopoliciaco*.[64]

The Hispanic detective novel has matured in generic terms: from its mimetic beginnings, through a critical, parodic stage, to its current manifestation as a mode of reflection and judgment on a society that is declining "as if darkness were its destiny."[65] Leonardo Padura, Paco Ignacio Taibo II, and their colleagues have created a version of the Hispanic detective novel with its own mythology and its own discursive spaces; it stands on its own merits, independent of models and past critical methods. The Anglo-Saxon detective novel escaped the reach of modernist critical methods by developing its own hermeneutic system: it begged the troublesome question of whether, rather than using literary criticism to critique the detective novel, it wouldn't be more useful to use the detective novel to critique the ethical underpinnings of literature. Alejo Carpentier intuited this when he wrote that "the detective is to the delinquent what the art critic is to the artist: the delinquent *invents*, the detective *explains*."[66] Today, the Latin American detective novel also stands outside the modernist paradigm: overcoming the symptoms of an elusive modernity, it has sidestepped the merely postmodern and become authentically, autochthonously post-modern. The Latin American detective genre exemplifies the primary hermeneutic predicament facing the intellectual subject: how to interpret a reality that fundamentally resists ontological commitments. The premises of the *neopoliciaco* advance it toward a resolution of two ostensibly competing frameworks of meaning—the aesthetic/personal and the ethical/social—in a literature of ideological and creative dissent.

and vigilance over editorial policy during that time. When new literary journals, publishing houses, and artists' organizations were created, they were often subject to ideological pressures, whether explicitly, as in the case of official cultural directives, or implicitly in the form of distribution of jobs, fellowships, and awards, or intellectual and literary reactions in print. The 1970s, significantly, are sometimes referred to as the "the black decade" *(la década negra)* in Cuban letters, and the socialist detective novel is paradigmatic of the ideological excesses of the period.

The history of the socialist detective novel is linked to a program of persecution of individuals who were perceived as imperfectly integrated into revolutionary society. The revolutionary leadership harbored an increasing suspicion that "aesthetic" art was associated with homosexuality. The detective genre represented an aesthetic and ideological reaction to the perceived sophistication of the *boom* and earlier vanguards, some of which were also associated with homosexual intellectuals of the previous generation.[3] The modern association between literacy and degeneracy, or intellectualism and decadence, was reinforced in Cuba by the fact that, at the start of the Revolution, illiteracy was almost universal in rural areas. As the primary setting of the guerrilla movement, the countryside became associated with wholesomeness and virility—revolutionary fighters were called "guajiros machos"—while the city as intellectual center was supposed to be corrupt. At a certain level, ignorance was understood to be an integral part of manliness, while high levels of education or intellectual cultivation in a man signaled the possibility of effeminacy.

Through a series of connections that led from the prerevolutionary literary publications *Orígenes* and *Ciclón* back to *modernismo*, homosexuality, literary sophistication, and political subversiveness became linked in the socialist aesthetic. Homosexual writers affiliated with *Ciclón* and *Orígenes*—like José Lezama Lima, who wrote that "only what is difficult is stimulating"[4]; Virgilio Piñera, and Severo Sarduy, whose work the revolutionary critic Roberto Fernández Retamar described as "Neo-Barthesian faggotry" *(mariposeo neobartesiano)*[5]—had been the leading exponents of literary experimentation during the 1950s. Some, like Piñera, had become internationally famous in the pages of Carlos Franqui's *Lunes de Revolución*. Piñera himself was reported to have said, "Real men don't read books. Literature is for faggots and I am a pure faggot."[6] Later socialist discourse would point back to these writers as the epitome of prerevolutionary decadence. Cubans embraced the presumptive intellectual humbleness of the detective story as a corrective to this avant-garde erudition and what socialist critics referred to generically as "formalism," or literature that emphasized suspect formal experimentation—textual mechanics, subjectivity, and other ludic or escapist possibilities of literary discourse—over social content.

Formalism in this context goes beyond the definition set forth by Roman Jakobson and the Russian Formalists as "organized violence committed on everyday speech."[7] It refers to any text that is self-consciously artistic, linguistically alienated, or nonmimetic in form, as well as texts with no didactic message or ideological content. According to socialist literary theory, formalism and realism are antithetical modes of expression, since formalism is supposed to be subjective and realism is supposed to be objective. In Cuba "formalism" became a catch-all designation for the literary production of the "self-involved aesthetes" *(escritores ensimismados y estetistas)*—as the influential critic José Antonio Portuondo called them—who dominated the literary scene in the years leading up to and immediately following the Revolution, and who were influenced by existentialism (especially following Sartre's visit to Cuba in 1960), surrealism, and other European avant-garde movements.[8]

Spanish American *modernismo*, which was a point of origin for many literary manifestations of formalism, had been accused in the past of decadence and excessive eroticism, especially homosexuality. Fernández Retamar's famous 1971 essay *Calibán* linked the sociological discussion of the fin de siècle inextricably with contemporary literary discourse. A response to José Enrique Rodó's seminal *Ariel* (1900), *Calibán* emphasized the decadence of the United States and the raw vigor of the Caribbean nation. Fernández Retamar defended the "volcanic violence" of Castro's speech closing the 1971 Primer Congreso Nacional de Educación y Cultura, which condemned homosexuality and formalism, against the criticism of intellectuals who saw it as a deformation of revolutionary zeal. Realism, insisted Retamar, would combat the "aberrations typical of bourgeois culture."[9]

During the early revolutionary period (from 1959 until about 1968, the year of Che Guevara's death), many intellectuals both inside and outside Cuba were inspired by the goals of the Revolution and felt committed to expressing their solidarity through art. They also believed that freedom of aesthetic expression (including the formal experimentation associated with the avant-gardes) served the ideal of freedom under socialism. On the extraliterary front, during the first years of the Revolution many ambitious and successful educational initiatives were undertaken, such as the literacy campaign in the countryside and the retraining of former prostitutes in the city. Following the Playa Girón (Bay of Pigs) invasion in 1961 and the October missile crisis the following year, revolutionary authorities saw the need to define a new society in opposition to the decadent, prerevolutionary one; to disseminate revolutionary culture and morality; and to defend the Island from the harassment visited on it by the United States and the Cuban exile community. The perceived need for political and social unity created an environment in which the authorities increasingly resorted to coercion with nonconformist and minority social populations, especially homosexuals. The most egregious example was the establishment of the Unidades Militares de Ayuda de la Producción (UMAPs), which ran from 1965 to 1967.[10] The CDRs or Comités de Defensa de la Revolución, locally based vigilance organizations, were also established, and volunteerism was strongly encouraged.

As part of its effort to effect change on public consciousness, the new revolutionary government immediately took over the news and cultural media. The international literary center Casa de las Américas, established in 1959, began publication of its extremely influential eponymous journal in 1960. By the summer of 1961—following the Playa Girón invasion—publishing initiatives were subordinated to specific cultural and political imperatives with increasing frequency. Guillermo Cabrera Infante and Heberto Padilla (both of whom would resurface in the debate on intellectual freedom in a much more explosive way seven years later) were dismissed as editors of the literary supplement *Lunes de Revolución* for being insufficiently dedicated to socialism; Sabá Cabrera's film *P.M.* showing the diverse nightlife of Havana was confiscated; and Fidel Castro announced in a series of speeches known as the "Words to the Intellectuals" *(Palabras a los intelectuales)* that artists and writers would be free to express themselves only in support of the Revolution, which had recently been redefined as Marxist-Leninist: "within the Revolution, anything; against the Revolution, nothing."[11] The Unión de Escritores y Artistas de Cuba (UNEAC) was established the same year and began publication of the journals *Unión* and the *Gaceta de Cuba* the following year. A system of prizes sponsored by the UNEAC, MININT (Ministry of the Interior), MINFAR (the Ministry of Armed Forces), and the Casa de las Américas effectively guided (and still guides) editorial policy by guaranteeing publication for selected novels.[12] After 1961 the "critical consciousness" *(conciencia crítica)* of the artist was increasingly subordinated to the "constructive consciousness" *(conciencia constructiva)* of the Revolution. Indeed, the aesthetically critical attitude of the intellectual was perceived as nothing more than a masked version of his own ingrained prerevolutionary ideologies.

The second, increasingly militant phase of the Revolution started in 1968 with the "Revolutionary Offensive," which entailed the centralization of virtually all private enterprise, the substitution of "moral" for material incentives to production, and the intensification of vigilance, ideological dogmatism, and militarism. The Cuban population began to show signs of cynicism toward the Revolution, and there was an increase in petty crimes such as truancy and absenteeism, types of delinquency that the socialist government described as demonstrations of "individualism" and "materialism." The spectacular failure to meet Castro's projected "ten-million ton" sugar harvest in 1970 came amid a general malaise caused by rationing, shortages, and pessimism about the Revolution, and the government realized that strong measures would be required to combat them.

The literary community was strongly affected by the tightening of cultural controls. The notorious Padilla affair, which began to heat up in 1967, was an index of the increasing strictures developing around cultural production, particularly that of literature.[13] At the end of the 1960s there was a retrenchment of attitudes among the writing community in Cuba, driven primarily by political pressure. The 1968 UNEAC congress called for increased ideological integration on the part of writers. At a round table discussion on the role of the intellectual in society held in 1969, Roque Dalton, René Depestre, Edmundo Desnoes, Roberto Fernández Retamar, Ambrosio Fornet, and Carlos María Gutiérrez discussed the responsibilities of the intellectual toward the Revolution. Fernández Retamar opened the discussion with the question "is it possible for an intellectual to exist outside the Revolution?" (es posible un intelectual fuera de la Revolución?) and in successive discourses by the other participants it became evident that this discussion was to mark a turning point in Cuban letters.[14] Dalton suggested (singling out José Lezama Lima several times) that literature up to this point had been a bourgeois activity, aimed solely at a cosmopolitan audience. Some authors "confessed" that their own intellectualism was a drawback in the revolutionary context, since only in capitalist countries could the intellectual consider himself superior to the masses. In a socialist context, the duty of the revolutionary artist was to submerge himself in the "social bath" (baño social) of the working collective and relinquish all claims to intellectual power, individualism, or superiority.[15] Desnoes's statement condemned the literary excesses and lack of political consciousness of the first years of the Revolution: "I believe that, to begin with, we have to recognize that many of us have been responsible for creating an illusion, the illusion that in Cuba there was absolute liberty to express ourselves freely, without recognizing the requirements of a society in revolution."[16] The meeting amounted to a formal repudiation of this "illusion": the initial revolutionary moment of agitation for aesthetic freedom and experimentation had ended. Fornet censured his own earlier work, and that of his colleagues, as "fundamentally aesthetic" and "decorative"; he regretted his dependence on external literary movements that were formalistic and therefore constitutionally nonrevolutionary. He explicitly linked sexual deviance with counterrevolutionary and decadent behaviors, characterizing his own former mode of expression as "deformed," and the UNEAC's denunciation of homosexual persecution (UNEAC had protested the UMAPs) as diversionary scandalizing on the part of "gays" *(mariposas)*.[17]

This meeting and the Padilla affair, which culminated in a bitter international polemic in 1971, marked the beginning of a period of increased government intervention in literary production, ultimately leading to the creation of didactic, formulaic, and artistically inferior novels. Fernández Retamar concluded the 1969 roundtable discussion with a summation of the role of the artist as a servant of the Revolution: "we must *invent* reality" (hay que *inventar* la realidad), he declared, under the ideological guidance of the socialist leadership. He emphasized the need to invent new genres to depict the newly invented reality.[18] Realism was considered an expression of "objective" reality and the only truly revolutionary mode of literary expression, while "formalism" was universally censured as effeminate, decadent, and counterrevolutionary. Revisionist histories of Cuban literature praised the "virile prose" of Félix Varela and José Martí, designating them as precursors of Fidel Castro and Che Guevara—whose "Palabras a los intelectuales" and "El socialismo y el hombre en Cuba" were best-sellers. Works by homosexual writers such as Virgilio Piñera were marginalized as "petit-bourgeois," "escapist," or "deformist"; Lezama Lima's masterpiece *Paradiso* (1966) was reduced to "prerevolutionary" status in literary manuals.[19] Marxist critic Ambrosio Fornet denounced the work of writers associated with the literary journal *Orígenes* as "pure aesthetic evasion" *(pura evasión estética)* and Lezama's "Oda a Julián del Casal" further strengthened suspicions of a link between homosexuality and "difficulty" in literature.[20] In 1977 the Cuban Minister of Culture, Armando Hart, declared that the purpose of literature in Cuba was, and *always had been*, the promotion of social progress and revolution.

While the Russian model of socialist realism was generally recognized as excessively reductive, critical realism as defined by Lukács had been a guiding light for some novelists of the first decade of the Revolution.[21] Nonetheless, as a result of changes in the ideological climate in the late 1960s and early 1970s, a version of socialist realism began to seriously overtake the vanguards represented by the *boom*. The police novel represented a return to pure, realistic prose fiction after an age in which narrative had threatened to move wholly into lyricism or regress to the epic.[22] In this context, the socialist detective genre became the most popular literature in Cuba.

Although the socialist detective novel was part of a general trend toward the imposition of a more rigid socialist ideology that culminated in the early 1970s, the literary climate that produced it began to form much earlier. At the turn of the twentieth century, the Uruguayan essayist José Enrique Rodó criticized the *modernista* movement for its frivolity, overadornment, and eroticism. In a spiritual antecedent to the Cuban socialist program, Rodó projected a utopian vision of solidarity based on virile comradeship (or male comradeship; his vision was fundamentally noncorporeal), intellectual preeminence, and moral purity. Regarded as part of a continuum that starts with Domingo F. Sarmiento's *Facundo* (or perhaps with Andrés Bello's "Agricultura de la zona tórrida"), Rodó's *Ariel* revisits the well-known Spanish American dichotomy of civilization and barbarism, spirituality and physicality or sensuality, and, by later extension (although this was almost certainly not Rodó's intention), weakness and strength, femininity and masculinity, preciosity and simplicity.

Rodó's depiction of the North American Goliath as a gross, materialistic Caliban—in opposition to the spiritually pure Latin American Ariel—was a starting point for the Cuban redefinition of its rhetorical relationship with the United States after the Revolution. In the fin de siècle context, readings of Rodó equated North American *utilitarismo* or *materialismo* with a dangerous and unbridled sensuality. This interpretation had particular resonance for Cubans fighting for the right to self-determination at the moment when *Ariel* was published in 1900. Because of Rodó's vaguely aristocratic viewpoint, *Arielismo* eventually came to be associated by some readers with extreme conservatism, and even fascism. Fernández Retamar's Marxist critique stands out among many responses to *Arielismo* for its vehemence. *Calibán* applies the Shakespearean paradigm to the discursive territory of the Cuban socialist project, modifying Rodó's aristocratic proclivities and reversing the referents in the Ariel/Caliban duality.

Fernández Retamar has sometimes been called the official cultural voice of the Cuban Revolution, and his reassessment of this duality had distinct repercussions for the socialist detective novel. Like Rodó's *Ariel*, Retamar's *Calibán* was a protest against North American hegemony in which he denounced "the crude, unjust and decadent character of the United States, and the continuous existence there of every kind of violence, discord, immorality and disorder."[23] Retamar linked the United States to Prospero, describing it as a nation of white Europeans who systematically exterminated the indigenous population and marginalized the black population, thus becoming a model for Nazism.[24]

Calibán realigned the Caliban figure with the Caribbean and described Mannoni's "Prospero complex," the subversive fear that the colonized slave produces in the colonizing master: "defined as a complex of unconscious neurotic tendencies that combine 'the figure of the colonial paternalism' and 'the portrait of a racist whose daughter has been the victim of an (imaginary) attempted rape by an inferior being.'"[25] The *mestizo* Caliban uses the language taught to him by Prospero to curse him but also to proclaim his own potency in contrast to the other's decadence. Fernández Retamar's essay linked Caliban to blackness, *mestizaje*, rebellion, masculinity, and authenticity, and the Caliban question to the legacy of *modernismo*. His essentially antimodernist stance had some points in common with the anti-*modernista* exchanges of the late nineteenth century, especially when seen as an adjunct to the nationalist project. Just as the closet homosexual was made into a metaphor for the cancerous or adulterated aspect of society, for many critics of European and Latin American modernist movements, the equivocal signification— or "effeminacy"—of *modernismo* weakened cultural identity, threatening the integrity of the body politic.[26] Retamar also denounced avant-garde criticism as "impressionist": "it is nothing but another version of impressionism . . . . But this 'type of creation' (I refer to the genus and not the species) was characteristic of another time: that of Walter Pater and Oscar Wilde: this is the 'creative criticism,' the 'artist as critic.'"[27] By choosing Pater and Wilde as the emblems of modernism, Retamar drew a clear connection between that movement, prerevolutionary values, fin de siècle decadence, and homosexuality. In Cuba, the postrevolutionary cult of realism was reinforced by the perceived need to strip away this "contaminating" ornament from literary production, leaving only the virile discourse of revolutionary truth.[28]

In his rationale of the detective novel, Luis Rogelio Nogueras also alluded to the union of formalist criticism, prerevolutionary homosexuality, and decadence. He described the traditional enigma novel as "dandyish": "Crime is a matter for the upper classes—this type of crime: exquisite, difficult, ingenious—and it is for them to commit it and resolve it. We are faced, in short, with detective dandyism."[29] The modernist "formalism" decried by Marxist Cuban critics can thus be understood from within this continuum as the defining characteristic of a literature (including classical detective literature) that is not only elitist but also effeminate. The new socialist detective genre projected the inverted Caliban paradigm, depicting the CIA and the Cuban delinquent alike as pale, effete, emasculated Prospero types or as immoral, brutish, and given to sexual disorders (desórdenes). In contrast, the Cuban forces of justice represented a newly civilized, militaristic, virile Caliban.

In 1972 a new, ideologically strategic literary genre was born under the auspices of the Cuban Ministry of the Interior: the socialist detective novel. With the inauguration of the *Concurso Aniversario del Triunfo de la Revolución*, the Ministry of the Interior broadcast the principles of the new genre. It was to be a medium for advancing government ideology, promoting conformity with revolutionary norms, and reinforcing the unmasking and suppression of antisocial tendencies:

> The competition is directed at developing this genre in our country, so the works that are presented will be on police themes and will have a didactic character, serving at the same time as a stimulus to prevention and vigilance over all activities that are antisocial and counter to the interests of the people.[30]

"Antisocial activities" was a nomenclature that covered a multitude of sins, mostly based on the pathologization of "deformed" character types also known as "nonintegrated" or "individualists" (*desintegrados* and *individualistas*). Homosexuality, acquisitiveness, intellectualism, secrecy, or a simple lack of enthusiasm for an endless series of volunteer projects could lead to being labeled antisocial.

The socialist detective novel was part of a project of ideological retrenchment that is often referred to as the "consolidation" of the Revolution. The effort to mandate cultural and ideological change intensified during this period, as illustrated by a number of initiatives. The most momentous of these was the *Primer Congreso de Educación y Cultura* in 1971, which reaffirmed the obligation of art to further ideological goals. As part of this project, the Congress denounced homosexuality and "intellectualism," which were tacitly linked in the revolutionary worldview under the rubric of "ideological diversionism": "The cultural media cannot serve as a framework for the proliferation of false intellectuals, isolated from the masses and from the spirit of our revolution, who want to convert snobbism, extravagance, homosexualism and other social aberrations into expressions of revolutionary art."[31] At the same time, in what Guillermo Cabrera Infante later described as a "strange history, almost clinical, of a government's obsession" (extraña historia, casi clínica, de una obsesión de un gobierno), homosexuals were prohibited from holding positions that put them in contact with the media.[32] A new policy was announced to exclude homosexuals from types of cultural activity that would give them influence over young people. The same year saw the eruption of the Padilla case and the publication of the first socialist detective novel, *Enigma para un domingo* by Ignacio Cárdenas Acuña. At that moment, homophobia was officially sanctioned in Cuban letters.

The new genre traced the root causes of criminal behavior to pre- and counterrevolutionary values and attitudes. The writers emphasized the virtues of "integration" and collective action through an adaptation of the police procedural, which allowed for detailed descriptions of the police hierarchy and the day-to-day activities and interactions of the police as a group. Aesthetically, the new detective novel represented a return to a plainer, more externalized kind of narrative.

Many Cuban detective novelists were journalists, poets, or critics. Leonardo Padura writes short stories and criticism; Luis Rogelio Nogueras and Guillermo Rodríguez Rivera were both poets before embarking on their detective-novelist careers. Nogueras was part of the so-called El Puente generation of revolutionary writers, who later were associated with the journal *El Caimán Barbudo.* The purpose of the Cuban detective novel was to advance party tenets using a traditionally popular medium, and writers, however conditioned they were to social commitment, struggled to justify the genre on aesthetic and literary grounds. As Luis Rogelio Nogueras, one of the most dedicated promoters of the genre, observed, "The Cuban detective novel, without disdaining its entertainment function—Brecht didn't disdain it in his rigorous conception of the theater—puts forward at the same time an educational function: to delve into the causes of criminality, socially and psychologically."[33]

Theodor Adorno argued that mass culture was a manufacturing project that he called the "culture industry," conceived by the capitalist ruling class for profit and ideological manipulation. The culture industry destroyed art, which was inherently critical and dehumanized—in the Orteguian sense—by replacing it with a noncritical, inherently conservative, and fraudulently realistic vision of humanity.[34] This "standardization" of art, Adorno conjectured, supported bourgeois values by promoting conformity and appropriating potential avenues of dissent for the dissemination of bourgeois values. Walter Benjamin expressed a similar concern, deploring the loss of artistic "aura" or authenticity. He feared that the mechanical reproduction and proliferation of art would lead to its appropriation by totalitarian forces for the purpose of manipulating a passive and uneducated public. Antonio Gramsci likewise posited that popular culture, including prosaic, realistic, or nonartistic literature, was a vehicle for "naturalizing" hegemonic views by subtly inserting them into the common sense of the public. The Marxist dramatist Bertolt Brecht advocated the insertion of formal elements into drama to keep audiences "alienated" and provoke independent reflection on the subject-object relationship. The Russian Formalists also equated "literary" with "deformed" or nonrealistic language: Roman Jakobson believed that language must be "made strange" in relation to its discursive context. For these thinkers, then, the denaturalized language of the avant-gardes represented the liberation of the mind from false consciousness.[35]

Cuban Marxists tried to reconcile these arguments in their theorization of the socialist detective novel. They wanted to curtail the popularity of British and North American detective novels in Cuba, which, they believed, "served, and serve, to stupify the masses and to distract them from the real social and political issues of our time."[36] The genre mystery story was an exemplar of the culture industry's tactics of obfuscation. At the same time, socialists felt an obligation to the aesthetic dictates of Brecht and the Frankfurt School, to aesthetic experimentation as antibourgeois. The socialist detective genre would combine entertainment value with the formal rigor necessary to achieve a Brechtian state of self-reflection (and self-improvement) in the reader.

Cuban debates on detective literature thus pitted formalism against representationalism, aestheticism against utilitarianism, elitism against socialism, and most importantly, escapism against realism. These dichotomies stemmed from a revisionist assessment of the modernist aesthetic, which, as Adorno's Frankfurt School colleague and adversary Georg Lukács believed, emphasizes the sensual, sensational perception of events as an essentially static phenomenon, in opposition to the "dynamic and developmental," or historical, vision posed by realism.[37] Lukács criticized the modernist/formalist project as inherently bourgeois. The implications of this split were twofold for later Marxist thinkers: first, aesthetic form was to be subject to the necessities of content, which is always centered on man as a social entity; and second, the realist worldview presumed that "potentiality" or change, which is effected through the interaction of man and environment, was both possible and positive. On the other hand, the socialist detective novel should be a realistic representation of society, rather than a flight into a bourgeois fantasyland: Lukács described the classic mystery as a falsely realist literature inspired by an escapist agenda: "an ideology of security, of exaltation, of the omniscience of those who guard the tranquility of bourgeois life."[38] The revised Marxist framework assumed a dialectical relationship between realist mimesis and formalist metaphor. Realism was the ethical mode of expression; formalism the "escapist" one. Following Lukács, many associated modernism and aestheticism with fascism, or at the very least, as a Spanish critic wrote, "a conservative moral stance" (una postura moral conservadora).[39] Lukács's theory of "objective reality" appealed to Cuban critics militating for "a stable conception of the world upon which to base value systems."[40] They saw representational literature as a more accessible and democratic form of art than the abstruse, metaphorical creations of the avant-gardes. The new detective novel was envisioned as a compass by which man would be able to orient himself; in short, "a representation of life, in which men accept themselves and their destinies, interpreted with greater scope, more profoundly, and with a much more orienting clarity than life itself usually gives them."[41]

The promulgation of the socialist detective novel was a kind of aesthetic warfare. The creators of the socialist detective novel felt it was their mission to undermine Anglo-American hegemony over the genre, which from the revolutionary perspective enshrined bourgeois imperialist values. Even though the focus of the genre was nominally on crime, the majority of the first and second wave of detective novelists minimized the presence and impact of the criminal element, presenting an idealized view of socialist society: police and popular vigilance, the cooperative spirit of the citizenry, and in particular the obvious perversity of the criminals. At a certain moment in each story, a revolutionary moral, called the *teque*, would be produced in case the reader had failed to grasp the ideological message.[42] The genre was a perfect example of what Fredric Jameson calls "the form of content": there were no "characters" but only "effects of system."[43] System, in this case, denoted both the aesthetic system, the socialist detective genre, and the ideological system, Cuban Marxism, to which the genre was mapped. Given the exigencies of didacticism in an already formulaic genre (not to mention that many of the authors weren't novelists at all but policemen and government functionaries), the result was often lackluster and predictable.

Despite its often dubious quality, the socialist detective novel enjoyed an unusually prominent position within Cuban literature as a whole. From 1971 to 1983 it accounted for 25 to 40 percent of published titles, and editions of between 20,000 and 200,000 copies routinely sold out within the first few days of publication.[44] However, with the escalation of the economic crisis in Cuba following the breakup of the Soviet Union in 1989, the relationship of the detective novel to official discourse changed. Publishing within Cuba was significantly disrupted due to paper shortages, and established systems of censorship began to ease somewhat in certain areas due to scarcity and, in general, the complications surrounding transport, communications, and all types of manufacturing, including literary production. As Cuban authors came into contact with other original detective novels in Spanish, they became increasingly critical of the trade-off between quality and ideology in the genre. In 1989 Leonardo Padura Fuentes took on what he perceived to be the weaknesses of his precursors—one-dimensional characters, lack of suspense, and paucity of literary art—and created a new type of Cuban detective novel. The development of the *neopoliciaco* genre in Spain and Mexico influenced the evolution of this new Cuban version, transforming it into a more critical, and at times even subversive, literature. Padura's Four Seasons tetralogy represents the first group of detective novels to openly express disappointment in the Revolution and is a sign of the new, more critical role of detective fiction in Cuba. Padura is virtually alone in this endeavor, although Pablo Bergues, a member of the National Assembly, has written novels critical of corruption in government, and Luis Adrián Betancourt acknowledges popular disillusionment with police and public vigilance in his recent, unpublished set of short stories "Un policía para la ciudad." Another interesting case is José Latour, whose anomalous English-language novel *Outcast* is discussed at some length in the following chapter.

While Padura's *neopoliciaco* retains many features of the original socialist detective novel, it is a much less dogmatic genre that questions the achievements of the Revolution by disrupting the stable, hegemonic notion of "objective reality" proposed by socialist literary theorists in the 1970s. Padura condemns the nurturing of this vision through the promulgation of narrowly defined social norms, such as those concerning gender identity, that have perpetuated intolerance and hypocrisy among leaders and citizens alike. He also depicts the delinquent as internal to the socialist community, as opposed to the externalized CIA or blatantly "antisocial" type, whose freakishness generally helped single him out as the criminal within the transparent socialist society.

Several critics (most notably Padura himself) have recently attempted to resituate the detective novel in the context of Cuban literary and social postmodernity. The approach is useful because it allows for an exploration and delineation of the parameters of postmodernity in both formal and ideological terms with respect to the unique circumstances of Cuban history: its late colonial status, its traditional literary preeminence, and the modernizing efforts of the Revolution. On the aesthetic front, postmodern literary theory typically offers a more hospitable forum for the study of popular literature—a fact that, whether they acknowledged it or not, most early practitioners of the socialist detective novel seem to have recognized, as the intrinsic intertextuality of the genre in Cuba demonstrates.

Padura has argued that his novels depict the clash of premodern society and postmodern knowledge. In many ways, the Cuban Revolution rapidly imposed a layer of scientific modernity over what was still largely (outside of Havana) an agrarian, preindustrial culture. The Revolution embraced modernizing and scientific paradigms: for the first time "population" became a quantifiable entity; the study of demographics came into vogue, and new ideas about youth formation and sex education gained currency as socialist goals. Sociological and scientific developments that had emerged in much of eighteenth- and nineteenth-century Europe and North America, and that can be traced in some of the foundational fictions of other areas of Latin America, had come to Cuba at the moment of its birth as a newly postcolonial nation.[45] The government's efforts to change or modernize sexual norms and behaviors, when they came into contact with the much older discourses of machismo and Catholicism, epitomized this conflict.[46]

Revolutionaries wanted to recreate Cuban society in a way that would not only redress the injustices of the previous regimes but instill new ideologies and values. As a contemporary sociologist put it, the Revolution aimed to create "a new basic personality" (una nueva personalidad básica).[47] The decadent past, epitomized in the revolutionary imagination by the American-run casinos and prostitutes of Havana, would be eradicated by literacy campaigns, job training, and the inculcation of the new socialist morality espoused by Ernesto "Che" Guevara. This morality was founded on the sacrifice and integration of the individual to society, as well as a constant process of self-questioning, evaluation, and improvement.

Though perfectly distinct from each other, both the cerebral detective and the tough guy were symbols of alienation. They represented superior beings in the Nietzschean sense, whose intellect, omniscience, exotic talents, or physical strength placed them above the rest of humanity. The protagonist of the new genre was constructed as a function of socialist ideology: he was undifferentiated by values, talents, or external attributes from the masses. He was supported in his efforts by socialist institutions, including government offices, and neighborhood vigilance organizations like the CDRs, Comités de Defensa de la Revolución. The socialist detective novel also attempted to construct heroes who were unmistakably masculine, yet free of the testosterone-driven impulses of the *macho*. From the beginning this identity was taken as a point of departure for the development of a novel of "impeccable morality" *(moral intachable)*[48] and it was embraced idealistically as an aesthetics of identity.[49]

As part of their confrontation with modernity, Latin American thinkers from José Enrique Rodó onward viewed the United States as the epitome of materialism. Socialist critics believed that the basic motivating factor in the classic mystery was greed: "in the detective novel the well-known motto *cherchez la femme* is replaced by the prosaic "look for the heir."[50] Agatha Christie was described as "poisonous and 'apolitical'" *(venenosa y 'apolítica').*[51] They also saw the North American hard-boiled novel as a realistic genre built around a central critique of the capitalist system. They emphasized the hard-boiled novel's emergence amid the spread of public corruption and gangsterism under Prohibition, the class and racial inequities exacerbated by the Depression years, and an ensuing disillusionment with the capitalist system as exemplified by mechanization, mass production, consumerism, and a burgeoning love affair with the automobile. According to this scheme, the hard-boiled detective was nothing more than a selfish and cynical man of business, and the criminal a predator amid the alienated, unconscious *lumpen*:

> The criminal wanders loose in the jungle of the city, his face blending with the indistinct faces of seven or ten million men and women, and the detective is a professional who charges for his work and for whom an unresolved crime is, not an insult to his intelligence, but bad business. Nothing more.[52]

Rejecting the hard-boiled formula as vicious, sensationalizing, and overly violent, the enigma story as effeminate, and both types as incompatible with their economic circumstances, Cuban writers redefined the genre according to Marxist literary and social theory. The effort to differentiate their detective novel both structurally and ideologically from the Anglo-Saxon type thus developed around both gender representations and economic differences. The outcome of this experiment was a hybrid, combining elements of the enigma novel, the spy novel, and especially the police procedural.

Although critics like Portuondo and Nogueras would claim that the form was entirely new, police procedurals had been in existence since the late 1950s, when the first dozen 87th Precinct novels by Ed McBain came out. After the Revolution, Cubans were also exposed to a great deal more of Georges Simenon's Inspector Maigret, in addition to mystery writers and critics from other communist countries, such as Bogomil Rainov, who placed more emphasis on police procedure than serendipitous genius. The police procedural, with its emphasis on organization and teamwork, proved to be a perfect vehicle for showcasing the smooth workings of the socialist system.

The two basic categories within the socialist detective novel—the detective novel or *novela policial* (e.g., Nogueras and Guillermo Rodríguez Rivera's *El cuarto círculo*, 1976) and the spy novel or *novela de contraespionaje* (e.g., Nogueras's *Y si muero mañana*)—were essentially quite similar.

The assumption that there was an inherent, metonymic affiliation between the individual and the nation under socialism united the spy and detective novels, since all crime, whether individual or corporate, was considered an assault on the integrity of the state. Even petty offenses such as absenteeism or pilfering from the workplace were potentially seditious, because they were indices of disaffection.

Despite their avowed distaste for the effeminate, reactionary whodunit formula, Cubans conformed far more closely to that type than they cared to admit. Unlike the alienated hard-boiled formula, both the whodunit formula (excluding Chesterton's) and the Cuban detective formula are based on a presumption of order and an unambiguous moral agenda. The Cubans did away with the eccentric genius but replaced him with an equally improbable selfless revolutionary. Until Padura's stories came along, rarely would evident rivalries or tensions disturb the relations among the ideally heterogeneous members of the force.

The spy and police stories intentionally reversed sociological metaphors appropriated from U.S. popular culture. As a socialist riposte to Cold War superhero fantasies, the Cuban spy story often resembled the idealistic, morally unambiguous works of writers prior to the Second World War, like those of Eric Ambler (himself a leftist).[53] The point of departure for this subgenre was its critical opposition to the "bourgeois capitalist" model represented by the James Bond stories, whose primary purpose was to "incite hatred against communism and distance the masses from revolutionary activity to convert them into 'silent majorities.'"[54]

Some of the better-known spy novels, like *Joy* and *Allá ellos* by Daniel Chavarría and *Y si muero mañana* by Luis Rogelio Nogueras, are relatively experimental in structure, using documentary techniques, innovative temporal paradigms, and narrative strategies such as testimonial, stream of consciousness, and the indirect style to describe the motives and actions of the CIA. Both writers present a subtler version of the positive/negative character duality, and critics such as Fernández Pequeño and Padura consider their novels superior specimens of the genre.

Popular culture theorist John Cawelti believes that clandestinity is the most salient element of the spy story because its transgressive nature makes it naturally fascinating.[55] The invisibility of the spy creates an atmosphere that allows the reader a voyeuristic participation, from an omniscient position, in an elaborate masquerade. (Although, as Chesterton's terrifying vision in *The Man Who Was Thursday* illustrates, the same sensations can easily cross the border into schizophrenia, abulia, and anomie.) However, true clandestinity is a secondary consideration in most Cuban spy novels. The Cuban spy genre depicts infiltration from the outside, usually by the CIA. The novelistic Cuban spy rarely suffers the ethical isolation of John Le Carré's or Graham Greene's spies. Like James Bond, he is supported by an army of professionals whose ideology matches his own. He demonstrates none of the frivolity of the gentleman spy, nor, on the face of things, Bond's implicit misogyny (like hard-boiled femmes fatales, the women in Bond novels die in large numbers).

The French critic Thomas Narcejac, often cited by Cuban critics, recognizes that sometimes the element of mystery and the element of investigation are at odds in the detective story.[56] This is certainly true of the Cuban detective novel, where the emphasis on the effectiveness of police procedure, on one hand, and the visibility of the criminal on the other rules out the use of traditional devices such as the red herring that protect the true solution from the reader. The role of the reader in the Cuban novel is also different from the traditional one: rather than being excluded by the author from the secrets of the mystery, the reader is meant to identify with the protagonists as they search for evidence against a more or less obvious miscreant (aside from having clear distinguishing features, the suspects usually give themselves away during interrogations by sweating profusely, swallowing dryly, or other cowardly behavior). Whereas the crime in the traditional mystery is usually committed by an insider—a member of the same family, class, or social group—whose guilt is to all practical purposes invisible, the criminal in the Cuban detective novel is deliberately externalized. He is literally labeled as nonintegrated, like Teo in *El cuarto círculo*, of whom his boss says, "he doesn't have much integration."[57] Murder is less prominent than other crimes, such as black-market activity, homosexual tendencies, or even absenteeism. And if murder is the crime in question, chances are that the murderer will also have perpetrated one of the pettier antirevolutionary crimes or "actividades antisociales" described by the Ministry of the Interior. The idealized vision of a perfectly transparent socialist society sacrifices suspense to didacticism.

The preoccupation with social concerns—and the corresponding devaluation of aesthetic elements—that writers were obliged to assume under the guidance of the socialist government ultimately prepared the way for the decline of the socialist detective genre, the centerpiece of governmental intervention in literary production. As the genre declined in popularity, its fortunes mirrored those of the Cuban revolution.

3.
Masking, Unmasking, and the Return to Signification

> "We all wear masks."
> —*Batman*
> *(Leonardo Padura Fuentes,* Máscaras*)*

*T*he socialist detective novel was part of an institutional program of nation building and national defense. Because it originated as a specifically ideological genre, the trajectory of its development over time exposes clearly the underlying social and political issues that motivated its invention. It also reveals the affiliations between ideology and gender in this process and demonstrates the ambivalence concerning gender roles within the newly defined socialist culture. Fidel Castro's regime associated bourgeois power structures with problematic sexualities and differentiated itself from them according to unambiguous gender norms. In attempting to portray the idealized, progressive society that the leadership was trying to create, the socialist detective genre nevertheless betrayed the continuing dominance of traditional gender roles.

The role of sexuality and gender (and genre) in nationalist projects is a topic that has been studied in depth by scholars outside Latin American letters, as well as within the Latin American context by David William Foster, Daniel Balderston, and Donna Guy, among others.[1] As they have pointed out, the building of a cultural identity often requires the identification and exclusion of undesirable elements of society. A complementary process is the construction of an imaginary exemplar or the seeking of an overarching commonality. An important part of the overall ideological project of the Cuban Revolution involved the interrogation and redefinition of gender roles under socialist ideals, the identification of certain sexualities with subversive or counterrevolutionary tendencies, and persecution based on sexual preference. This process was reflected in the propagandistic detective novel.

Because of the capitalist system's association with the sexual excesses of prerevolutionary Cuba, revolutionary rhetoric identified it with abnormal sexual behaviors and identities. These were represented in the Anglo-Saxon detective novel by the "crepuscular" Hercule Poirot and Nero Wolfe on one hand, and the excessively macho "imperialist" figures such as Ian Fleming's James Bond and Mickey Spillane's Mike Hammer on the other.[2] The "exquisite aficionados" (as critic Luis Rogelio Nogueras called Poirot) of the Anglo-Saxon mystery novel often exhibited suspiciously effeminate characteristics, such as Poirot's foppishness and Philo Vance's inordinate love for Etruscan pottery. Another critic described Poirot as "unquestionably homosexual," indicated by his "stubborn bachelorhood, his penchant for gossiping with aristocratic ladies, his impeccable *toilette,* his taste for perfumes and gourmet pleasures, and his domestic tendencies."[3] He also elaborated a convincing theory that Rex Stout's detectives Archie Goodwin and Nero Wolfe are the *macho* and *maricón* of a gay couple: Archie's physical, "hard-boiled" role contrasting with the effeminate habits of Nero Wolfe, an obsessive misogynist who cultivates orchids and gourmet cooking (Stout himself was the author of an article titled "Watson Was a Woman").

While one of the most significant revolutionary goals was to modernize deeply rooted social attitudes—especially those dealing with gender—through education, persuasion, and eventually coercion, the goals of the revolutionary leadership were sometimes at odds with its reality. The Revolution itself was defined by *machista* images and values that would not only prove resistant to change but became a built-in part of the increasingly militarized revolutionary culture.[4] As the (admittedly anti-Castro) journalist and historian Carlos Alberto Montaner has observed:

> The Cuban Revolution is the business of machos. . . . Machos drive jeeps, have big pistols, and make revolutions. . . . The Revolution, like certain brandies, is only for men. All that rhetoric of "assault brigades against the tomato," "the guerrilla fighters of the potatoes" and other belligerent formulas to get people to work, reflect the epic-machismo background of the Revolution. . . . [Each leader], each time he zips up his olive green fly and checks the lock in his pistol, reinforces his male ego and congratulates himself for being such a macho.[5]

Machismo is a complex set of cultural behaviors that associates masculinity with the ability to subordinate others. The relationship between Fidel Castro and the Cuban people was paternalistic and sexualized, positing a feminine "mass" who "vibrated" to the words of the virile leader. As Che Guevara described it: "Fidel and the masses begin to vibrate in a dialogue of growing intensity until they reach an abrupt climax, crowned by our shout of struggle and victory."[6] The same masses, represented as submissive and domesticated, thrived under Fidel's fatherly tutelage: "the masses carry out with unequaled enthusiasm and discipline the tasks set them by the government."[7] Guevara believed that the socialist consciousness (conciencia) of the individual within the masses was in a state of incompleteness. The revolutionary vanguard would always be ahead of the masses in the development and realization of conciencia, while the masses, less evolved, "must be submitted to stimuli and pressures of a certain intensity" (deben ser sometidos a estímulos y presiones de cierta intensidad) in order to develop their consciousness.[8]

Cuban revolutionary machismo connoted a conventionalized masculinity whose principal symbols (or symptoms) are physical courage, the ability to march long hours and use a machete, a predilection for coffee and big cigars, and a vociferous, if not totally physical, aversion toward homosexuality. The macho factor, with its connotation of physical prowess, was of fundamental importance to Castro, who linked virility, courage, and physical strength to the capacity to sustain a guerrilla war in the mountains. The revolutionary fighters were called "barbudos" in reference to their rugged, bearded character, and it was said that if an ordinary man could cross a room in nine paces, Fidel himself would need only three. In short, the image of "los barbudos" did not admit effeminacy.

Even though the Revolution itself was inherently a machista entity captained by the quintessential macho himself, leaders recognized that some aspects of machismo were counterproductive, particularly those that discouraged women from working. The official terminology attempted to reorient the word "machismo" or "male-ism" by inventing a complementary, pseudoscientific "hembrismo" or "female-ism."[9] This ingenuous nomenclature would supposedly transform machismo from a dominating ethos to a force for social equality. This construct represented a break with the old, prerevolutionary machismo, which was identified as egotistical and atavistic. The detective writer Justo Vasco emphasized that this old form of machismo contributed to "the socially negative" (lo socialmente negativo) that the detective novel had to combat.[10] Often, counterrevolutionary figures in the socialist detective novel are depicted as overly macho, as in Javier Morán's Choque de leyendas (1993), where the actions of Tony Saunders signal cowardice, lack of discipline, and a quasi-sexual pleasure in shooting that leads only to premature ejaculation:

An expert with steady nerves would have concentrated the first barrage on one flank, then on another and finally on the third, but the artillery-man was no expert, he lacked thousands of hours of patient dedication to the theory and practice of combat, he was overexcited, and the chaotic emission of projectiles had little effect.[11]

Vasco's *El muro* (1990) also attests to efforts to change the prejudice against women working, by condemning absenteeism and the small-mindedness of stay-at-home housewives. At the same time it betrays a deeper ambivalence with respect to the professional woman. The junction of these two sets of values is represented by a woman psychologist—who is described as "a mix of doctor and mother" *(entre doctoral y maternal)*—who suggests that housewives are bad citizens, bad wives, bad neighbors, and bad mothers: "In general they aren't aware of much. They live in queues, what they got here or there, suspecting their husbands of infidel-ity, envying their neighbors and doing the same thing day after day. And they never understand their kids."[12]

To promote women's rights and combat machismo, the Federation of Cuban Women (FMC), led by Raúl Castro's wife Vilma Espín until 1991, promoted the creation of day care centers; the Family Code of 1975, which stated that both partners in a marriage must share household and child-rearing duties; and a national curriculum for sex education. Machismo was officially rejected as counterproductive to the new ethic of equal partnership and reflective of prerevolutionary immorality.[13] Starting in the late 1970s, under the direction of Celestino Álvarez Lajonchere and Monika Krause, the National Working Group on Sex Education (GNTES) attempted to promote equal rights for women, as well as to depathologize homosexuality in its official teachings by distrib-uting the manual *Man and Woman Together (El hombre y la mujer en la in-timidad)* by East German Siegfried Schnabl. The final chapter explained that homosexuals "do not 'suffer' from homosexuality; they suffer from the difficulties that their condition causes them in society."[14]

The Cuban attitude toward male homosexuality has roots in both the traditional machista culture, which despises effeminacy, and the particu-lar ills of prerevolutionary Cuba, when the U.S. mafia and Batista's cro-nies had turned Havana into a tourist playground catering to decadent tastes of all kinds.[15] The image of Havana before the Revolution was of a city controlled by organized crime and plagued by prostitution, drugs, and gambling. Over 200,000 people in Havana alone worked as casino employees, servants, entertainers, and so on; of these, at least half were in the sex trades, including female, male, and gay prostitutes.[16] After the Revolution, these aspects of the past were the first to be attacked in the many campaigns to create a new, morally unadulterated Cuba, with homosexuality at the forefront of problems to be eradicated. Marriage and reproduction were still considered to be the ultimate goals for young people, and prostitution, homosexuality, and "free love" were condemned in textbooks as counterrevolutionary.[17]

Detective literature in Cuba thus reflected both official ventures toward tolerance and equality for women and, on a less overt level, deeply held *machista* beliefs about women's roles and especially about male sexual identity. Homosexuality was believed to be caused by environmental factors and was specifically associated with the city, where these "remnants" of prerevolutionary society persisted. The Cuban government was particularly concerned about the influence of counterrevolutionary "pederasts" over the youth of the Revolution.

Officially, teachers were seen as quite influential regarding the sexuality of their pupils. Thus, when a teenage girl commits suicide in Justo Vasco's *El muro*, the investigator goes to her chemistry teacher to find out about her sex life. He then consults a psychologist and they speculate about her "late" blooming and compare her sexual activity with the statistically and normatively acceptable behaviors advocated by sex manuals. Given the programmatic emphasis on training teachers in sex education, extramarital sex was particularly frowned on when it occurred within a pedagogical or mentoring relationship. Teachers were thus especially suspect as possible disseminators of homosexuality among Cuban youth, and many detective novels depict questionable relationships between teachers—both men and women—and their teenage students. In Leonardo Padura's *Vientos de cuaresma* (1993), a young teacher has sexual relations with her teenage students. The outcome is predictably catastrophic for all parties, but the teacher, whose corruptive, marijuana-smoking, counterrevolutionary morality is made blatantly evident by her expensive stereo equipment and designer clothes, is the one who is most severely punished: she is the murder victim. (A promiscuous single woman is also the murder victim in *La voz de las huellas* [1981] by Edmundo Mas and Isabel Ramírez.)

These ideas on education, environment, and homosexuality were not limited to, nor even necessarily original to, Cuba: sociologists, pedagogues, and psychologists abundantly cited American and European sources. To a certain extent, too, Cuban attitudes have changed along with those of the rest of the world: homosexuality has for the most part been decriminalized and is much less persecuted today than it was in the days of the UMAPs or the 1980 Mariel exodus.[18] Peculiar to Cuba, however, and crucial to the Cuban manifestation of homophobia, was the linkage of nationalism and sexuality in the tradition of machismo, reinforced by the newer, Fidelist brand of Marxism-Leninism.

Two foundational texts on sexuality and nationalism are George Mosse's *Nationalism and Sexuality* and Michel Foucault's *History of Sexuality*.[19] Both Mosse and Foucault link the construction of stereotypes of masculinity and femininity with the modern project of nation building and identity. In his *History of Sexuality*, Foucault questions the "repressive hypothesis" of public and nonreproductive sexual behaviors with the advent of bourgeois society in the seventeenth century. Capitalism, according to this hypothesis, was a natural ally of sexual taboos that excluded any activity that did not multiply the race; while on the other hand, repression was accompanied by the desire to transgress the silence surrounding taboos through discussion and analysis of sex. Rejecting this theory of repression, Foucault instead suspects that the "discourse of sex" is in fact an instrument of power wherein those who appear to transgress may in fact be controlling the uses of pleasure itself: "I do not maintain that the prohibition of sex is a ruse; but it is a ruse to make prohibition into the basic and constitutive element from which one would be able to write the history of what has been said concerning sex starting from the modern epoch."[20] The modern era was characterized by increasing regulatory discussion about sex: starting with the efforts of the Counter-Reformation to criminalize everything pertaining to "the flesh" by transforming acts and thoughts into the language of confession; and proceeding in the nineteenth century through medicine, education, sociology, and psychology. This proliferation of discourse was aimed primarily at promoting reproduction through the pathologization of nonreproductive sex, including homosexual, onanist, or recreational activities.[21]

One outcome of this process was the definition of homosexuality (among other pathologies) as an essential trait marked by externally visible characterological defects, rather than as a variable set of activities: for the first time, individuals could be identified and categorized according to their sexual activity. Foucault thus replaces the repressive hypothesis, rooted in the perception of nineteenth-century repression/reproduction and twentieth-century enlightenment or tolerance, with one based on the increased volume of the discourse itself over the last three centuries. Moreover, he emphasizes that the focus of the discourse was not the population as a whole, but the bourgeois family, and was intended, first, to promote health and longevity, and hence hegemony, among that class. Later it would be used to suppress the same behaviors in the lower classes.

The pathologization of sexual behaviors accompanied the same modern developments that led to the birth of the detective genre, described here by Thomas Narcejac:

> First and foremost, the sociological conditions: in the first place, you have the "disturbing event"; that is, the mysterious crime described in the newspaper, the drama turned into spectacle. . . . In second place, the scientific conditions. Analysis of fingerprints, clues, physiognamy or phrenology to determine an individual's character according to his facial features. In the third place, a picturesque or prosaic "subject," the case, articulated in a rigorous "form": the detective investigation; finally, as nexus connecting all these elements, the detective, half scoundrel and half wise man.[22]

Like Foucault's "medicine of sex," the conversion of crime into public spectacle pathologizes the "disturbing event," while the disciplines of forensic medicine and physiognomy are concerned with its visible traces. Revealing crime in this way therefore depends very much on its visible aspect.

As Amelia Simpson points out, a significant characteristic of the socialist detective novel is "the extreme visibility of the criminal against the background of actively mobilized, ever vigilant masses."[23] In a similar vein, Justo Vasco wrote in 1983 that the job of the socialist detective novel was to unmask or make evident the negative elements of society: "to constantly assume the duty of unmasking any social or individual entity that permits the commission of a crime or an aggression against the Security of the proletarian State."[24] Vasco describes the socialist detective genre as the space of a contest between "the socially positive" and "the socially negative": socially positive behavior is that which is integrated—and thus attracts minimal attention—while socially negative behavior is that which is differentiated or alienated, as indexed by primarily external markers such as an odd physical appearance, flamboyant behavior, or unusual possessions. The detective novel nominally explores crime from within Cuban society, but the criminal, by his very nature, cannot truly be a part of that society. First and foremost, the Cuban delinquent is Other, a nonconformist.

Cuban detective novels and spy stories thus emphasize the external aspect of a person as a key to his character. As Vasco affirms, "it is obvious that each of these characters requires a different treatment, the same in literature as in life. But all require the same attention, the same vigilance on the part of society."[25] As a result, the novelistic delinquent is by necessity "deformed," usually both morally and physically; his identity is an outcome of the pathologization of undesirable types: *desintegrados, individualistas*, prostitutes, blacks and mulattos (despite the official anti-racist stance), Cubans of Chinese descent and Jews, and above all, homosexuals. The last are usually referred to as *antisociales*, a term that encompasses other crimes as well. These ingredients were meant to provoke aversion in the reader, as well as to advertise the infallibility of vigilance. Indeed, the detective protagonists were often so flat and schematic that critics worried that readers would sympathize with the negative characters, because they were portrayed with more realism and detail.[26]

It is important to understand the nature of the idealized collective, for which individual consciousness, creativity, infiltration, immorality, and nonconformism can all be construed as crimes against the state. During the first decades of the socialist regime, the U.S. government tried no less than thirty times to assassinate Fidel Castro. Biological and other types of sabotage were a constant threat, as was military incursion, confirmed by the attack at Playa Girón in 1961. However, contrary to the widely accepted theory that the detective novel (especially the hard-boiled variety) was a reaction to a surge in crime, the birth of the Cuban detective novel apparently corresponded to a drastic decrease in everyday crime.[27] The Cuban socialist novel, indeed, responded much more to a need to foster national solidarity against external threats than to an actual internal crisis.

Because Marxism privileges the well-being of the social organism as the desired outcome of individual perfection, crime in the Cuban socialist model violates the norms cultivated by the Revolution. The new state founded its strength on social conformity as a way of promoting solidarity against the imperialist enemy. External signs of nonconformity were discouraged.[28] The UMAPs held homosexuals and other nonconformists, especially those who appeared overly concerned with their clothing and external appearance. Thus ideas about antisocial activities, integration, and disintegration, as defined by juridical and sociological norms, provide a revealing background for the constructs of delinquency that appear in the Cuban detective novel.

The perception of homosexuality in Cuba, as in Latin America as a whole, has typically been limited to the "passive" or "feminine" participant—the *maricón* or *loca*—who is the more visible in a homosexual pair. Scholars of homosexual cultures in Latin America are unanimous in pointing out the presumptive connection between effeminacy, signaled by behavior that is visibly passive, weak, lazy, frivolous, melodramatic, or "hysterical," and male homosexuality in Latin American societies.[29] Conversely, physical prowess and a taste for sports signify heterosexuality. Fidel Castro himself obliquely endorsed this perspective in a 1965 interview:

Homosexuals must not be allowed in positions where they are able to exert influence over young people . . . we must inculcate our youth with the spirit of discipline, of struggle, of work. In my opinion, everything that tends to promote in our youth the strongest possible spirit, activities related in some way with the defense of the country, such as sports, must be promoted.[30]

As a means of portraying either (positive) militancy or (negative) lack of integration, detective novelists characterized both detectives and delinquents according to nineteenth-century forensic theory. Cesare Lombroso's influential writings on criminology related mental state to biological condition. According to this type of theory, visible good health reflected moral rectitude and was measured according to positivist tenets (including those describing racial hierarchies).[31] Even if he was one-dimensional or nondescript, the socialist protagonist often revealed a mania for physical development, as in the following example from one of the best-known novels of the genre, Daniel Chavarría's *Joy* (1977):

His daily workout was tough: twenty-five minutes of jumping rope, forty chin-ups, one hundred squats, a hundred sit-ups with two kilograms of counterweight at his neck, forty push-ups, all preceeded by a five-minute warm-up and followed by five minutes of stretching. It wasn't anything exceptional, but it was enough to keep him in magnificent physical shape.[32]

All Cuban heroes smoke extreme quantities of tobacco, an index of both manliness and patriotic consumerism.

In contrast to the aberrant but intellectually superior criminals of nineteenth-century detective literature, criminals in Cuban detective novels were often depicted as pathetic, weak, inept, or simply banal. Physical infirmity signaled mental, nervous, and/or moral weakness, due either to degeneration (associated with homosexuality) or a monstrous atavism (associated with excessive machismo). The villain in *La voz de las huellas* is described by the local CDR (Comités de Defensa de la Revolución) representative, or *cederista*, as a compendium of repellant characteristics that suggest both homosexuality and criminality: "a really weird guy, blonde, tall, with really long arms, with bulging eyes like a toad. Those two always go around together in the car. So much . . . that it makes you wonder!"[33] The CIA Colonel in *Joy* is of the atavistic and bestial persuasion: "a giant gray dog came to him, and the Colonel caressed him with a childish, inanely sentimental gesture."[34]

Effeminacy is synonymous with cowardice and subterfuge. Once identified as a homosexual, a character will inevitably turn out to be involved in (other) criminal activities. The following descriptions are from one of the first socialist detective novels, Armando Cristóbal Pérez's *La ronda de los rubíes* (1973), which became something of a model text for the genre:

> They have a friend named Luisito from before [the Revolution] . . . very delicate type, you know what I mean? He wears those fancy clothes . . . And one afternoon, well, this mulatto comes to see him. He asked me where he was, a big strong mulatto, looked like a working guy, but I don't know, all fixed up.[35]

Not only is Luisito effeminate but he is also manifestly feeble and poorly developed, at only five feet four inches. Added to his debility is what the speaker obviously considers a perverse taste for big strong mulatto men. The detective, being a good macho, feels extremely uncomfortable while searching for the delicate one, perhaps because he is concerned about being *quemado*—condemned by association: "every time he asked for information about him, he had a hard time describing him without putting himself in an embarassing situation."[36]

In addition to external threats, internal ideological factors within the Revolution favored conformity to gender norms. The brand of Marxism-Leninism that Castro embraced had never been sympathetic to alternative sexualities or lifestyles. Stalin had interned homosexuals in camps, and he outlawed homosexuality in the Soviet Union in 1934, enacting particularly stiff penalties for male prostitution. Homosexuality was also explicitly associated with class, specifically the "degeneracy of the fascist bourgeoisie."[37] And the repression of homosexuality under Stalin, as later in Cuba, was accompanied by a glorification of the family and individuals in terms of their reproductive potential.

The persecution of homosexuality under the Revolution thus came from a variety of traditions, including adherence to Stalinist tenets, Catholicism, machismo, male prostitution under Batista, and the deliberate politicization of gayness as a holdover from prerevolutionary, presocialist society. After the Revolution, homosexuality came to be associated with male prostitution for American tourists in prerevolutionary Havana and therefore served as a grotesque expression of the colonial relationship and of decadence under capitalism.[38]

Two novels in particular, *Y si muero mañana* by Luis Rogelio Nogueras (1978), and *Máscaras* (1997) by Leonardo Padura Fuentes, show the trajectory of the gendered metaphor of the Revolution from the apogee of the Cuban detective novel in the mid-1970s to a kind of renaissance in the 1990s. In the former, the Revolution is represented both metaphorically and metonymically as a virile, heroic entity, momentarily threatened by an effeminate, decadent CIA.[39] The latter deals rather sympathetically with the marginalized life of transvestites and homosexuals in Havana at the end of the 1980s. Padura's policeman protagonist is himself a somewhat marginalized being, in stark contrast to the integrated police figures of his precursors. His macho identity is drawn into question when he comes into contact with the gay underworld, which holds a perverse fascination for him. His questioning of the Revolution takes place through the metaphor of a problematic sexuality that involves, as the title indicates, the masking of identity, role playing, and the exhumation of specific symbols of Cuban literary culture (like the members of Orígenes) that have been buried by homophobic revolutionary discourse.

Y si muero mañana is a counterespionage story. The protagonist is named Ricardo, but his nom de guerre is Bruno, a possible allusion to Manuel Cofiño's hero of the same name in *La última mujer y el próximo combate* (the 1971 Casa de las Américas prizewinner). Both sacrifice not only marriage but their lives for the Revolution. Ricardo is a revolutionary who has been sent to live in Miami to spy on the CIA and the Cuban exile community, referred to invariably as *gusanos*. This community, for its part, is concocting a plot to invade the Island. The novel focuses on the activities of Ricardo in Miami, New York, and California, those of his colleagues in Havana, and the machinations of the CIA.[40]

Nogueras uses distinctly gendered, Lombrosian descriptions to represent the enemy as soulless and effeminate. In the first place (and contrary to North American cinematic representations), almost all the agents of the CIA are Jewish.[41] A few short descriptions of the agent Harry Tertz demonstrate that Jewishness is tantamount to weakness and decadence: "In the eyes of the tired old man, in his obstinate Jewish face, there appeared a look of uncertainty."[42] Tertz has an unusually small head, and when praised he is "grateful like a dog" (agradecido como un perro). In contrast to the virile solidarity of the Cubans, the CIA officers display "typical" feminine behaviors: back-stabbing competition, gossip, betrayal, and mutual contempt. Like Ian Fleming's supervillains (Blofeld, Goldfinger, Dr. No), the younger agents depend, not on physical courage, but on the use of technology. Their methods are distinguished by clandestinity, subterfuge, and cowardice, as exemplified by the main villain, Mickey Normand:

> The Marine Corps had toughened him, but what had really made him hard was his work in the secret development center for chemical, biological and psychological weapons in Dugway, Utah. There, attached to the CIA, he had seen first-hand the face of modern warfare, a kind of warfare

that guys like Duke (and even Kaplan) weren't ready for: aerosols that could induce hallucinations and death, ultrasounds that drove people insane, microbes that a single genetic mutation would transform into deadly weapons. Total, invisible war.[43]

Normand is hardened emotionally and morally, but he is physically passive and sends subordinates to do his dirty work. While Ricardo, a man of action, has sacrificed love of a woman for that of the Revolution, Normand views women as commodities and passes his time idly watching Playboy Bunnies.

Clandestinity was irrelevant to the early socialist detective novel, because the alienated individual, by his very nature, had to stand out from the integrated masses. Conversely, the detective or spy figure, as an integrated member of society, was often quite nondescript. It often happened that, as opposed to the conventionally named detectives, *cederistas,* and general populace, criminals were given nicknames like "Lefty" (el Zurdo), "the Gimp" (el Cojo), "Skinny" (el Flaco), "Twenty Bucks" (Veinte Pesos), or even "Sweet Eyes" (Ojos bellos) that drew attention to distinguishing or abnormal physical features.[44] Diminutives also denoted effeminacy, weakness, and criminal tendencies: thus Luisito, Alfonsito, Carlitos, etc., as "mariconcitos," were all suspect. The very process of description, in fact, performed an unmasking, often feminizing function in the socialist detective novel, as Nogueras stated in a discussion of *El cuarto círculo*:

> The only character who is not described is the detective, Hector Roman (we only know his age: 35 years old in 1973). Sherlock Holmes is thin, with a hook-nose and a high forehead; Poirot uses hairspray, has a handlebar mustache and looks basically like a foppishly-dressed toad; Maigret has gray hair, stooped shoulders and is on the tall side. But Hector Roman . . . is however you want to imagine him.[45]

In Ángel Cardi's *El American Way of Death* (1980), the two detectives don't even have names. *Y si muero mañana* makes this technique even more explicit. Ricardo is a lone hero; he is relatively invisible: a function of action rather than qualities. His physical description is sketchy but masculine—we only know that he is "tall, thin, and very un-Latin looking" (alto, delgado, y de rostro muy poco latino) so that he can more easily blend into his North American milieu, but Normand is minutely described and distinctly feminized. He has a "sharp face" (rostro afilado), "very well-groomed hair" (una cabeza muy bien peinada), his hands are "white as chalk" (blancas como el yeso).[46] He smokes light cigarettes, an obvious sign of frailty in a genre whose protagonists chain-smoke Cuban cigars and cigarettes.

The counterrevolutionaries are, if possible, even less attractive than the North Americans, and Nogueras inserts thinly disguised references to real people, often homosexuals in exile: "Lunch in the house of the obese, flaccid Leon Ortiz was prolonged by the presence of a certain Arnaldo Rodiles, a 'worm' who had emigrated to Paris after publishing a moderately successful novel in Cuba."[47] The *gusanos* (the term used by patriotic Islanders to describe the exiles) are not overtly effeminate: they are unreformed machistas whose counterrevolutionary lust is due to an excess of testosterone. Ortiz is a purveyor of pornography and has, as well as a "greasy face" *(cara sebosa)*, a promiscuous daughter who runs around "in a sweater without a bra, as if to show off her big nipples."[48] His friend's name—Winston "Macho" Barroso—combines slavish consumerism (to American tobacco), macho arrogance, and the connotation that his face is covered with pimples. Another character is "a big strong guy, who looked like a butcher and sounded like a drill sergeant" (un hombre fornido, con aspecto de carnicero y voz de sargento político). Like Ortiz and Barroso, he too has dermatological problems; his face is "lardy" *(mantecoso)*. This greasy, overly hormonal machismo masks an essential cowardice among the exiles: the latter, when confronted with a CIA agent (who, predictably, has "delicate lips" *[labios finos]*), is overcome with fear: "he was so terrrified that he submitted docilely to the needle. His bull-like body trembled like jello."[49] All visible signs of virility—strong bodies, physical strength—are modified by other, even more evident symptoms of moral atavism, such as obesity or greasy skin.

Nogueras's protagonist is carefully portrayed as a regular guy, whose appetites conform to masculine norms without being extreme. In spite of the fact that he is accustomed to drinking heavily before noon, Ricardo is not presented as an alcoholic. Nor is he a machista of the same type as the *gusanos*. But, as a "normal" guy, he can't help spending a certain amount of time observing the breasts of the women he comes across: in addition to the breasty *gusana (tetona)*, the second woman he sees is described only as "a nondescript face, some sagging breasts under a housecoat" (un rostro vulgar, unos senos flojos bajo la bata de casa). In another scene Ricardo goes out with his former lover, and her breasts vibrate with emotion. Nonetheless, the "true" sexist is the primitive *gusano* who objectifies women in the street by yelling comments about their behinds, or the soulless agent of the CIA, who identifies a former one night stand by looking at her breasts.[50]

In nineteenth-century sociological discourse, certain character traits or behaviors were considered an indication of criminal tendencies. This discourse was still quite active in the first decades of the Revolution, as the work of sociologist José Ángel Bustamante confirms. Loquacity, for one, was associated with the need for subterfuge, or indirectness, on the part of Afro-Cuban slaves and therefore could be taken as an indication of dishonest or servile character.[51] In the revolutionary view, excessive talkativeness was a sign of laziness in an atmosphere where silent productivity equaled patriotism. It was also seen as a sign of possible subversive activity: in one short story by Eduardo Heras León, Rosendo el Cojo is a talkative factory saboteur whose words infect others with his own discontent. By contrast, both the detective Héctor Román and the spy Ricardo are predominantly uncommunicative, while the CIA agents' words are carefully recorded, as is the disjunction between their words and their perfidious thoughts.

Parallel to the treatment of his protagonists' taciturnity, Nogueras's image of Cuba is hazy and conspicuously lacks the obsessive detail communicated in his portrayal of life in the United States. The cumulative effect of English words and phrases—the repetition of details, clichés, brand names, and long descriptive passages—is overwhelming and kaleidoscopic and vividly evokes the corrupting nature of capitalism: *business, free-lance, drugstore, porno shop, dirty work, yellow cab, bunker, plus tax* (Cubans were not taxed until the mid-1990s). Numerous brand names signify the unbridled consumerism of the North but also titillate the deprived Cuban reader: *Playboy Bunny, Ford Torino, Rolex GMT, Hertz,* and of course the vital accoutrements of the manly spy: liquor *(Martell, Courvoisier Reserve, gin-and-tonic, manhattan),* tobacco *(Camel, Tareyton),* and guns *(Browning, Magnum, Star 9mm).* This relentless enumeration links mindless consumerism with the brand-conscious James Bond, with whose elitist tastes in cars, wine, and women we are all familiar.[52] Because of the general state of necessity in Cuba, the possession of material objects is generally portrayed as the projection of effeminacy on an economic plane. In *Joy,* Chavarría's *gusano* villain recalls the luxury of his wealthy prerevolutionary days: "He remembered that in Cuba he always had the finest objects, even a little faggy, like a worked-gold cigarette case with a little music box, or that long marble cigarette holder he had used the night of the party Papa Batista's girlfriend threw."[53] North Americans often favor German products and icons—German Shepherds, German beer, even German food—an allusion to their fascist tendencies and their general sociopathy.

For Nogueras, the materialism of North American culture is greatly exacerbated in the exile community of Miami, where the Americanized

Cubans suffer a pathological need to acquire property, the obscene pro-liferation of which serves "every commodity, every taste, at all hours, all styles, every whim" (todas las comodidades, todos los gustos, todas las horas, todos los usos, todos los caprichos). The insistent repetition of the word *todos* lets the reader imagine a gamut of perversions, sexual or otherwise. Even the language of Miami has become corrupted: "a half-fossilized Spanish . . . that in its twists and inversions had been frozen somewhere between English and the street slang of Pila and Colón" (un español en conserva . . . que, en sus giros y modismos, se había quedado detenido a medio camino entre el inglés y el caló de Pila y Colón). It is a patently degenerate language, contaminated by Spanglish words like *hamanhuevo* and *fokear*.[54]

Nogueras, the revolutionary and nominal supporter of a parame-trizable society, is paradoxically disgusted by "the heterogeneous mass" *(la masa heterogénea)* in Miami, precisely because the old signifiers of class and occupation have disappeared in the new medium:

> The double agent mixes with the pimp, the erstwhile girl of a good family with the Colón Street whore, the unlicensed doctor with the thirty-year old pretty-boy, the Batista supporter with the radical nationalist, the mediocre singer with the politician, the loiterer with the soldier of for-tune . . . the fanatical Catholic with the gangster.[55]

This "strange fusion" *(extraña fusión)* perturbs Ricardo not only as a sort of political miscegenation, but also because of its element of masquerade. Just as a whore can mingle with (or hide among) the "good girls," the enemy (the dandyish, implicitly homosexual *pepillo*) can conceal himself behind the heterosexual mask.

One of the great claims of the socialist detective genre is that it com-bats the undeniable xenophobia of the Bond model.[56] Yet Nogueras's anti-Semitism, implicit in the portrayal of the CIA, extends to overt racism in an encounter with a Chinese Shaolin hit man whose "squinty eyes" *(ojillos)* are, predictably, inscrutable. The Chinese assassin also ex-hibits homosexual characteristics. Chinese workers were imported to the Island without their families; and, as it was prohibited for them to marry into other ethnic groups, they acquired a reputation as homosexuals. This particular Chinaman is also a Shaolin priest and therefore known to abstain from female company, deriving his sensual pleasures from the art of killing.

Nogueras's novel was published in 1978, during a time of relative economic and ideological stability. A new phase of the Cuban Revolution began in 1986, when economic crisis, a growing black market, deteriorating relationships with the Soviet Union and Eastern bloc countries, and the apparent failure of government policy to improve the *conciencia* of many Cubans provoked the initiation of the "Rectification Campaign." Private enterprise was again restricted while foreign investment, particularly in tourism, was encouraged. The use of moral incentives returned as the shortage of material goods worsened.

An unexpected result of the deepening crisis was a relaxation of some aspects of political control. The Partido Socialista Popular allowed members of religious organizations to join the party as of 1991; the use of dollars was legalized; and private enterprise, for example the renting of rooms to tourists, was officially recognized as legitimate, even if, as some Cubans believe, only for the purposes of taxation. At the same time, a movement to restore the work of homosexual writers to its rightful place in Cuban literature took hold in the late 1980s. A volume of Piñera's short stories was published in 1987 (stories with homosexual content were expurgated); Lezama Lima's *Paradiso* was reprinted there for the first time since its limited run in 1966; Senel Paz's "El lobo, el bosque y el hombre nuevo" was published; Severo Sarduy was restored to the literary canon. On the other hand, crime and juvenile delinquency increased drastically, especially prostitution, theft, and black market activities (it still does not approach the crime rate in the United States or other Latin American countries).

Coincident with the start of the economic crisis, Cuban writers began to question the necessity of strict adherence to ideological utility and socialist realism in literature. In the late 1980s Cubans began to participate in international discussions about the detective genre at conferences like the *Semana Negra* in Gijón, Spain (founded by Paco Ignacio Taibo II in 1988). Manuel Vázquez Montalbán, Taibo, and other *neopoliciaco* writers showed Cubans a viable Spanish-language alternative to the Anglo-Saxon model.

As they were exposed to international currents in crime literature, Cubans became intensely self-critical. Justo Vasco, Leonardo Padura, and José M. Fernández Pequeño censured the schematic characters and the general lack of writerly prose in the socialist detective novel. Padura complained that, in spite of having the virtue of depicting events of the 1970s that were real and immediate for most Cubans, the genre typically represented a false reality: "The Cuban detective novel of the 70s was apologist, schematic, permeated with ideas of a socialist realism that was all socialist but very little realist."[57] Part of the problem stemmed from the uncritical climate created by political pressures, which he called "conformist and laudatory to an extreme" (conformista y laudatoria en extremo).[58] Even so, critics including Padura consider Nogueras's *Y si muero mañana* (winner of the 1978 UNEAC prize) and Daniel Chavarría's *Joy* the two best examples of the socialist detective novel.

In 1989 the dramatic arrest and execution of the distinguished General Arnaldo Ochoa Sánchez provided a final disillusionment for many in Padura's generation. Ochoa and other high-ranking officers were condemned for drug-trafficking, hard currency appropriation, and negligence of duty; they were executed by firing squad. Known as "Causa 1" (Case #1 of 1989), the Ochoa trial was widely regarded as a sham intended to eliminate some independent-minded officers amid political uncertainties provoked by the fall of the Berlin Wall. Ochoa was an officially designated "Hero of the Revolution," uncomfortably well-connected abroad, and apparently given to flippancy on ideological matters. One analyst noted that throughout the affair both Fidel and Raúl Castro commented repeatedly on his "mask":

> A rather bizarre facet of the Ochoa case was the official assessment of the military officer's conduct and attitude. In strong terms, he was accused of hiding aspects of his activities "beneath certain features of his personality" which made it difficult to discern his "true thoughts." In other words, Ochoa may have been dissimulating or "wearing the mask."[59]

The Ochoa affair marked the unofficial death of the socialist detective novel; it allowed Raúl Castro's MINFAR (Cuban Revolutionary Armed Forces) to absorb the MININT, which had sponsored the genre, and at the same time discredited the intelligence community and the armed forces, which had provided its heroes.

Inspired by multiple disenchantments with the detective novel and the political and economic situation in Cuba, Padura began writing the Four Seasons tetralogy of detective novels set in 1989. His intention was not only to improve on the existing detective stories but to create a more accurate, realistic vision of Cuban life, showing the imperfections of the Revolution as well as its positive side. A member of the "invisible generation" of Cubans born just before the Revolution, Padura and his contemporaries missed all the promise of its early days, living through constant hardships and disappointments that made them skeptical toward official discourse and its organs in literature. Frustrated with schematic socialist novels, they were nostalgic for the literary artistry of the *Orígenes* generation.

To begin his renovation of the socialist detective novel, Padura had to break with the hegemonic "positive/negative" character dichotomy by creating more complex, multidimensional characters. His policeman protagonist, Mario Conde, is "a solitary guy, gloomy, skeptical, pensive, a heavy drinker" (un tipo solitario, triste, escéptico, reconcentrado, bastante borracho).[60] As the protagonists became more realistic and multifaceted, the delinquents ceased to be mere petty thieves, degenerates, and *gusanos*: for the first time, Padura described corrupt officials, dirty policemen, the black market, *jineteras* (prostitutes), and other facts of life that had been glossed over by previous novelists. His detective novels share the critical ethic of the North American hard-boiled novel, combined with literary techniques derived from his thinking on Cuban postmodernity.

Padura considers his own writing to be aesthetically postmodern, in the sense that it uses intertextuality (in *Máscaras*, the Piñera subtext, among other things); incorporates elements from popular culture (baseball, pop music); focuses on all aspects, desirable and undesirable, of Cuban society; and subordinates the rationalist elements of the mystery to social criticism and novelistic art. Perhaps the most postmodern feature is his fully realized, slightly decentered hero, Mario Conde, who has much more in common with Philip Marlowe and Vázquez Montalbán's Pepe Carvalho than most of his sketchily idealized predecessors (Justo Vasco's detective, Calderón, prefigured some of Conde's depth of character, but within a more rigidly ideological framework). Conde's job is to apply rational deductive techniques to an irrational society in which scientifically defined enterprises have broken down; which seems to have lost the heart of its ideology; and which is patently selling itself back into a colonial condition. Cuba's present condition is postmodern in the sense that the scientific, ideologically consistent discourse of the Marxist Revolution (that is, its modernity) is collapsing. Revolutionary functionaries and tourism workers are becoming flourishing dollar capitalists; while loyal state-paid professionals starve in the peso economy.

As a representation of the ideological and social fragmentation taking place in Cuba, as well as of a decentered subject—in this case, both delinquent and detective—Padura's work undermines the rationalist construct of "objective reality" proposed by Lukács and promoted in the Cuban literature of the 1970s and early 1980s. He hints at a return to Lukács's negative vision of the modernist man: "Man, for these writers, is by nature solitary, asocial, unable to enter into relationships with other beings."[61] El Conde's drunkenness, his dysfunctional womanizing, and his skepticism hint at the same inherent lack of meaning that, as Bataille and Lacan noticed, afflicts the North American or Spanish hard-boiled protagonist. While he does not exhibit the same nihilism as Pepe Carvalho, he is nostalgic for the freedoms of the early days of the Revolution and depressed about Cuba's future.

Like el Conde himself, his friends all have slightly subversive or vaguely counterrevolutionary nicknames. In a reference to the criminals of yore, one is slyly named el Flaco and another, el Cojo. Whereas a negative character in Vasco's 1986 *El muro* is called "el Bitle," an allusion to his long hair and subversive taste for music by the Beatles, the Conde and his friends are dedicated Beatles fans. They all commit petty larceny on an almost daily basis to survive (this was known in the earlier stories by the pseudoscientific term "operativity" *[operatividad]*), and they share his irreverence for institutional wisdom. El Flaco is a paraplegic from the Angola war: a monument to Cuba's misguided foreign policy that parallels the United States' experience in Vietnam.

Máscaras, the third of Padura's four detective novels, refers obliquely to the Ochoa affair as an exemplar of Cuba's intolerance of ambiguity. It deals with the prejudices and hypocrisies of official revolutionary culture; in Padura's words, it is "a story of homosexuals, of masks, centered on the phenomenon of moral transvestitism that has been the Cuban experience during this period."[62] The plot centers on the murder of the homosexual son of a high-up party functionary. His body is found strangled in a park, dressed in drag in the costume of Virgilio Piñera's *Electra Garrigó*. In his search for the murderer, el Conde becomes fascinated with the gay underworld of Havana: specifically, the life of the notorious homosexual dramatist Alberto Marqués, a figure modeled primarily after Piñera. El Conde's friends jokingly call him by this pseudoaristocratic nickname, but, despite his initial repugnance, he finds out that he has much in common with "el Marqués."

Padura chose to use the discourse of homosexuality and transvestitism as a political metaphor, and not an investigation into sexuality itself. Nonetheless, the issue of homosexuality that has always been an integral component of the socialist detective novel, and of the revolutionary metaphor, is of paramount importance for Padura. As the protagonist becomes increasingly disturbed by his own changing attitudes toward homosexuality, the virile metaphor of the Revolution, formerly equated with the "objective" representation of reality, also becomes destabilized.

El Conde is a typical Cuban-style *machista*: to this end, he is portrayed as a "man's man": he and his friends drink and smoke together in epic proportions, they affectionately call each other *salvaje* or *bestia*—a common terminology that contrasts with *civilizado*, the term used by gays to describe a person who is not homophobic. El Conde keeps an album of his sexual conquests to tide him over the dry spells. He divides the male sex into categories based on their sexuality: "real men" *(hombres-hombres)*, "passive homosexuals" (homosexuales pasivos), and the nefarious "active homosexuals, hidden behind an impenetrable façade of the real man, a tough guy, a bugger."[63] He has never liked "sissies" *(maricones)*: his macho egotism makes him imagine that every gay man he sees desires him, and, like Pérez's policeman, he suffers a terrible paranoia when he has to interview homosexual suspects.

El Conde is also a marginalized figure within the revolutionary hierarchy: he is openly rebellious, fights with his boss (in *Máscaras* he is technically suspended from the force), and operates under a cloud of suspicion and recrimination. Worst of all, he is a policeman in a state where the police have clearly become the enemy. His encounters with the CDR are subtly hostile. His friends and the young men of the neighborhood avoid public contact with him for fear of being *quemados*, or that he will catch them in one of the myriad daily violations of the law that are necessary for survival in Cuba today. When el Conde visits the house of his paralyzed best friend, he has to refrain from asking where el Flaco's mother gets the ingredients for the gourmet meals she prepares for them. Her culinary inventiveness amid chronic shortages is a metaphor for resistance to a system that criminalizes its citizens.

When el Conde's own department initiates a series of internal political witch hunts, he recognizes a parallel between his situation and that of gays under the Revolution. His attitude is complicated by his homophobia. The main suspect in the murder, Alberto Marqués, is a compendium of homosexual and counterrevolutionary vices:

> A homosexual of vast predatory experience, politically uncommitted and ideologically deviant, confrontational and a provocateur, xenophile, hermetic, Baroque, a potential user of marihuana and other drugs, protector of dissolute faggots, a man of questionable philosophical associations, full of petit-bourgeois, classist prejudices.[64]

This description parodies the rigid ideology of previous novels, and el Conde, like the author, evidently dislikes this kind of extreme rhetoric.[65] Nevertheless, he cannot avoid his own prejudices: he suspects Marqués of spying on him when he goes to the bathroom and believes that he wants to seduce him. But little by little, el Conde begins to feel respect for this broken-down dramatist whose persecutions haven't erased his dignity. In fact, suffering has lent him a certain quasi-virile legitimacy: "because the real truth was that this faggot that shits himself if someone yells at him, he's got balls all the way to his ankles. He took it like a man and stayed here on the Island."[66]

In contemplating the victim Alexis and the suspect Marqués, el Conde begins to explore the phenomenon of representation. As he ponders the revolutionary equation of sexuality and ideology, he is led to question the usefulness of the visibility factor in understanding either. He asks himself whether the victim was a real transvestite, or only an apparent one: "the problem . . . wasn't essence, but appearance; it wasn't the action, but the representation."[67] The answer seems less and less relevant as he begins to understand that for him personally, the problem of Alexis Arayán lies not in what he is but in the transparency of his masquerade: the visible manifestation of his rejection of a particular masculine identity known as machismo. Transvestitism is thus a challenge to the Revolution because it provokes the inevitable question of whether revolutionary identity itself is only a mask. The notion of the *travesti* combines the elements of disguise and burlesque with an essential rejection of the self. Mario Conde intuitively makes a connection between transvestitism and the reversal of roles that characterizes revolution.

And in spite of his repugnance for homosexuals, he is attracted by the gay underworld of Havana. He speculates pruriently about the manner of Alexis's death, which starts to acquire a sort of erotic fascination in his imagination: "Maybe they kissed, even caressed each other, and Alexis went down on his knees, like a penitent, surely with the intention of satisfying his companion's desire with the nearest orifice."[68]

The character of Alberto Marqués is an amalgam of Piñera and other "pederast poets" (as Piñera famously referred to himself). His sexual tastes run to the scandalous—like Piñera, he pays rough men to attack him in his house—but unlike Piñera he is an avowed bibliophile and collector (and book thief) whose home is a shrine to Cuban literature. As his name suggests, he lives in his own glorious past, reminiscing about dinners with Sartre, Simone de Beauvoir, and "el Recio" (a figure resembling Severo Sarduy, alluded to by the wordplay *recio/severo*).

Máscaras is, of course, an allegorical story. The history of el Marqués, persecuted, dismissed from his job in the theater, and effectively prevented from working by the Revolution, is the story of Virgilio Piñera and all the *parametrados*, but it is also a story that represents the Revolution itself. El Conde's generic doubts and speculations coincide with his political disillusionment: he discovers that the secretary in his office, with whom he has flirted for years, is a government informer, and one of his colleagues is suspended for corruption. His political misgivings come to a crisis when he accompanies el Marqués to a gay party, where he anxiously imagines the "oily leers" (*miradas aceitosas*) of "little faggots of the languid variety, who seemed to lament his immaculate heterosexuality."[69] Despite his professed disgust with their behavior, el Conde takes home a girl whom he suspects is a male transsexual. In a symbolically homoerotic gesture, instead of copulating in accordance with revolutionary (hetero-sexual) norms, he sodomizes her.

The link between government corruption, the persecution of homo-sexuals, and the political disillusionment of el Conde portrayed in this novel presents a harsh critique of the Revolution by undermining the macho metaphor and replacing it with another: that of the sexual mas-querade. The feminist critic Nelly Richard has posited that the question-ing of "hegemonic gender identity formations" may constitute the most radical form of postmodernism in Latin America. She suggests that the Bakhtinian notion of the festival entails a fetishization of cultural differ-ence that denies the "different" one the "right to negotiate its own con-ditions of discursive control."[70] Padura's deployment of the masquerade also goes beyond a binary discourse of subversion and creates the begin-nings of a space for complication, ambiguity, and diversity. In short, el Conde's investigation of the masquerade leads him to the recognition, if not actual acceptance, of an alternative masculine "essence" that goes beyond the simple desire or compulsion to be visible: "transvestitism was something more essential and biological than the simple faggotish exhi-bitionism of going out dressed up as a woman."[71]

Foucault's notion of the "medicine of sex" is one of many post-modernist analyses of the social consequences of imposing modern norms or "disciplines" on a phenomenon like sexuality. Neil Larson, a scholar of Latin American postmodernisms, would include this critique in his theory of left postmodernism. "Left postmodernism" establishes itself as specifically anticolonial and anti-imperialist, privileging the subaltern, the decentered, and historically Other. Larson sees Retamar's *Calibán* as an expression of this posture, which denies that modern uni-versals can be applied to "the radical alterity of 'Nuestra America.'"[72] The problem with this approach is that it ultimately creates, as in the case of Cuba, a new center, a new *"nosotros,"* a new universalizing model from which differences and aberrations can be measured and disciplines imposed. The masking of difference is one response to this condition; another is the defiant masquerade, the parading of anomaly.

Through an epigraph quoting Batman, "we all wear masks" (todos usamos máscaras), Padura renders homage to G. K. Chesterton's asser-tion that the detective story is like a masked ball, where nothing is what it seems, and the game of representation itself is foregrounded.[73] As el Marqués explains to el Conde, transvestitism is the nexus of three kinds of mimesis: creation through aesthetic representation, intimidation of the upholders of the status quo, and effacement of the macho identity. At the same time, Padura recognizes and rejects the high-contrast morality of his precursors' production. Good and evil were represented in the earlier socialist detective novel as clearly marked, gendered, and generic counterpoints. The mask, for Nogueras, Vasco, Pérez Valero, and others, signified a menacing equivocation of signs, a threat to the norms that protected the Revolution. Padura's detective stories attempt to recover the tolerance for masquerade that characterizes the traditional mystery, as well as the moral ambiguity found in the old hard-boiled novel and the *neopoliciacos* of Vázquez Montalbán and Taibo.

Padura's criticism of the Revolution is as much based on aesthetics as politics. He resists compromising aesthetic value for the sake of conforming to an ill-conceived, crumbling norm. His protagonist sheds the anodyne, collectivist, *machista* mask of earlier detectives of the genre and rejects its models, the masks of revolutionary zeal:

> That moral masquerade that so many people have lived with at some
> point in their lives: homosexuals that give the impression of being
> straight, embittered people who smile in bad times, witch-doctors with
> Marxist pamphlets under their arms, wolfish opportunists disguised as
> docile lambs, ideological cynics with their handy Party membership card
> in their pockets.[74]

Instead, he symbolically embraces the subversive mask that reveals: the tragic burlesque mask of the *travesti*. In doing so, he faces the complexity of his own gendered identity and of his uneasy relationship with his Revolution.

Mexico: Crimes against Persons

4.
Contesting
"la mexicanidad"

This country, our homeland, closed itself to us, reduced
to the spoils of petty opportunists, cheats and liars,
a cynicism dressed up in words that no one
believed anymore, words spoken out of habit.
—*Paco Ignacio Taibo II,* No Happy Endings

*F*rom Sarmiento forward, the Latin American relationship to European models for modernity has been characterized by the violence exercised by the "civilized" on the "barbarous." Straying far from their liberal origins, proponents of modernization have advanced eugenic projects,
condoned bossism or *caciquismo*, and authorized dictatorship and police
terrorism. These enterprises excuse an essential irrationality in the pursuit of progress, order, and economic stability. In recent decades, critics
like the liberation theologist Enrique Dussel have rejected the "irrationality of violence generated by the myth of modernity."[1] Latin American
postmodernist theorists have organized themselves behind a rejection
of neoliberalism, a commitment to voicing subaltern perspectives, and a
critique of nationalizing discourses as subservient to the interests of an
oppressive minority. The Mexican detective novelists discussed in this
chapter laid the groundwork for the contemporary novel's critique of the
traps of modernity and concomitant abuses of power, specifically those
brought about by globalization and neoliberalism.

In the 1970s and 1980s, critics like Carlos Monsiváis and Jorge Ibargüengoitia in Mexico began to explore the problem of situating the detective novel, which they saw as an essentially modern, Anglo-Saxon,
middle-class literature, within the political and social context of Mexico.
The Enlightenment paradigms that underpinned the detective story had
little applicability, they felt, in the Mexican context. Even the imitative
or parodic approach was irrelevant, since Mexican political reality itself

was a kind of farce. As Monsiváis asked, "who would think of parody in a baroque country?"[2]

In the Cuban detective novel, individuals do violence to the state by undermining its institutions. In the Mexican detective novel, it is the institutions—police, government, unions—who are the criminals. They attack individuals who threaten their hegemony, brutalizing whole sectors of society in their drive for money and power. As Paco Ignacio Taibo II puts it, the primary element of the *neopoliciaco* is "the characterization of the police as a force of chaos, of the barbarous system ready to suffocate its citizens in violence."[3] Since order is the instrument of tyranny and subjugation, the Mexican detective hero rejects ratiocination, legal process, and the scientific method as means to truth, offering his physical body as both a catalyst and a stage for the battle between good and evil.

The detective novel has another important function in Mexico: it contests the nihilistic rhetoric of the "Mexican national character" as savage and a friend of death that has historically justified the government's brutal treatment of minority and dissenting voices. The so-called Mexican love for death has provided a convenient rationale for a discourse of power based on Octavio Paz's famous dictum: "chingar o ser chingado." The detective novel reveals the mechanisms of control that drive this thinking and asserts an alternative view of Mexican identity that privileges humanity, individual responsibility, and heterogeneity.

Carlos Monsiváis's important essay "Los viajeros y la invención de México" (Travelers and the Invention of Mexico) presents an alternative theory about the origins of the Mexico's official history and the much-debated "Mexican national character." During the nineteenth century, he maintains, thrill-seeking tourists from the United States and England (cradles of modernity) began to flow into Mexico. Their prejudices, racial, religious, and otherwise, confronted with the chaotic aftermath of the Independence movement, produced an image of Mexico as savage, hermetic, and backwards. From Frances Calderón de la Barca to D. H. Lawrence, these travelers found solitude instead of peace, folly instead of innocence, and cruelty instead of ambition. This vision was absorbed and internalized by the upper classes, becoming an integral part of the myths of "Mexican identity" propagated in histories, fictions, and popular culture.

For Monsiváis, then, Mexican identity is a totalizing construct conceived by foreigners in collusion with the Mexican right: "the ideologues of the Mexican right and almost all tourists construct that 'Mexico' and they colonize it with prejudices that will become judgments, in fantasy-driven observations about the national psychology that turn into attitudes and behaviors."[4] The discourses of tourism and Manifest Destiny manufactured the necessary barbarous Other, which would be characterized in the imagination of the future by "the use of key words: mystery, primitivism, barbarism, innocence, paradise lost, atavism, sensuality, cruelty. . . . The impression of a vanished beauty expressed in the colonial monuments, prehispanic ruins, that which has no continuity or descendants equal to its grandeur."[5]

Monsiváis's orientalized Other corresponds to Octavio Paz's description of Mexican identity, though Paz's construction of Mexicanness originates with Mexican history rather than the views of covetous foreign travelers. In the famous essays that make up *The Labyrinth of Solitude* *(El laberinto de la soledad)*, Paz probed the essence behind the so-called Mexican mask: the internalized "otherness" that leads the Mexican to call himself an "hijo de la Chingada." The origin of the Mexican is also the root of his nihilism. Paz believed that the detective novel could never flourish in Mexico because of this essential nihilism and because Mexico is inherently antimodern. If a Mexican commits murder, Paz asserted, he kills another human being rather than a scientifically objectified Other. Living daily with death, he has no need for hygienic or technical solutions for confronting it: "modern technical skills and the popularity of crime stories are, like concentration camps and collective extermination, the results of an optimistic, unilateral conception of existence."[6]

Despite Paz's ostensible affirmation of the humanity of the Mexican, his thesis was essentially the opposite: that the Mexican is inherently Other, to himself and to other Mexicans. Monsiváis understood that otherness, or *lo otro*, is always the name used by the intellectual to describe the "pueblo popular." Since the middle classes long to separate themselves from the masses, they invent the myth of "the picturesque, the dense and obscurely symbolic."[7] Under the regime of Miguel de Alemán, Marxist and revolutionary rhetoric founded on this conception of *el pueblo* was appropriated to legitimize the state, while the myth of a *mestizo* destiny was enshrined (and embalmed) in institutions like the Museo Nacional de la Antropología.

Paz saw the government's 1968 student massacre at the Plaza de Tres Culturas as a confirmation of his nihilistic vision. However, Monsiváis considers the massacre, the events leading up to it, and the ensuing mass disillusionment with authority as the beginnings of an emergence from "la fiesta desarrollista" (an oblique reference to Paz's explosive *fiesta nacional*) and the sign of a nascent culture of dissidence.[8] Known as the *Onda* generation, the writers who came of age after the massacre used literature to express this dissidence by violating traditional barriers between high and popular culture, author and reader, fiction and nonfiction. They foregrounded Mexico City as a physical and psychological presence, home to a multitude of cultures and voices. These features are common to the Mexican detective novel, which one critic characterizes as "the daughter of *la Onda*."[9]

Mexican detective novels certainly became a much more powerful cultural presence after the events of 1968. Innovation in the detective story has coincided with political upheaval from its beginnings: Poe's detective stories, set in Paris, with European revolutionary movements of 1848; Chesterton's early Father Brown stories (1911, 1914) with the beginning of World War I; Biorges's *Don Isidro Parodi* (1942) with World War II and Argentina's difficult neutrality; and the Spanish *novela negra* with the post-Franco transition. Like the literature of the *Onda*, the *neopoliciaco* is multivoiced and strongly urban, where the city serves as both the scene of the crime and refuge of the persecuted. But, although the post-1968 Mexican *neopoliciaco* owes its existence to the values of the *Onda* generation, it is a riskier and more marginal proposition altogether. Many of its salient characteristics can be found in the stories of three precursors: Antonio Helú (1900–1972), Jorge Ibargüengoitia (1928–1983), and Rafael Bernal (1915–1972).

Helú, Ibargüengoitia, and Bernal each contributed an essential attribute to the development of the Mexican *neopoliciaco*: Helú an unabashed cynicism about law and authority; Ibargüengoitia a critique of the tabloid news, or *nota roja* (which presented crime as a consumable for the masses) and an irreverence for official revolutionary rhetoric; and Bernal a sense of the defrauding of the Mexican people by their government and institutions. Taibo brought these elements together in the Belascoarán novels; and the younger generation is building on his innovations. Mexican detective novelists Juan Hernández Luna, Gabriel Trujillo, and others are completely remaking the detective genre to depict a world devoid of reason and justice. In the apocalyptic, antirational Mexico of the twenty-first century, Hernández Luna maintains, moral outrage is the writer's only alternative. But ethics must not be grounded in rationalism, or it would merely justify the neocapitalist system: "the only defenses are rage and passion."[10]

Antonio Helú: The Detective Is a Thief

During the 1940s and 1950s, Antonio Helú edited the Mexican version of *Ellery Queen's Mystery Magazine*, *Selecciones Policiacas y de Misterio* (founded in 1946), which was a counterpart to Borges's *Séptimo Circulo* series.

An erstwhile follower of the Mexican pedagogue and philosopher José Vasconcelos, Helú also directed films but dedicated most of his energy to detective literature. His stories feature the comical buffoon Carlos Miranda and the elegant and ironical Máximo Roldán, both thieves whose criminal activities tend to place them at the scene of a murder.

Helú's plots and settings lack a distinct regionalist flavor in the sense that they depict neither social injustices nor problems unique to Mexico, but they are nonetheless distinctly Mexican and political. Helú had no illusions about the "courtly or devastating proceedings" (procedimientos exterminadores o cortesanos) of the mechanisms of justice in Mexico, and his protagonists echo this cynicism in *La obligación de asesinar*.[11] On discovering a nest of criminals, Roldán is astounded at their firepower and concludes that they must be corrupt government officials: "another .45 Special . . . Damn! Are you guys government officials?"[12] When they angrily deny this, he apologizes for having insulted them.

Helú's stories are not parodies of the traditional detective novel but parodies of bourgeois Mexican manners structured around a detective-centered conundrum. The settings don't expose the "real" Mexico; instead they open doors into the curiously hermetic drawing rooms, clubs, and salons of the wealthy. The complete helplessness of Miranda and Roldán when faced with rapidly mounting piles of corpses creates an atmosphere of farcical irreality that foregrounds the suspects' callous egotism. It is Helú's very silence on political matters that lends such authority to his portrait of the upper classes, a portrait as critical as that of any of his contemporaries.

Rafael Bernal's *Complot mongol*

Filiberto García, the protagonist of Rafael Bernal's *The Mongolian Plot* (*El complot mongol*, 1969) is a gunman or *pistolero*: a paid killer for the police (precursor of the apelike strongman, or *guarura*). A former soldier of the Revolution, García is disgusted with the fossilized bureaucracy that it has become, or "the Revolution turned Government" (*la Revolución hecha Gobierno*). He is not disillusioned only about the failure of revolutionary hopes for equality and justice. His nostalgia is more for the life of the soldier, where rape, pillage, and murder didn't need to hide themselves behind a bureaucratic mask.

Although it was published in 1969, *El complot mongol* only began to receive critical attention in Mexico in the 1980s. According to Bernal's widow, there may have been an effort to suppress the book when it first appeared, due to the resemblance between the characters and actual political figures.[13] The plot is an elaborately designed xenophobic spy conspiracy in which Maoist terrorists disguised as tourists are supposedly coming from Outer Mongolia to kill the president of the United States, who is to visit Mexico in a few days. The real plot, revealed in onionlike layers, is the assassination of the Mexican president with the object of installing a military regime. A secondary intrigue, disguised behind a Chinese drug ring, involves a Chinese plan to displace Russia's influence in Cuba (the Latin American version of the Yellow Peril).

Bernal underlines both the ferocity of the Mexican police and their ineptitude. Because he is a policeman, García's work, even if it is of a criminal nature, is protected by the law. Recognizing this coldly as a fact of the corrupted institution that employs him, he contrasts the function of Mexican law with that of United States law: "And the police from the other side are always talking about respect for the Law but I say that the Law is one of those things they put there for losers. Maybe the gringos are losers. Because the Law leads no place."[14] García is assigned to work with an FBI agent and a Russian agent to track down the would-be assassins. As he sees it, he (as a representative of Mexico) suffers from a lack of finesse in comparison to the other agents. While the Russians and Americans "know judo, karate and how to garrote with silk cords . . . in Mexico they don't teach us those fancy things. They teach us to kill. Maybe not even that. They hire us because we already know how to kill. We're not experts, just enthusiasts."[15]

Filiberto García is an "expert in fucking up the other guy" (experto en joder al prójimo) who, despite his lack of ideology, finds himself forced to take sides against the law, personified by corrupt military officers and politicians, in order to serve justice. (While the novel highlights police corruption, both García and his commanding officer, identified only as the "fucking Colonel" (pinche Coronel), are on the side of justice. García ultimately recognizes the irony of his situation as a protector of the public good who kills the very people he is charged with protecting: "we're losers and we kill the customers."[16]) García's lack of ideological loyalty—he sides neither with the Russians nor with the Americans, although the Russian saves his life at the end—is identical to that of Raymond Chandler's Johnny Dalmas or Philip Marlowe, Dashiell Hammett's Continental Op or Sam Spade. But García also has a Mexican pedigree: he bears a striking resemblance to Carlos Fuentes's most notorious exponent of realpolitik, Artemio Cruz.

While García may seem to be a sociopath and antihero, the real trajectory of the novel is his gradual, painful conversion from a mercenary serving all masters to a man with a conscience. In order to effect this metamorphosis, García must resort to the moral subterfuge of "following orders," orders he follows to the letter rather than the spirit. Despite his past as a rapist and womanizer, he falls in love with a Chinese girl, Martita, in whom he finds a chance for redemption. So, despite García's cynicism, *El complot mongol* is more of a tragic tale than a cynical one. Filiberto García wins the sympathy of the reader because, in spite of his efforts to remain corrupt and cynical, he is irredeemably drawn to good. Like many of the best hard-boiled tales, this novel is essentially pathetic.

Like Carlos Fuentes's Artemio Cruz, García is a disillusioned revolutionary from the provinces who has no patience with bureaucracy and official pretension. He even resembles Cruz physically:

> His dark face was expressionless, the mouth almost always immobile, even when he spoke. There was life only in his large green almond-shaped eyes. When he was young, in Yurécuaro, they called him the Cat and a woman in Tampico called him My Gentle Tiger. (Fucking Gentle Tiger!) But even if his eyes encouraged nicknames like that, the rest of his face, especially the rictus of his mouth, didn't encourage anyone to use nicknames with him.[17]

As happens to Artemio Cruz, García's only true love, Martita, is killed along with his chance for redemption, not in the crossfire of the Revolution but in the equally senseless postrevolutionary "spy" game. It is the nature of the hard-boiled detective to suffer tragedy and disillusionment—even disfigurement, as Héctor Belascoarán Shayne does in *Cosa fácil*. (James Bond's wife is murdered at the end of *On Her Majesty's Secret Service*.)

Rafael Bernal worked as a war correspondent in Paris during the Second World War, after which he spent a year in Hollywood writing for the movies. In 1959 he began a career in the Servicio Exterior Mexicano, which took him to Lima (where he wrote *El complot mongol*), the Philippines, and ultimately to Switzerland where he died in 1972. He was a Catholic who devoted much of his life to synarchism (conservative religious activism) and who read Agatha Christie and Chesterton to relax. According to his wife, he considered detective novels disposable and always left them behind when he moved from post to post. He was an individualist in other ways: he was the first Spanish-speaking writer to publish a story ("A Poetic Death" [La muerte poética, 1947]) in Helú's *Selecciones policiacas y de misterio*.[18] He was the author of the don Teódulo Batanes mystery stories and *A Corpse in the Grave* (*Un muerto en la tumba: Novela policiaca*, 1946), a tribute to G. K. Chesterton with a priest-detective.

El complot mongol combines Bernal's passion for detective stories with his pessimism about Mexico's future. In it, Bernal sets out for posterity the vital subject of the Mexican detective novel: the failed Mexican Revolution. The novel mixes the hard-boiled and spy genres in a new and completely original way, one that Carlos Fuentes would later take up—much less successfully—in *The Hydra-Head* (*La cabeza de la hidra*, 1978). Carlos Fuentes's spy novel depicts Mexico as a pawn of various international petroleum interests. This situation involves a complicated revisiting of the legacy of Lázaro Cárdenas, whose patriotic expropriation of British and U.S. oil holdings in 1938 remains a high point in Mexican foreign policy. Cárdenas's presidency represented the delayed—and truncated—realization of many of the goals of the Mexican Revolution, including land reform, a move toward social justice, and freedom from the foreign domination fostered by the *Porfiriato*. The novel's Shakespearean subtext alludes to the Prospero/Caliban paradigm that dominated Latin American political discussions in the 1970s. Fuentes's detective novel is unusually obvious in both its symbolism and its ideology and should be considered as Fuentes's contribution to the socially conscious literature of that period. His choice of the spy genre is a comment on the increasing cultural dominance of the United States and allows him to portray Mexican politics as an intricate and self-perpetuating series of internal betrayals.

Jorge Ibargüengoitia: Anatomy of the *nota roja*

Jorge Ibargüengoitia did not approve of the traditional mystery novel, which he claimed was unreadable. He found it utterly incompatible with his Mexican existence, in which solutions to mysteries were not the rule but the anomaly: "When I examine my life the opposite happens to me than to Poirot: I see in the shadow of the past a forest of unresolved cases."[19] Ibargüengoitia's contribution to the Mexican detective genre consists of two novels, both of which have received high critical praise: *Two crimes* (*Dos crímenes*, 1979), an inverted tale of murder and chicanery; and *The Dead Girls* (*Las muertas*, 1977), a fictionalization of the notorious mass murder of a group of prostitutes by three madames known as Las Poquianchis.[20] A precursor of present-day detective writers in Mexico (Argen-Mex writers Myriam Laurini and Rolo Diez, and especially Juan Hernández Luna), Ibargüengoitia addressed the outrageous news of the day by turning it into a kind of fiction that emphasized both the farcical irreality and heinousness of the crimes themselves, and the sensationalizing excesses committed by crime reporters in what is known as the *nota roja*.

Ibargüengoitia's weekly columns for *Excelsior* were often apolitical, and he has been criticized as a conservative. However, much of his writing is undeniably critical of Mexican institutions, particularly his quasi-detective novel *Las muertas*. A hybrid text that is half fiction and half documentary, *Las muertas* corresponds most closely to the true-crime or testimonial genre exemplified by Truman Capote's *In Cold Blood* (1965); Miguel Barnet's *Biography of a Runaway Slave* (*Biografía de un cimarrón*, 1968); and Elena Poniatowska's *Massacre in Mexico* (*La noche de Tlatelolco*, 1971), which documented the events surrounding the Tlatelolco massacre.

Testimonial is a literature of protest, designed to make injustice known and demand a remedy. Its structure of chronicle and confession suggests its origins in the tradition of jurisprudence, and as Josefina Ludmer points out, chronicle "can function simultaneously as 'history' and 'legal chronicle' of a culture founded on a belief in the veracity of confession and in palpable subjectivities."[21] The testimonial has been particularly valued in Latin America as a literature that circumvents official discourse and provides an outlet for subaltern viewpoints. Doris Sommer observed, regarding its truth-seeking function, that "to doubt referentiality in testimonials would be an irresponsible luxury given the urgency of the call to action."[22]

Written during the critical apogee of the testimonial genre, *Las muertas* questions its validity and proposes instead a discursive space where the testimonial voice is deprived of all ethical and rhetorical authority. Ibargüengoitia underlines the urgency of discovery (in the juridical sense) and rectification, but also the impossibility of realizing them. The notion of a "palpable subjectivity" loses its vitality when confronted with the systematic introduction of multiple reservations regarding the victims, the witnesses, and the delinquents. The author deliberately violates the formulas testimonial = real and art = fiction to reveal the essential fragility of this dichotomy.

Las muertas describes the hermeneutic and moral anomie that characterizes crime and its witnesses at the end of the twentieth century. In retelling the details of the Poquianchis case, Ibargüengoitia's text suggests that Mexican "reality" is a literary construct that denies its readers the opportunity to approach either the subject or any notion of "objective" truth. The text is a technology of fallacies, contradictions, and ambiguities: an antiexegetical machine that even when it manages to expose the facts (as in the detective novel) cannot illuminate them (as in the documentary true-crime narrative). The truth-seeking testimonial genre becomes an instrument of falsehood, dehumanization, and the erasure of the very subjectivity it strives to recognize. In the end, the enormity of the crimes (approximately sixteen girls are murdered and ten are sold off) is such that the reader's credulity is overtaxed. The crimes are compounded and travestied by the windy rhetoric of local politicians and the media frenzy that greet its discovery.

As Ibargüengoitia himself pointed out, the true-crime genre implies a rigorous process of research and psychological probing, while his own method was cursory and even frivolous: "Truman Capote . . . interviewed them for hours and days on end and then reconstructed their lives. I did the opposite. . . . I invented the characters because if I went to interview the Poquianchis they would tell me to go to hell."[23] He thus reveals an extreme skepticism about the possibility of ascertaining historical truth, whether official (as in the interspersed news reports) or intrahistorical. Ibargüengoitia discards the close focus, the articulation of the subaltern perspective, and the act of transcription—essential ingredients of the testimonial—at the outset. His antiscientific method asserts the artifice of literature—especially popular and journalistic literature that purports to be "of the people."

In *Las muertas,* Ibargüengoitia juxtaposes fact and fiction in such a way that they often appear transposed. In addition, various devices simultaneously proclaim and undermine the apparent authority of his tale. In the traditional detective novel, there is a detective-*sujet* through whose intelligence impressions, facts, and clues are transmitted to the reader. Walter Benjamin described this mechanism as necessary to providing a central, authoritative filter for the various suspects' stories. Whether a Watson or a Belascoarán, this figure constitutes an organizing force for the narrative. It is through this authoritative view that the reader accesses the delinquent's "text" and begins to structure his or her own theories about the identity and actions of the criminal.

Las muertas distorts this detecting eye: the narrative itself precludes a coherent reading. Rather than ordering the evidence, the author/narrator presents the details of the case haphazardly, aligning himself with the reader and sharing the reader's confusion. His intervention engenders both structural and temporal instabilities in the narrative. His narrative alternates with the first-person sworn statements of many of the other characters, so that the authoritative "I" becomes a fluid and unreliable voice.

The opening sentence draws the narrator's reliability into question. Instead of describing a series of events, he appears to be merely speculating about events he has no way of discovering: "One can picture them: all four wearing dark glasses, Ladder, driving, hunched over the wheel, Brave Nicolás, beside him, reading Strength magazine, the woman, gazing out of the window, and Captain Bedoya, asleep, his head bobbing."[24]

From the vantage point of 1976, the narrator describes a crime, the burning of a bakery twelve years previously, that led to the eventual discovery that the accused, Serafina Baladro, and the victim, Simón Corona, had been lovers and that he had helped her bury a corpse in 1960, four years prior to the crime in question and sixteen years before the narrator begins (for unknown motives) to recount the history.

The narrator's fundamental uncertainty resurfaces repeatedly at crucial moments throughout the text: in describing a double homicide he says, "the scene is more or less like this" (la imagen es más o menos así, 100) or "it could have happened that way" (así pudo ser, 104). He has a poor grasp of the names of the protagonists and does not understand their motives. The motives of the investigators are equally opaque to him: "It should be noted that Chief Cueto's motives . . . are obscure"; "Chief Cueto's role in the apprehension of the Baladro sisters is one of the obscure parts of this story. The following hypothesis seems reasonable."[25] In this way the narrator widens the psychological distance between the reader and the "real" detective, at the same time problematizing the truth-telling pretensions of the nonfiction genre.

Since the stability of the observing subject is the organizing element of both detective and testimonial literature, the reader of *Las muertas* can be under no illusion of having reliable access to the particulars of the case and must try to constitute a coherent narrative without this knowledge. The multiplicity of contentious subject voices make this virtually impossible. Even the names of the characters are perverse, misleading, or equivocal. While the identity of the criminals, the two (distinctly demonic) matrons of the México Lindo brothel, Serafina and Arcángela Baladros, is quite firmly established, that of their victims is often questionable. In the chapter "El caso de Ernestina, Helda, o Elena," one of the characters gives sworn testimony about the first victim. Not only is he operating from hearsay (made even less trustworthy by the passage of time) but the facts themselves are patently unverifiable: "according to what I heard, her name was Ernestina, Helda, or Elena."[26] Besides the mysterious Ernestina/Helda/Elena, other characters travel under aliases or partial names such as "Juana Cornejo, alias la Calavera" or "Herminia X." (In all cases the testimony is notable for its grotesque lack of sentiment or remorse.)

Ibargüengoitia's text systematically denies the credibility of the testimonial subject. He emphasizes the temporal disjunction between the events and the present time, as well as the possible mendacity or forgetfulness of the witnesses, by prefacing supposedly legal testimony with phrases like "she says that" (ella dice que . . .) and "she now says that" (ella dice ahora que . . .). The crimes themselves are one of the most perplexing ingredients of the case, since they are almost without exception bizarre, ill-conceived, and/or accidental. Motives are obscure, nonexistent, or completely out of keeping with the crimes. In most cases they are so trivial that they would never justify a fictional murder.

To please the wealthy elite of the state of Plan de Abajo (a play on Plan de Ayala), the Governor mandates the closing of all the bordellos, thus breaking the ties of mutual support and obligation between the madams, the police, and the bureaucrats of the state. The madams, awaiting better days, lock up the prostitutes. As time passes, the prostitutes become rebellious and initiate a series of strange, ill-conceived, and even accidental aggressions. They kill one of their colleagues with hot irons while trying to cure her of a mysterious paralysis. Another is shoved into a latrine but turns out to be too fat to fit through the opening. One is beaten to death with the high heels of their shoes, and two more die falling through a poorly constructed balcony while fighting over the gold teeth of yet another dead girl. When the madams run out of money, they can no longer feed their employees and begin to slowly starve them. Two are shot trying to escape. In every case, and in stark contrast to the meticulous planning that characterizes crime in a typical mystery, the deaths occur in a vacuum of irreflexivity: more from lack of imagination than from malice.

If the crimes are mainly incidental, their discovery is no less casual. Evidence is discovered by accident—the Inspector discovers the hand of one of the victims by literally tripping over it—and at all times the police reveal themselves to be corrupt, incompetent, and totally implicated in the suppression of the truth. Even the legal documents are misleading: "The terms in which the document is couched are definitive. Anybody unfamiliar with the story who read it might assume that the investigation must have ended at this point."[27] The surviving prostitutes frequently change their testimony, adding trivial details or trying to discredit the Baladros; one claims "that she saw the sisters Serafina and Arcángela Baladro push the two women who fell off the balcony on September 14."[28] In the majority of cases it is obvious that the changes are a reaction to public outcry and tabloid hysteria, as the prostitutes try to capitalize on their misfortune by rewriting it.

The narrator seems concerned, not with verifying what happened, but why. Ibargüengoitia brings together interviews and depositions by the surviving protagonists, creating a polyphonic text that mutilates and deauthorizes the voices that compose it. The court transcripts and news clippings that supplement the narrative are marred by lacunae that the reader could attribute equally to the narrator, the press, or the corrupt judicial process. In this way, Ibargüengoitia exposes a reality that foils both the prestige and the authority of the first-person testimonial genre. The sworn testimony of the prostitutes and others involved, presented in the first person and filtered through the speculations, contradictions, doubts, and equivocations of the narrator, compete among themselves and against the narrator, obscuring their individual stories and the coherence of the whole. Contrasting with the narrator's florid speculations—analogous to the "interpretive aspirations" of a Capote or a Poniatowska[29]—the individual stories are almost grotesquely inflectionless due to the lack of education and imagination of the claimants. Victims, delinquents, and witnesses are erased from the narrative: suppressed by the narrator, the corruption of the judicial process, and the salaciousness of the *nota roja* journalists who pretend to lament their victimization. The privileged orality of testimonial becomes an accomplice to deception and self-interest.

Ibargüengoitia invented the documentary farce. He discerned the burlesque intrinsic to the daily news, the discourse of Mexican history, and the myths of *mexicanidad*. Master of the Brechtian aside, Ibargüengoitia endeavored to create an alienating effect as much in his narrative as in his drama. In the case of *Las muertas*, the alienation provoked by the fragmented, mutilated narrative is surpassed only by the simple brutality of the actual events.

Although *Las muertas* is by no means a typical detective story, Ibargüengoitia brings together in one text many of the most salient ingredients of the Mexican genre: institutional degeneracy; the corruption of history by power; the presentation of a mass or serial murder, rather than a single murder; and levels of intrigue so complex, and at the same time so ferocious, that they appear burlesque. By using real news as the basis of his fiction, he sets a precedent for later detective writers, who almost inevitably will turn to Mexican current events in their search for the bizarre, the outrageous, and the depraved. The unstable subject that constitutes the novel's most fundamental innovation anticipates the radical detective novels of the 1990s, whose chaotic narrative style and sordid (but fact-based) plots ultimately threaten to efface the subject entirely.

If modernity produced the crime as text and the detective as reader (as Jameson proposed), Ibargüengoitia presents the Poquianchis case as a hermetic and illegible text, and the detective as essentially pathetic, as ignorant and illiterate as the victims. In contrast to the classical detective story, *Las muertas* is not a modernizing text. It has no internal logic to counterbalance the chaotic fact of violence. In contrast to the true-crime or testimonial narrative, Ibargüengoitia's novel militates against the possibility of accessing the viewpoint of the Other with exemplary or rectificatory intent. Truth exists only in fragments, and they are unverifiable.

Nevertheless, Ibargüengoitia is not criticizing rationalism but the official discourses and their organs—press, police, and government—that depend on it for their authority. Through *Las muertas* he warns the reader that the epistemological conditions necessary for the pursuit of justice no longer exist, because the state has inculcated a program of discursive dehumanization that leaves no space for the politics of identity.

Underlying all of Ibargüengoitia's cultural commentary was his early recognition of the programmatic nature of Mexican popular culture. Critics in the area of cultural studies would later identify this as "a pact between state-aligned elites who promoted import-substitution industrialization and an equally state-aligned popular nationalism that sought state welfare, delivered in corporatist forms since the 1920s and 1930s."[30] Ibargüengoitia wrote numerous critical articles on the Mexican film industry and its totalizing portrayal of Mexican culture.

Like the detective writers who came after him, Ibargüengoitia refused to commit himself to a prefabricated version of reality. He saw culture (both high and low) as an instrument of control and shared Monsiváis's *Onda*-bred skepticism about the *mestizo* myth. He preferred to protest the minor indignities of middle-class life in Mexico by poking fun at the bombastic rhetoric of "la mexicanidad":

> We're imperturbable, tough, all Indians . . . who suffered in silence the oppression of the middle class, we'll rise up in arms and in the end we will triumph—we'll nationalize petroleum and the land will be for whomever works it—. The implicit corollary of this vision is that we're living in the Golden Age: final fruition of the seeds sown by Cuauhtémoc, the priest Hidalgo, Juárez, Madero and Zapata.[31]

Ibargüengoitia linked all these themes in a short article, "Homage to James Bond" (Homenaje a James Bond):

> James Bond arrives in Munich and he knows where to get the best liverwürst in the city. At a certain moment he says, "I feel like a cocktail." That is, he's a guy who always knows what he wants, always knows where to get it, and always has the cash to pay for it. . . . He's the best shot in the Secret Service . . . he drinks like a fish and never gets drunk . . . . What I say is, why don't we Mexicans do something like that?[32]

Bond is the modern hero par excellence, the quasi-surgical Black Hand of Anglo-Saxon security. A license to kill, the eternal apparatus proffered by Q, the incessant flirting with the long-suffering but emancipated secretary Moneypenny, the martinis, the love affairs, the hypertechnological villains: all are indices of an Anglo-Saxon modernity and its hygienic xenophobia. According to Ibargüengoitia, Bond could never exist in a country like Mexico, where the organs of modern security, the police and the bureaucrats, are assassins whose xenophobia is directed internally, at the Mexican people. The image of the Mexican secret police lends itself neither to heroism nor to comedy. In all of Ibargüengoitia's copious journalistic production, this is one of his few overtly political pieces. His comments address the incongruity between the Nietzschean Superman, grist of the classic detective and spy novel, and the cult of national heroes in Mexico: el Pípila in Guanajuato or the statues of Morelos and Juárez that dot the highways.[33] Ibargüengoitia's criticisms of the *nota roja*, the Mexican film industry, and Mexican hero culture all reflect his reservations about the morality of converting crime into a consumable commodity, and his awareness that the struggle for representation in the public arena has already been lost.

5.
The Dismembered City

"There is only hope in action."
—Jean Paul Sartre
(PIT II), An Easy Thing

*T*he hard-boiled genre is based on an essentially antisocial view of society; the detective often operates outside the law, using the techniques of criminals against the criminals themselves. In the Mexican *neopoliciaco,* the criminals are invariably those in power: the wealthy, the government, and the police. The villain is corporate: the pervasive discourses of a "barbaric pseudodemocracy."[1] The outcome of the clash between the detective's personal ideals and the corporate reality is inevitably violent and dramatizes a greater battle for discursive territory, or what Homi Bhabha calls "the 'right' to signify from the periphery of authorized power."[2]

Paco Ignacio Taibo II
Paco Ignacio Taibo II, Carmen Boullosa, and a handful of other writers have used the detective genre to assert the rights of civilians against the corrupt hegemony of institutions. The detective novels of Paco Ignacio Taibo II assert a space of enunciation through the demarcation of an alternative, virtual *patria* where the poor, the hopeless, and the marginalized gather in mutual solidarity and solace. Taibo's detective hero Héctor Belascoarán Shayne rejects ratiocination, offering his physical body as both a catalyst and a stage for the battle between good and evil. His scars symbolize the futility of metaphysical inquiry, and his continued physical existence is a declaration of protest. He stubbornly lives in his city as a member of the unwashed millions, but his

Taibo's *neopoliciaco* novels amalgamate the hard-boiled genre with a healthy dose of Cuban-style populism; they even include what can only be called a *teque*, or ideological sermonette. The epigraph from Sartre in Taibo's second Belascoarán novel, *An Easy Thing (Cosa fácil)*, which is also the epigraph to this chapter, connects Belascoarán's actions specifically to Sartre's late shift to Marxism, when he advocated collective revolutionary action. As Glen Close observes, "Taibo's protagonists are private investigators in the tradition of Sam Spade and Phillip Marlowe, but their concerns are far from private and their effectiveness depends almost entirely on the collaboration of the friends, acquaintances and strangers who constitute *la raza*."[12] Through Belascoarán, Taibo observes all the external ingredients of the hard-boiled genre, down to the detective's trench coat. His insistence on these details doesn't constitute parody; instead, it is an important aspect of a dedicated intertextuality that ultimately generates a parallel commentary on the genre, its roots in the urban landscape, and the dismembered space of the millennial *Defe*. Taibo's self-conscious rendering of formulaic details like the 1940s office furniture in Belascoarán's office is counterbalanced on a generic level by his deep commitment to the art and mission of storytelling; to excavating and retelling the morally pure "sequences" of Mexican history, many of which would otherwise disappear. Bruno Bosteels explains:

> The anarchist struggles of the 20s, the student movement of 68, the re-emergence of syndicalist struggles in the 70s, the popular response to the earthquake in 1985, and the promise of a new left under Cárdenas since 1988, are more than simply the background of Taibo II's stories. They are, in fact, what really matters but only if we understand that it is not until history becomes a story, or perhaps even a myth, that the true subjective potential of these political struggles becomes effectively visible. Writing, in other words, involves above all a fidelity to political events which, without this intervention, risk vanishing or merely becoming one of the many ghosts that roam around the streets of Mexico City.[13]

The detective novel functions as an intrachronicle: an unofficial, parallel history of the Mexican people; at a generic level, its outsider status (mirroring the outsider status of the detective protagonist) enables Taibo to advance a critical agenda. Taibo employs abundant references to actual history, news, and people. Belascoarán's cases include a search for Emiliano Zapata (rumored to be still living and fighting in various leftist causes throughout Latin America), an investigation of strike breaking, an investigation into the *Halcones* (a paramilitary group who massacred a group of students in 1971), and other populist scenarios.

Belascoarán is a literary detective. He constantly signals his awareness of himself as a literary construction at the risk of succumbing to his
own clichés. Likewise, his desire to recover radical and popular history
from its fossilized state in institutionalized discourse is expressed inter-
textually through constant allusions to the detective's reading habits. In
one story, Belascoarán acquires two novels by Chester Himes, the black
American writer whose Harlem detective stories are a critical antecedent
to Taibo's construction of the terrorist detective.

The problematic relationship of the hard-boiled genre to "main-
stream" novelistic production is epitomized in the person and oeuvre of
Chester Himes. Himes was very influential in the development of the *novela negra* in Spain.[14] Taibo explains how Chester Himes's radical take on the
hard-boiled genre influenced both the Spanish genre and his own writing:

> Their thematics weren't comparable to those of the American hard-boiled
> novel, although they were very influenced by the most radical voices of the
> genre (curiously also the latest) Himes and Thompson, who were more
> substantial than the classics of the genre. The irrationality of violence,
> shown as a presence in the cities they described, that unleashed itself at
> the slightest provocation, the edginess of their settings, the colloquialism
> of the dialogues, had passed from Himes and Thompson to the aaforemen-
> tioned authors.[15]

For G. K. Chesterton, criticism of society and its institutions was the
first duty of a true patriot. Taibo and Himes are patriots in the sense
that, as writers of detective fiction, they adhere to an ideal of locating
community in the face of institutional acts that dislocate their respective
constituencies. Their advocacy of illegal and violent action in the pursuit
of this goal represents a patriotic stance analogous to that of the IRA or
the ETA, in that it attempts to claim discursive space through the representation of chaotic practices. Himes and Taibo use violence to foreground the absurd nature of their basic premise—the detective's pursuit
of truth and justice amid the posthermeneutic, dismembered reality of
Harlem and Mexico.

Chester Himes's detective novels run little risk of being parodies, since
he was basically ignorant of the genre and its conventions when he was
asked to start writing detective novels in the 1950s. He adopted instead the
term "absurd" to identify his detectives' predicament as agents of the law
in a subculture that suffers from a continual state of injustice. Absurdity
also describes the divergence of expectation and realization experienced
by black people in a racist society. The violence in the Harlem novels
is exaggerated, cartoonlike, and macabre. Himes's two black detectives,

Coffin Ed Johnson and Grave Digger Jones, are so tough that "it was said in Harlem that Coffin Ed's pistol would kill a rock and Grave Digger's would bury it."[16] Their method of detection is elemental and they are frequently suspended for police brutality, but almost as often they themselves are the victims of violence. After a thug throws acid in his face in the first novel, Coffin Ed becomes distinctly volatile toward criminals, uncooperative witnesses, and racist white policemen and must periodically be restrained by his partner.

The formula for a traditional detective story, whether it is hard-boiled or a classic whodunit, is basically a stable one: "crime + clues + deduction = solution." If the hard-boiled model substitutes action for reason as a deductive method, it generally also offers some version of truth seeking. Clues and deduction play very little part in the process of detection in these texts, however. Criminal motives can be opaque to the conventional logic of detection, reflecting Himes's conviction that black culture was opaque to white authority. Criminals are rarely punished according to conventional processes; instead, the detectives seek exposure of the criminals or restitution to their victims: Coffin and Digger steal the profits from a spurious Back-to-Africa group to give to neighborhood families and children and let a murderer go when they believe the victim deserved to die. Knowing in advance that his targets will probably be beyond the reach of justice, Taibo's detective describes his mission as follows: "I'm going to find out as much as I can, and fuck with them as much as I can."[17]

Rational, scientific, or even traditional hard-boiled methods (strong-arming, chatting up the local police lieutenant) are ineffective in Mexico and Harlem because neither operates according to the rationalist/positivist tenets that (at least nominally) governed detective narrative in its earlier incarnations. Grave Digger and Coffin Ed acknowledge that "the Medical Examiner's report, photographs, fingerprints, the findings of the criminal laboratory and all the results of modern police techniques—including police theories—were generally useless in solving murders in Harlem."[18] Taibo, too, states unequivocally that "there is no science that can help a Mexican discover the truth."[19] When his detective finds himself in a typical Chandler-style confrontation, even standard hard-boiled methods are rendered inoperable:

> It had all seemed so simple: take out gun, kick door down, rush into room. Now, according to the script, he ought to either beat the shit out of the fat man until he gave the name of the hotel on Zaragoza Boulevard, or lure him into a conversation and trick him into spilling the beans that way. Hector didn't feel capable of either one.[20]

The relationship of the detective to the criminal in the hard-boiled novel is an inherently unstable one, in which the detective's actions provoke an escalation of violence as the criminal tries to remain undetected. Belascoarán's "method" of detection is the inverse: he deliberately provokes the escalation of violence by harassing or assaulting his suspects. Rather than rage, as in Coffin Ed's case, Héctor's violent actions are the result of a vague impulse to provocation that he himself does not fully understand and that he observes with some detachment: "Because happy endings weren't made for Mexico. . . . Hector was impelled by these, and other, more obscure motivations, toward the finale."[21]

Hard-boiled solutions are often bloody, disillusioning, and complex, but the central mystery is explained; loose ends are tied up, and corrupt or not, an underlying order is revealed. Both Taibo and Himes depart radically from this model in their treatment of solutions, which may have little or no causal relationship with the original crime. Survival alone is an achievement, as Belascoarán observes in *Cosa fácil*:

> It was crazy. There was nothing else like it, nothing else to compare it to. But when, in the course of six short months, there had been six different attempts on his life (with a scar to show for every one of them) . . . then, and only then, did the joke cease to be a joke on him alone, and it became part and parcel of the city itself, of the whole damn country even.[22]

Defending Belascoarán's resuscitation in his forth novel of the group, Taibo claims that "resurrection is a Mexican phenomenon" (la resurrección es un fenómeno mexicano) (Ramirez, 'Paco Ignacio Taibo II," 44); that is, the readers willingly suspend their disbelief in order to continue sharing Belascoarán's adventures. But resurrection has another, more political role, as Chester Himes said: "When America kills a nigger it expects him to remain dead. . . . But I didn't know I was supposed to die." Himes's metaphorical death in the critical press, like Taibo's, is analogous to Hector's death at the end of *No habrá final feliz*; he simply refuses to cooperate with conventional expectations.[23] In Himes's final novel, *Plan B*, which is not part of the Harlem domestic series, Ed kills Digger before being murdered himself.

Taibo's detective is conditionally optimistic in that he believes himself to be acting on behalf of a specific community—"los nativos" or "chilangos": the natives of the D.F., as opposed to "las autoridades"—but Himes is undeniably a pessimist. There is little sympathy for the victims: Harlem is populated by a cannibalistic mélange of pushers, gangsters, whores, and pimps who routinely sell each other out to white policemen, perverts, and politicians. Community and well-being themselves are

members of a linguistic community that is hermetic to outsiders.[34] Harlem residents speak in a code that multiplies meaning and, at the same time, redirects discourse to the rawness of actuality. "You is going to be happy," says Sister Heavenly, a heroin pusher who masquerades as a faith healer, to a sick man. "You is going to be happy if you got the faith." He replies as she jabs him with the needle, "I is got the faith."[35] A drug peddler masquerading as a Sister of Mercy quotes equivocal scripture as he sells two "tickets to heaven" to a little girl: "And I saw heaven opened, and beheld a white horse."[36]

Chester Himes's Harlem is not only a fragmented urban space; it, like its population, exists in complete segregation from the rest of New York. It is a city within a city, just as the two black detectives are a separate unit within the (then white) New York metropolitan police force. White policemen are unable to function effectively in Harlem because they do not understand the language and all black people look alike to them. Black fugitives panic on leaving Harlem, and respectable citizens change their clothes to cross its boundaries. This geographical boundary echoes the racial one. Belascoarán is also afraid of leaving the D.F.: "that outside of the D.F. he was a dead man" (que fuera del DF era cadáver).[37]

In "Chester Himes: Black Guns and Words," Nora Alter traces a trajectory from the detectives' function as mediators between the black and white spheres in the early novels to one of complete rejection by both, which renders them completely ineffective by the final novel, *Blind Man with a Pistol*, in 1969. This trajectory follows major events in race relations, from school desegregation and other civil rights actions in the early 1960s to increasingly militant movements like Back-to-Africa, Black Power, and the Black Muslims. But Chester Himes's political views appear to have been fully radicalized from the beginning: only his external points of reference change. His portrayal of black religious or militant movements as large-scale scams clearly demonstrates his belief that they are merely secondary attributes of racism. As he states in his autobiography, violent action, not language, is the sole viable response to a discourse that is already controlled by the enemy.[38]

Ultimately, the confusion of identities, multiplied by linguistic games, equivocal gender signification, scams, and masquerades, resolves itself in the universal epithets "nigger" and "mother-raper," the verbal equivalents of the physical violence with which they alternate. Violence, then, is to be regarded as a response not only to racism but also to a generic confusion emanating from problems of identity, nationality, and cultural affiliation. In a world where beauty and wealth usually signal evil, the hard-boiled detective is conspicuously ugly: scarred, lame, or otherwise disfigured.[39] In keeping with this tradition, Héctor Belascoarán is one-eyed, lame, and covered with scars. Coffin Ed's face is disfigured from acid, and Grave Digger's hairline is marked by a finger-size scar where a bullet took off his hair. All three detectives have been shot repeatedly. More than mere battle scars, these marks are the physical inscriptions of the bearers' marginalized, absurd engagement with a brutal society: the scars of the vigilante who combats an overwhelmingly powerful enemy."[40]

Like Himes, Taibo enjoys critical success mostly outside his own country and considers Mexican literary criticism to be just another form of hegemonic discourse. His detective Belascoarán is likewise not native to Mexico: rather, he willfully uses his profession to insert himself into its social, political, and historical discourses. As an antidote to official history and the sacred myths and icons of Mexican nationality, Taibo's hero engages in the interstitial experiences of popular urban culture: frequenting street vendors and taquerías (where he often gets sick), shopping at the Medellín market, taking merengue lessons in a local arts center, riding the subway, walking the streets at night, injecting his cases into radio talk shows, TV quiz shows, and other popular media. His physical, or "horizontal," interaction with and traversal of the city compliments his use of the "vertical" mass media to assert cultural bonds.[41] Héctor and his friends speak a distinct Mexico City argot laced with profanity, malapropisms, and bad grammar, addressing each other, ridiculously, with the formal "usted." His officemates' professions are laughably prosaic but symbolize the multilayered corruption of Mexican politics. A plumber, an upholsterer, and a sewage engineer, they all deal with the hind end of society and its excrement, like Héctor.

Himes's Harlem stories dramatize the predicament of thinking black men in a racist society. The violence in Taibo's Mexico occurs in a much more overtly wholesale manner, is primarily institutional in nature, and assaults the citizenry as a whole: *Algunas nubes* recounts the true story of fourteen drug traffickers who were robbed and assassinated by police and dumped in a sewer; *No habrá final feliz* revisits the Halcones; *Adiós Madrid* recounts the theft of Moctezuma's breastplate from the national museum. Most of the crimes can be traced to the police, who are brutal and arbitrary: as Taibo says, "they are loyal to no one . . . they like to fuck with people. There is nothing in the world they like more than the power they wield when they terrorize someone."[42]

Beyond his own self-defense, Belascoarán's violent acts appropriate this institutional barbarism and reorganize it on an individual level, in the same way that his individualized historical investigations aim to recover history from textbooks written by the power elite. Belascoarán personifies Taibo's interrogation of institutionalized patriotism: he chases down reports of "un tal Zapata, de nombre don Emiliano" reputed to be living in a cave; visits the house of one of Pancho Villa's twenty-five wives; and rescues the stolen breastplate of Moctezuma. Taibo's interest in radical history, workers' movements, and detective novels all fit together in "una especie de lógica de resistencia del ciudadano contra el sistema."[43] His willed enactment of revolutionary ideals melds with the detective project in *Cosa fácil*, where Héctor is assisted by El Cuervo, a nighttime deejay who alludes to the possibilities of a collective venture into deduction: "the folks out there'll do what they can. You can't imagine how many people are out there listening just waiting for a chance to help out, to be a part of something."[44]

Both Taibo and Himes attempt to combat the rhetoric of victimization through which marginalized peoples are often represented. In Mexico, the image of the savage, hermetic Mexican popularized by Octavio Paz (among others) led to the cultural binarism of "chingar o ser chingado." Taibo counters the construct of Mexico as a nation of victims by transforming victimization into a fulcrum for resistance. Belascoarán's personal identity as a Mexican of the masses—a victim who complains about the price of tortillas and the corruption of the transit police—is the source of his energy and diligence as a detective. Through it the powerlessness and suffering of the everyday citizen reconstructs itself as a critical stance that facilitates resistance and even action:

> This social conscience that emerged from a primitive, elemental humanism, from an eminently superficial evaluation of the situation, from a political consciousness constructed from within the detective's own personal world, let him at the very least envision Mexico with mordant penetration, from a critical vantage-point, from outside power and privilege.[45]

Balancing his utopian vision of fraternity, however, is Belascoarán's realization that the exercise of his profession is inherently absurd in Mexico, where the revelation of truth does not necessarily alter the fact of injustice. In this context, his identification with the everyday Mexican citizen, formerly a source of empowerment, becomes the source of dislocation and expatriation. Belascoarán's prayer to the goddess of night (whom he implicitly offers as an alternative to other national female icons such as the Virgin of Guadalupe or "la chingada," La Malinche) reveals his despair of ever realizing his ephemeral *patria*:

Our lady of the lightless hours, protect us, lady of the night, watch over us.

Watch over us, because we are not among the worst that is left to this city, and yet we have nothing, we are worth nothing. We aren't of this place, nor do we renounce this place, nor do we know how to go to another place from which to yearn for these abandoned streets, the afternoon sun, banana *liquados*, tacos with salsa verde, the Zócalo on the sixteenth of September, the baseball diamond in Cuauhtémoc Stadium, the Christmas specials on Channel 4, this terrible loneliness that torments us with its stubborn pursuit. And this awful fear that forgives nothing.[46]

The culture of victimization was also problematic for Chester Himes. While he always perceived himself as a victim of racism, Himes wanted his detective novels to show black life as absurd, rather than pathetic. In contrast, Himes intended his texts to be "a protest against racism itself excusing all their sins and major faults."[47] The brutality of Coffin Ed and Grave Digger is directed primarily toward the black community and is meant to illustrate this attitude, which refuses to excuse criminals on the basis of oppression alone. The criminals who evoke the most rage and hatred are those who ally themselves with white criminals to prey on Harlem.

For Taibo's Belascoarán, violence is an inescapable part of Mexican experience. Belascoarán's choice to be a detective, like Ed and Digger's choice to be policemen, results less from his commitment to an abstract notion of justice than to an imagined community. As isolated as they are by their seemingly absurd choice of profession, it is only by the exercise of that profession—whose symbiotic relationship with crime licenses their use of violence—that they are empowered to pursue this patriotic ideal. But in order to do this, Belascoarán, like Coffin Ed and Grave Digger, must "embrace the demonic."[48] In the end, he admits, a terrorist detective is not necessarily any better than a criminal:

When he thought about it, it seemed to Hector that he'd gotten away with as much as any of the others. Hadn't he thrown sticks of dynamite, blown up station wagons, shot down gunmen, without having anything happen to him in return?

He was almost ready to accept the upholsterer's dictum, heard over and over again in their shared office: "In Mexico nothing happens, and even if something does, still nothing happened."[49]

Fredric Jameson believes that the detective story foregrounds the significance of fragmentary, everyday acts in a way that "high" literature does not, by revealing interstitial, extraofficial realities to the half-focused mind. The "right to signify" or construct history from an unprivileged position is the political analogue to the interstitial niche occupied by genre fiction: an ideological objective whose formal modes of expression are to be found in the cross-cultural phenomena of popular culture. Taibo asserts this right to signify through a popular genre; likewise, he asserts the existence of a community of detective-novelist activists through references to his international colleagues: Leonardo Padura Fuentes and Juan Hernández Luna appear in *La bicicleta de Leonardo*; Rolo Diez and Manuel Vázquez Montalbán in *La vida misma*. This impulse to solidarity reinserts the genre, subversively, into the cultural discussion that tries to ignore it.

If Chester Himes was initially ambivalent about writing genre fiction and only agreed to do so for financial reasons, Taibo was clearer about his adoption of a traditionally "low" genre and resists attempts to describe the Belascoarán Shayne novels as parodic (which would tend to legitimize them in the Latin American tradition). His transplantation of the genre to a seemingly hostile environment, rather than attenuating this generic connection, enriches the genre by reasserting its popular roots.

Carmen Boullosa's Media Megametropolis

The Belascoarán novels represent Taibo's attempt to inscribe a discursive space from the margins of cultural endeavor. He admits that the odds are against him: the absurd rumors of Zapata's survival may be simply a counterdiscourse arising from the desperation of the masses systematically deprived of access to the truth: "it was a natural defense against an enemy that controlled both media and myth."[50] Carmen Boullosa's novel *The Miracle-Worker* (*La Milagrosa*, 1993) uses a variation on the detective formula to reveal the mechanisms of this control.

La Milagrosa is concerned with the struggle for representation. Its two primary, interconnected narratives describe the predicament of women as symbols to be described, disfigured, and consumed by men; and the power of the *Partido Revolucionario Institucional* (PRI) and its systematic manipulation of the public through mass-media images. The novel's fragmented, polyphonic texture defies easy decipherment, commenting on the detective genre's putative legibility to suggest that the narratives of public life are totalizing literary constructions that obscure a complex and contested reality.

The figure of La Milagrosa alludes to the Virgin of Guadalupe, Mexico's patron saint and one of its most important popular cultural icons. A virgin who works miracles in her dreams, the Milagrosa has become the center of the communal life of her barrio. The space of the barrio Santa Fe, where the Milagrosa lives, represents a nonmodern, nonrational, faith-driven episteme that is strongly associated with the feminine through the metonymic figure of the Milagrosa. Although outsiders are afraid of entering this space, the community improvements (schools, parks, etc.) that have come about through La Milagrosa's presence suggest that rationality is not a requisite to well-being.

The Milagrosa is engaged in a struggle to maintain her spiritual and psychic (and physical) integrity amid all the claims on her persona and to sustain herself as "one in the face of a temptation of a dozen different fractions."[51] After being tricked by a conservative presidential candidate into rehabilitating his image, she falls in love with a detective and sheds her iconic identity as Virgin/Miracle Worker to become the flesh and blood woman, Elena. Simultaneously, she leaves the domesticated space of the barrio Santa Fe for the megametropolis that is the modern-day D.F. The brightly lit, masculine, linear space of Insurgentes Avenue is associated with the ubiquitous media image of the dishonest candidate Felipe Morales on televisions and billboards. Like Raymond Chandler's Los Angeles, the D.F. is "a new, centerless city in which the various classes have lost touch with each other because each is isolated in [its] own geographical compartment."[52] The powerful exploit this fragmentation by pouring images into the vacuum where civic discourse once took place. Bombarded with media propaganda, the people forget the Milagrosa and, sheeplike in their consumerism, give their allegiance to the image of Morales. The Milagrosa's destruction as an icon, if only a popular one, is a necessary precursor to Morales's monopolistic takeover of the public imagination.

The novel's connection to the detective genre resides in the character of Aurelio Jiménez, a private detective who has been hired by a corrupt union to discredit the Milagrosa. The story begins with what is presumably his corpse (there are no certainties to be discovered in Boullosa's text), which inverts both the chronology and characterological functioning of the detective genre. Throughout the story, he is the subject of an ever more ominous police and media manhunt, having been framed (again, presumably) for brutalizing two women.

The problem of representation is reinforced by a system of doubles throughout the text. Minor doublings (a play on the names Jiménez / Giménez) reflect a much graver crisis of signification. Felipe Morales and his much younger lover Norma Juárez are doubled by a taxi driver from the City (mirrored by a Santa Fe taxi driver) and his much younger wife; Norma and the union secretary Lupe are beaten (actually, Norma's

para el puma takes place in the city of Puebla. It is a somewhat chaotic narrative that unites people-smuggling, murder, a secret cache of revolutionary artillery, popular protests against the Puebla electric company, and a mysterious entity called the "furtive hand" *(mano furtiva)*, reports of whose indecent gropings punctuate the story. The protagonists are a drunk, a magician, two young video artists, and sundry others, and the action is manic and fragmented. With each generation of writers, less and less of the mystery gets resolved, and Hernández Luna continues this trend.

Olivier Debroise is an anomalous but interesting case: a critic and art historian whose novel *Lo peor sucede al atardecer* (1990) is set in Acapulco and the D.F. The protagonist, symbolically named Mateo Osorio, is a European-trained criminologist in the Mexican police. His trust in forensic technology renders him virtually useless and even embarrassing to his superiors, because the "unsolvable crimes that require delicate investigations and have to be led with incredible discretion" do not exist in Mexico.[57] A man of infinite virtue and discipline, Mateo is a cultural and temporal misfit. However, when he gets sent to Acapulco to investigate a murder, he becomes involved with a group of decadent fashionistas, who gradually devour him spiritually. Obsessed by the investigation, Osorio disappears halfway through the book, literally consumed in a miasma of evil and mystery. He loses his family, his job, his life in the D.F., his identity, and, finally, he even alters his sexuality, as he drifts into a new life as a homosexual beach bum. The novel is unrelentingly cynical; as one jaded journalist says, evil is no longer the enemy but a sort of inoculation against mediocrity: "Evil is fashionable. But it's not even a moral thing anymore, but a way to defend yourself from mediocrity and tastelessness. From anguish and fear. . . . face the evil, make it yours, shape as an aesthethic of your times."[58]

Rolo Diez and Myriam Laurini are writers of what Taibo calls the "literatura policial Argen-Mex." Both are Argentines, detective writers, and journalists who have lived in Mexico City since 1980. *Nota roja 70's* and *Nota roja 80's*, on which they collaborated, are annotated compilations of news articles on true-crime cases of those two decades, such as the case of the Mummies of Tlatelolco, where the bodies of two murdered students were preserved in garbage inside a ventilation duct for seven years; the strangler of Coyoacán; the tamale maker who killed her husband, cut him up, and boiled his head in her tamale pot; the Chiapaneca maid who killed her mistress; the policemen who tortured and killed fourteen drug dealers and dumped them in the River Tula; and the killings of journalist Manuel Buendía and DEA agent Enrique Camarena. In most cases the ferocity and mindlessness of the crimes speaks for itself, but Diez and Laurini have added some background information and the occasional commentary.

Laurini's 1994 *Morena en rojo* is a meandering narrative that follows the peregrinations, loves, and losses of la Morena, a half-black Mexican woman, sometime *nota roja* journalist and part-time factory worker. The case that nominally unites the episodes involves child prostitution, but the protagonist becomes involved in other lives, such as those of the *maquileras* on the border, that are defined by ignorance, powerlessness, and exploitation. All the crimes are taken from actual news stories.

Rolo Diez is the author of *Los compañeros* (1987), *Vladimir Illich contra los uniformados* (1989), *Paso del tigre* (1992), *Una baldosa en el valle de la muerte* (1992), *Paso y voy* (1993), *Gatos de azotea* (1993), and *Luna de escarlata* (1994; it won the Hammett Prize for a detective novel in Spanish in 1995). Like that of Chester Himes, Diez's work has been extremely well received in France. His novels have an *esperpento* quality that goes beyond Taibo's reflective private eye. A chapter of *Luna de escarlata* opens: "The night I set fire to the Rat was the beginning of all my misfortunes."[59] Whereas Laurini's rather romantic novel emphasizes the life of the individual, Diez's replicate the chaos of present-day Mexico from a variety of perspectives, in order to show that no one is immune from its violence and corruption.

Taibo wrote of the *neopoliciaco* that "in this new Spanish-speaking detective genre, there wasn't a genre being nationalized, but a national genre being created."[60] Laurini and Diez have picked up where he, Rafael Bernal, and Jorge Ibargüengoitia left off. Eschewing the traditional detective, they concentrate on figures and events from real life in Mexico. Diez in particular draws a world so unspeakable that the reader would find it hard to believe, if it weren't already in the daily newspapers. The past and its failed Revolution are no longer his focus: instead, he draws us into the apocalyptic future of the biggest city in the world. No longer self-conscious about the limitations or origins of the genre, Diez's narrative combines black humor, pathos, and stark horror to evoke the dehumanizing effects of decades of cynicism and corruption. He dispenses with the single protagonist, shifting perspectives from predator to victim to Mexico City itself, a dark, menacing abyss where even the enclaves of the privileged are vulnerable to omnipotent criminal forces. Like cyberpunk, Diez's novels link present to future in a calamitous chain of inevitability.

Epilogue:
Globalization and Detective
Literature in Spanish

*W*alter Benjamin likened both the detective and the criminal predator to the alienated, modern figure of the *flâneur* in fin de siècle Paris, whose ability to read his surroundings is a function of his outsider status. Poe, wrote Benjamin, was the first writer to apply scientifically and aesthetically modern ideas to the messy phenomena of crime. His detective narratives were the original "exposition of pathological manifestations."[1] The inscrutable genius of a Dupin, Holmes, or Poirot represented the social decontextualization of modern man and the solitary, disengaged eminence of the artist. Raymond Chandler believed that a good hard-boiled detective never gets married. His lonely, alienated heroes represent the pyrrhic victory of modern individualism over democratic mediocrity. Georg Lukács also intuited that the modernist vision of man was that of an essentially solitary being, while the realist vision saw human existence as a social phenomenon wherein man functions as an integral part of his circumstances.

As opposed to Hercule Poirot or Hammett's faceless Continental Op, the *neopoliciaco* detective often enjoys a family or social life.[2] Nonetheless, his critical acuity and the moral credibility of his position depend on his alienation from authority and all its systems, in parallel with the alienation of man under capitalism. Through a genre that critiqued modernist ethics and aesthetics, Hispanic *neopoliciaco* writers move toward an ahistorical, alienated subjectivity. Manuel Vázquez Montalbán's book-burning detective Pepe Carvalho displays the sensual aestheticism of the modernist: the iconoclastic, solitary act of destroying his library suggests a deliberate act of estrangement from the intellectual and political fabric of his Marxist formation, and a renunciation of the Unamunian "problema de España." He rejects equally the crisis of modernity and the discursive lineage of *casticismo*, opting to reenact a daily fecal dialectic in its most literal sense: from each hunger pang to each bite of food consumed (organ meats predominate) to the equally detailed act of defecation, culminating in a wiping clean with pages from the day's arts editorials.

Paco Taibo's Héctor Belascoarán Shayne, despite his socialist fervor, has deliberately chosen the most solitary profession possible in his social and political milieu. His reading habits, which form an important subtext to the action of the novels, disclose a love for the ideals of socialism (Marx, Che Guevara, Bertolt Brecht, Fernández Retamar, Mario Benedetti) but also reveal his essential nihilism, articulated by an epigraph taken from Sartre: "There is only hope in action."[3] He is the embodiment of Octavio Paz's famous rendering of the Mexican national motto, "chingar o ser chingado"; however, while Paz's construal was essentially one of vulnerability, Belascoarán insistently reenacts this dictum in defiance of the postsocialist reality he inhabits. Padura's Mario Conde, who spends his conscious hours drinking himself into unconsciousness, represents the progressive psychological and social disintegration of a personality confronted with an attenuated ideology and an increasingly meaningless reality. His love affair with the decaying city of Havana mirrors his quixotic commitment to a defrauded ideal.

The detective novel's future in Cuba and Mexico is uncertain: generic markers like the serial detective are disappearing even as crime-fiction narratives proliferate. Leonardo Padura suggests that there is no more detective genre, only a *género negro*: a "black genre" that represents crime, chaos, and the alienation of a not quite modern condition. Chronic economic failures in Mexico, like the United States embargo on trade with Cuba and the resulting publishing crisis, have created a difficult climate for the production and diffusion of popular literature.

In Cuba, the loss of trade caused by the dissolution of the Soviet Union created a crisis in printing that drastically reduced the number of books published. Distribution of detective novels was reduced to editions of five and ten thousand.[4] The prize system that once signaled the immediate publication of a novel no longer provides that guarantee, and publication may take several years. The legalization of dollars has led to an even more difficult situation, since some bookstores now sell only in dollars, to which many Cubans have limited access in the two-tiered economy of the early twenty-first century. During the late 1980s and early 1990s many well-known detective writers (Justo Vasco, Alberto Molina, Bertha Recio Tenorio, Rodolfo Pérez Valero, Juan Carlos Fernández) emigrated to Spain and the United States. Paradoxically, it was the economic crisis, with all the attendant difficulties in communication and production, that permitted a relaxation of censorship in Cuba. Those who remained in Cuba saw the detective genre as an increasingly viable outlet for social criticism. Leonardo Padura, who appears to be firmly committed to staying in Cuba, also suggests that the crisis enabled some Cuban writers to risk being more outspoken, since they didn't know whether their work would ever get published.[5]

However, although by the late 1990s censorship had eased somewhat in Cuba (and smaller, more expensive editions reduced the availability and impact of books in general), the Castro government found a new impetus for repressing dissent in the Elián González affair of 1999–2000. "El niño Elián" became a rallying point for the ideology of embattlement. The call for national unity provided a justification for tightening many of the controls that had begun to relax under the "special period," and many writers now speak of the conditions of censorship "before and after Elián."

Leonardo Padura has said that he will not write any more Mario Conde novels. The Four Seasons tetralogy is currently in production as a series of four TV movies in Spain. Nonetheless, Padura's work has changed the way that Cuban detective writers view their relationship to, and responsibilities toward, official discourse. His latest novella, *Adiós Hemingway* (2000), is a Conde mystery in which Conde is no longer a policeman and has effectively become a private detective whom his former colleagues of the police must consult on a difficult, academic case.

Given Padura's success, perhaps more authors will eventually feel at liberty to write critically about a difficult period in the history of Cuba. Some Cubans now living outside Cuba, such as Justo Vasco, also continue to write crime fiction, as well as publishing texts that were considered too problematic or provocative by the Cuban publishing establishment. Vasco, while still committed to the ideals of the Revolution, rejects the rigidity and intolerance of its social agenda as expressed in the socialist detective novel. For many detective writers of his generation, he believes, initial fervor for the socialist project created the unintentional paradox of an exclusionary rhetoric. This view is one that must certainly prevail in a new group of Cuban detective novels being written from the perspective of exile. Another growing category of genre detective writers is Cuban American: Alex Abella's Charlie Morell and Carolina Aguilera-García's Lupe Solano are two popular Cuban American detective protagonists.

Unexpectedly, the decline of the Cuban detective novel within Cuba has coincided with its discovery by English-speaking audiences. Akashic Books is actively promoting Cuban noir in translation, with the publication of Uruguayan-Cuban Daniel Chavarría's *Adiós muchachos* (which won an Edgar in 2001) and *The Eye of Cybele* (2002); Arnaldo Correa's *Spy's Fate* (2002). Their Cuban noir collection was founded with the publication of José Latour's intriguing novel *Outcast* in 2001.

In 1999 an anomalous text was published by a small press in the United States. José Latour's *Outcast* was written in English, but the author lives in Cuba. An updated answer to Luis Rogelio Nogueras's *Y si muero mañana*, Latour's novel also spans the Straits of Florida. Like Nogueras, the author is harshly critical of United States consumerism and Miami Cuban culture, but he balances his criticism with an excruciatingly detailed portrait of the slow death by starvation—both physical and social—that faces apolitical Cubans on the island. As the title suggests, the novel's protagonist is an outcast in Cuban society: a frustrated English teacher who, because of his American father, lives as a third-class citizen in the supposedly classless state.

Elliot Steil loves Cuba's people, climate, and way of life, but when offered the opportunity, he feels he can't pass up the chance to escape his situation, in which "unknown persons behind closed doors could make, on an essentially political basis and with full impunity, irrevocable decisions on absent human beings."[6] In Cuba, all relationships are politicized: success or failure depends on the constant, jealous vigilance of colleagues, neighbors, and teachers. Even the "opportunistic political bastards"—members of the party who receive coveted jobs, housing, and other benefits—feel trapped in the system and embarrassed by their own self-interest.

Rather than any explicitly criminal activity (except the inevitable black-market food purchases, now tacitly and universally admitted), it is Steil's lack of political enthusiasm that is perceived as subversive. It results in his being passed over for promotion, ostracized, and ultimately starved for lack of access to the life-giving dollars that can buy cooking oil, soap, and other staples. He has lost forty pounds in the Special Period, and his passivity and resignation are a constant recrimination to his more political colleagues. His one marketable asset is his ability to speak English. The wealth of detail about the misery of day-to-day existence in Cuba in the middle 1990s far surpasses that in Padura's Four Seasons series. Latour injects anti-Fidel jokes into the dialogue and describes the ruinous effects of the two-tiered economy as it transforms the political elite into a capitalist one.

If Latour's criticisms of Cuba are harsh, Cuban Miami fares even worse in *Outcast*. Like Nogueras, Latour condemns the unbridled consumerism of the exiles in long lists of brand names (guns, cars, and liquor) and descriptions of testosterone-crazed low-lifes. Through a series of misadventures the mild-mannered Cuban teacher becomes a cold-blooded criminal in Miami. Compared with the intrusive regulation of Cuban life, the freedom of the United States is immoral and anarchical: "America confuses liberty with libertinism."[7] The plot is labyrinthine and slightly ridiculous (involving, among other things, a Jewish gang that traffics in illegal refrigerants), and marked by the protagonist's moments of prorevolutionary regret: he secretly would have loved to volunteer in Nicaragua, and he even misses the Cuban health system. Lamentably (proving that old habits die hard), the villain turns out to be a gay FBI agent.

Despite its overt political messages, the novel's ideological interest is perhaps more in the circumstances of its production than in its content. Latour's English-language novel is clearly aimed at a United States audience and, in fact, has been somewhat successful. It is an example of the kind of postnational market-seeking that the Cuban economic and political situation has inspired. As more and more successful authors publish outside Cuba and for specifically non-Cuban audiences, this formerly national literature becomes an effectively globalized one.

Following the innovations of Rafael Bernal and Jorge Ibargüengoitia, Paco Ignacio Taibo II paved the way for a new generation of Mexican detective writers who create authentic detective fiction without apology to either the Mexican literary establishment or to their North American precursors. Their challenge, once conceived in historical and literary terms, now must be framed within the context of the drastic increase in crime caused by the economic crisis that followed Carlos Salinas's disastrous devaluation of the peso in the early 1990s. As corruption and crime spin out of control, the Mexican detective novel has grown increasingly chaotic. Taibo himself writes that the City is beginning to escape his descriptive powers: "There is in this city a perverse condensation of madness and horror, mingled with a stack of myths. It's a frankly unstable city, full of malignant vibes and attempts at solidarity. Catastrophe pervades it and everyday protests nourish it. Lately it fucks me up, because it gets away from me, I can't get hold of it like I used to."[8]

In order to compete with reality itself, Mexican detective writers must transform the linguistic tools available to them, creating a new language to describe the violence and confusion of their times. Not surprisingly, many of the writers in this genre also write science fiction and horror stories.

Market appeal, which to a great extent defines genre fiction, favors conformity to generic norms, narrative simplicity, and the serial protagonist. However, the market is much less relevant in Mexico and Cuba than in countries like the United States or Spain. Mauricio-José Schwarz, a writer and critic of genre fiction, stresses the difference between the North American and Mexican book markets: with the exception of Taibo, most Mexican authors can't expect to see their works published in editions of more than two thousand. He attributes this to the "small but dwindling" number of Mexicans who read, as greatly straitened financial circumstances have combined with disastrous post-1968 government education policies to reduce literacy among the public at large.[9] Since the phenomenon itself depends on market success, the existence and survival of genre fiction under such circumstances is an anomaly at best. Taibo continues to run the yearly Semana Negra in Spain and works indefatigably to promote the genre, but he has not produced a Belascoarán Shayne novel since *Adiós Madrid* in 1993.

For writers in both Cuba and Mexico, however, international contacts offer a range of possibilities, including the potential to reach much wider audiences. Padura and Taibo are only two of the many Latin American detective writers whose books are increasingly published in Spain, thus circumventing economic limitations, an inhospitable critical climate, and the possibility of censorship. The yearly meeting in Gijón of the International Association of Detective Writers is both a stimulus and an outcome of this growing internationalism.

Between 1968 and the present, the detective novel in Spanish developed far beyond its mimetic origins, past the impulse to parody, and came to maturity as a genre with its own discursive spaces and mythologies. Paco Ignacio Taibo II acknowledges that this success depended on a departure from previous approaches: "See, the easy way out was using a Juan Martinez or Pedro Peres [sic], but you don't construct a national genre with these imitations."[10] A truly Mexican version of the detective novel wasn't just a matter of changing labels but of rethinking the formal and ontological relationships between the crime novel and real life. Like Mexicans themselves, the *neopoliciaco* detective is scarred and cynical. He manifestly embodies the phenomena of postmodern fragmentation and hermeneutical disarray. Yet, confronted with systematic attempts to silence or annihilate him, he persists in asserting the right to self-representation, reaching beyond the tyrannies of the national to an "impure" discursive arena. Néstor García Canclini's term "impure" describes a transcultural, hybrid, reterritorializing form of expression "destined to affirm presence and even possession over a neighborhood" (destinada a afirmar la presencia y hasta la posesión sobre un barrio). His terminology also alludes to the hybridity of texts that combine the visual and the alphabetical, like grafitti and the *historieta*; in the case of the detective novel, this hybridity is generic—combining fictional elements with history, chronicle, literary criticism, and the *nota roja*—as well as cultural.[11]

García Canclini has commented extensively on the positionality of the Latin American subject under globalization: deprived of traditional spaces of representation by the increasing hostility and segregation of the urban environment, citizens become consumers of a globalized cultural product.[12] García Canclini is not necessarily pessimistic about this consumption; rather, he sees it as a potential agent of democratization and a significant aspect of an adaptive strategy of hybridization affected by the transnational, postcolonial subject.[13] While detective novels are not, strictly speaking, an expression of Latin American "popular culture," they increasingly reflect an awareness of identity as hybrid, postnational, and postmodern. García Canclini's characterization of the anthropologist's revised approach to this identity also mirrors the Latin American detective's methodology: it is *postempirical* and *posthermeneutic*.[14]

While Anglo-European academies may have declared the demise of the postmodernist enterprise, the problematic nature of modernity in Latin America has kept the question of postmodernity in play among many of its intellectuals. Their position is preeminently an ideological one, grounded in the conviction that social justice is compatible with, and indeed necessary to, aesthetic excellence. French theorists of the postmodern originally rejected Marxism and liberalism as "essentialist," or based on the same rationalist episteme that underlay modernity. Critics like Fredric Jameson, however, introduced a new, more politicized understanding of postmodernity, one that embraced postcolonial and subaltern perspectives and seemed much more applicable to Latin American political and cultural issues.

Because the Hispanic detective novel developed in a constant dialogue with hegemonic models, its writers were forced to adopt a defensively critical, analytical attitude toward their production. Hispanic detective writers—on the whole, a much more literary group than their Anglo counterparts—are well informed in Gramscian cultural theory, Chestertonian ethics, and poststructuralist aesthetics, and they are conversant with all the main international currents in detective literature and analysis. Their novels reflect concerns about both the aesthetic and ethical responsibilities of the writer and explore ways to reconcile the

which helped popularize the *novela negra* in Spain. The Mexican "Caimán" and Argentine "Rastros" series brought the hard-boiled novel to Spain in the 1950s. The prestigious Spanish publishing house Alianza reissued classics by Dashiell Hammett (1967) and Raymond Chandler (1973) and new works by Ross Macdonald. In the 1970s the Serie Negra de Enlace (started just before Franco's death) and another series by Bruguera started a boom for the North American *novela negra* that inspired Spanish writers to create their own version. See Roger Caillois, *The Mystery Novel*; also Régis Messac, *Le "detective novel" et l'influence de la pensée scientifique*; François Fosca, *Histoire et technique du roman policier*; Pierre Boileau and Thomas Narcejac, *Le roman policier*; and Fereydoun Hoveyda (René Ballet), *Historia de la novela policial*.

7. Reyes, "Sobre la novela policial," 339.

8. The *pelado* is a complex Mexican stereotype that combines insecurity, arrogance, and machismo. For an elaboration of the stereotype, see Samuel Ramos, *Profile of Man and Culture in Mexico*, 58–63.

9. Ilán Stavans's *Antihéroes: México y su novela policial* is a critical history that goes from the tabloid journalism of the 1930s (known as *nota roja*) to the early 1990s, with emphasis on comics, magazines, and film adaptations (64–66). Gabriel Trujillo Muñoz's *Testigos de cargo* is the most up-to-date description of the genre in Mexico and includes a valuable discussion of detective writing along the U.S.-Mexico border.

10. La forma de expresión poética más representativa de nuestro tiempo. Portuondo, *Astrolabio*, 51.

11. Spain's detective tradition goes back to the nineteenth century, when British and French "true-crime" stories were widely published in the *folletín*, a supplement that accompanied magazines and other periodicals. American dime novels and British "penny dreadfuls" were also popular. The collection *La Novela Moderna*, published by the Sopena Publishing House in the 1910s, consisted exclusively of British mystery titles. Although few literary figures interested themselves in the genre, Pedro Antonio de Alarcón published *El clavo y otros relatos de misterio y crimen* in 1853 (it significantly predates Arthur Conan Doyle's first Sherlock Holmes story); Emilia Pardo Bazán published a mystery story called "La gota de sangre" in 1911; and Enrique Jardiel Poncela wrote a series of parodies of Sherlock Holmes titled *Las siete novísimas aventuras de Sherlock Holmes* in 1928. During the Second World War many Spanish publishers moved to Argentina but continued to publish for the Spanish market. Agatha Christie, Erle Stanley Gardner, and Rex Stout became staples in the more than a hundred Spanish and Latin American series in production. A handful of Spanish detective writers began to emerge; to avoid political repercussions they often used anglicized pseudonyms, or even set their novels in England, France, or the United States. In 1965 the first Pliny novel by Spaniard Francisco García Pavón was published; its detective continued to appear in novels and short stories until 1982. A general perception of greater modernity after Franco's death—"the spread of legality as a social mentality and its reflection in a more modern legal

system" (la generalización de la ideología jurídica como mentalidad social y su reflejo en una regulación legal más moderna)—also encouraged Spanish writers to begin writing detective stories (Valles Calatrava, *La novela criminal española*, 108). Manuel Vázquez Montalbán's first Pepe Carvalho novel, *Yo maté a Kennedy*, was published in 1972 (by coincidence this was the same year as the first Concurso Aniversario del Triunfo de la Revolución, the detective fiction competition sponsored by the Cuban Ministry of the Interior). Other *novela negra* writers of the post-Franco transition period include Eduardo Mendoza, Jaume Fuster, Andreu Martín, and Juan Madrid. Paradoxically, one of the most successful detective writers today, Arturo Pérez Reverte, has reverted to the more traditional mystery format in his best-selling intellectual puzzlers. Pérez Reverte, elected in January 2003 to the Real Academia Española, is one of the few Hispanic detective writers (along with Paco Ignacio Taibo II and Jorge Ibargüengoitia) who have crossed over to achieve a wide readership in English. Sources on the development of Spanish detective fiction include Patricia Hart's *The Spanish Sleuth*; Valles Calatrava, *La novela criminal española*; Vázquez de Parga, *La novela policiaca en España*; Colmeiro, *La novela policiaca española*; Landeira, *El género policiaco en la literatura del siglo XIX*; and Renée W. Craig-Odders, *The Detective Novel in Post-Franco Spain*. George Demko provides useful overviews of Hispanic, Mexican, and Argentine mysteries on the Web at http://www.dartmouth.edu/~gjdemko/intcolumns.html.

12. Con Franco vivíamos mejor. The majority of contemporary Spanish detective stories are set in the modern industrial centers of Madrid and Barcelona (many of the authors are Catalan). Like many Mexican and Cuban writers, Spanish writers see the *novela negra* as a realistic critique of society's problems: "The crime novel that has overcome its puzzle debt and its exclusively biological or psychotic explanations of crime has been transformed into a genre dedicated to exposing the double truth that rules contemporary social conduct: power and para-power, order and disorder, politics and crime, liberty and state terrorism." (La novela criminal que ha superado las hipotecas crucugrámicas y las explicaciones exclusivamente naturalistas o psicóticas del porqué de delito se ha convertido en una novela dedicada a la revelación de la doble verdad que guía la conducta social contemporánea: poder y parapoder, orden y desorden, política y delito, libertad y terrorismo de estado.) Manuel Vázquez Montalbán, in Valles Calatrava, *La novela criminal española*, 9.

13. Un género surgido del lodo y la sangre del capitalismo. Luis Rogelio Nogueras, *Por la novela policial*, 9.

14. Somos el decorado exótico de los crímenes de Agatha Christie, somos los criados de ojos rasgados, las bailarinas fogosas que sirven de cebo para atrapar ingenuos blancos; somos el detective mas depreciado de todo el género policial: Charlie Chan. . . . Los ojos de la viejísima y astutísima Agatha . . . son, en verdad, los ojos del imperio. Julio Miranda, "Para una novela policiaca del subdesarrollo," 614 ff.

15. The Argentine literary critic Enrique Anderson Imbert (who is unjustly

overlooked as a writer and aficionado of detective stories) implicitly stated the problem when he asked, "Why are detective stories written in English? Could it be because only in civilized countries is there an aversion to violent death?" Enrique Anderson Imbert, "The General Makes a Lovely Corpse," in Amelia Simpson, ed., *Detective Fiction from Latin America*. The Cuban critic Leonardo Acosta surmises that Latin America lacks a detective tradition because of its history of criminal leaders: "As any sane person can see, ours is a continent that has been under the rule of the worst criminals for decades, whether their names be Somoza, Trujillo, Castillo Armas, Ubico, Juan Vicente Gómez or Stroessner." (Como es evidente para cualquier persona en su sano juicio, se trata de un continente que ha estado durante decenios sometido a la férula de los peores criminales, llámense Somoza, Trujillo, Castillo Armas, Ubico, Juan Vicente Gómez o Stroessner.) Acosta, *Novela policial y medios masivos*, 129.

16. ¿A quién le importa quién mató a Roger Ackroyd . . . si nadie sabe (oficialmente) quién fue el responsable de la matanza de Tlatelolco o quién ordenó el asalto de los Halcones el 10 de junio? Monsiváis, "Ustedes que jamás han sido asesinados," 10.

17. Borges was among many who acknowledged the political incongruity of the British-style detective story in a Latin American context: "the Englishman knows the agitation of two incompatible passions: the strange appetite for adventure and the strange appetite for legality. I say 'strange,' because for the *criollo* they are." (El inglés conoce la agitación de dos incompatibles pasiones: el extraño apetito de aventuras y el extraño apetito de legalidad. Escribo 'extraño,' porque para el criollo lo son.) Jorge Luis Borges, "Los laberintos policiales y Chesterton," 92. In most cases, Borges's investigations were on a purely intellectual plane, but in the Parodi stories he ventured a comment on the more political aspects of modernity. His jailed detective (who had been framed by the police) was a symbol of the same fettered justice, corruption, and equivocation that later appeared in the *neopoliciaco*.

18. Carlos Alonso, *The Burden of Modernity*, 23.

19. See Borges, "Los laberintos policiales y Chesterton"; "Modos de G. K. Chesterton"; "Sobre Chesterton"; "Emma Zunz," in *El Aleph*; "La muerte y la brújula" and "El jardín de senderos que se bifurcan," in *Ficciones*; and *Historia universal de la infamia*. Enrique Anderson Imbert asserted disingenuously that "there is no fiction by Borges that derives directly from one by Chesterton, but there are reflections" (No hay ficción de Borges que derive directamente de otra de Chesterton, pero hay reflejos) ("Chesterton en Borges," 83). See also Emir Rodríguez Monegal, *Jorge Luis Borges*; John T. Irwin, *The Mystery to a Solution: Poe, Borges, and the Analytic Detective Story*; Sylvia Molloy, *Signs of Borges*; Julio Chiappini, *Borges y Chesterton*; Elmar Schenkel, "Circling the Cross, Crossing the Circle: On Borges and Chesterton"; Marta Susana Domínguez, "El detective en el cuarto cerrado"; Naomi Lindstrom, "The Argentine Reading of Chesterton"; Aden W. Hayes and Khachig Tololyan, "The Cross and the Compass: Patterns of Order in Chesterton and Borges."

20. Ese arrebato duradero de asombro (y de gratitud). Borges, "Modos de G. K. Chesterton," 52.

21. Cada cuento de Chesterton viene a ser de algún modo como un cuadro, luego, como una pieza de teatro; luego, como una parábola. También están los paisajes—los personajes aparecen como actores que entran en escena, y son siempre muy vívidos; visualmente vívidos. Y después está la solución, que es siempre ingeniosa. Emir Rodríguez Monegal, *Borges por él mismo*, 123. Borges also admired Chesterton as a literary critic. In his *Introduction to English Literature* (with María Esther Vázquez), a volume so slim (like his *Introduction to North American Literature*, it consists of sixty-six pages) that it seems either a cipher or a joke, Borges made a game of incorporating Chesterton's literary judgment into his own.

22. G. K. Chesterton, "The Defendant," 119.

23. Ibid.

24. Quiere explicar, mediante la sola razón, un hecho inexplicable. Borges, "Sobre Chesterton," 88.

25. G. K. Chesterton, *Lunacy and Letters*, 35. Edgar Allan Poe's detective C. Auguste Dupin himself points out the fallacies of abstract logic when applied to moral intrigue. Dupin bases his method on the simple proposition that once he has identified a suspect as either a poet or a mathematician, he can anticipate whether his actions will be limited by logic. Poetry is the result of a synthetic, creative process, whereas mathematics is usually regarded as the simple recognition and description of preexisting, absolute truths. His method of detection in "The Purloined Letter" is ultimately founded not on reason but on intuition, imagination, and empathy. At times Dupin's close observation of his environment leads him to "common-sense" conclusions (equivalent to Father Brown's faith), as when he guesses his companion's thoughts. Both detectives attempt at all times to understand the concrete reality of the objects around them. Yet, while Poe's epistemological premise is modern—the domination of the external world by the rational human mind—Chesterton's is premodern, suggesting a strict, causal correspondence between appearance and essence.

26. Pocas personas juzgan necesario o agradable el conocimiento de *Les palais nomades*; muchas, el del *Oráculo del perro*. Claro que en el estímulo peculiar de los nombres de Chesterton obra nuestra conciencia de que esos nombres no han sido invocados en vano. Sabemos que en los *Palais nomades* no hay palacios nómadas; sabemos que *The oracle of the dog* no carecerá de un perro y de un oráculo, o de un perro concreto y oracular. Borges, "Modos de G. K. Chesterton," 51–52.

27. G. K. Chesterton, *The Father Brown Omnibus*, 107.

28. Borges praised Chesterton for dispensing with forensic timetables and maps, ashes, burnt matches, and fingerprints: "For every reasoning 'detective'—every Ellery Queen or Father Brown—there are ten match-collectors and clue-decipherers. Toxicology, ballistics, secret diplomacy, anthropometry, locksmithing, topography, and even criminology, have despoiled the purity of the crime genre." (Por un "detective" razonador—por un Ellery Queen o padre Brown—

hay diez coleccionistas de fósforos y descifradores de rastros. La toxicología, la balística, la diplomacia secreta, la antropometría, la cerrajería, la topografía, y hasta la criminología, han ultrajado la pureza del género policial.) *Borges en El Hogar*, 77.

29. G. K. Chesterton, *The Father Brown Omnibus*, 161.

30. Un juego de vanas repeticiones. Borges, "Nathaniel Hawthorne," in *Otras inquisiciones*, 59.

31. Los últimos intuyen que las ideas son realidades; los primeros, que son generalizaciones; para éstos, el lenguaje no es otra cosa que un sistema de símbolos arbitrarios; para aquéllos, es el mapa del universo. El platónico sabe que el universo es de algún modo un cosmos, un orden; ese orden, para el aristotélico, puede ser un error o una ficción de nuestro conocimiento parcial. Borges, "De las alegorías a las novelas," 155.

32. Franz Kuhn, the supposed discoverer of the Chinese encyclopedia in Borges's "El idioma analítico de John Wilkins" (in *Otras inquisiciones*) becomes a casualty of this semiotic elasticity. Kuhn was a nineteenth-century folklorist and linguist whose studies, according to his entry in the famous thirteenth edition of the *Encyclopaedia Britannica*, led him to believe that myth was the result of linguistic duplication: "polynomy, or the giving of many names to the same thing; and homonymy, or many things having the same name." His mania for interchanging signs culminated in the creation of an aesthetically interesting but ultimately pointless synthetic language.

33. Fredric Jameson, "Postmodernism and Consumer Society."

34. Paul de Man, "A Modern Master: Jorge Luis Borges," 129. As de Man noticed, the *Universal History of Infamy* is a book of mimetic crimes: "misdeeds like plagiarism, impersonation, espionage, in which someone pretends to be what he is not, substitutes a misleading appearance for his actual being."

35. Chesterton named his *Thursday* protagonists according to their symbolic functions. Because each has three identities, each has at least three names: one "real" (which we never learn, implying that it might be the sacred, cabalistic sign that Borges alluded to); another professional, and a third, allegorical. The ordinary (and therefore angelic) protagonist is called Gabriel Syme, and his companions are named descriptively, according to their disguises: the Professor de Worms (decrepit and repulsive), Gogol ("a man obviously mad"), Dr. Bull (short, vigorous), and so on. The mystery of their anarchist *noms de guerre* (Sunday, Tuesday, Saturday, etc.) resolves itself as an allegory of creation, but one that displaces creation itself. The resident nonbeliever is named Lucian Gregory, an allusion to the fallen angel Lucifer. G. K. Chesterton, *The Man Who Was Thursday, a Nightmare*, 6.

36. This misinterpretation may arise from Alfonso Reyes's introduction to his 1938 translation of *The Man Who Was Thursday*, in which he described Chesterton's good humor. See Reyes, *El hombre que fue jueves*. While the text certainly contains farcical elements, the overall effect of these, as Borges understood, is a mounting sense of anxiety, apprehension, and irreality. The novel's

subtitle is *A Nightmare*. Chesterton's detective stories likewise elicit a sense of unease and discomfort, starting with Father Brown himself, the "beloved" detective who is actually quite repulsive. He has a "moon-calf simplicity" and a "foolishly large head"; he is excessively short and shapeless, and permanently "dusty-looking." His method of solving puzzles stems not from a complex intelligence but rather from an extreme simplicity, which rejects interpretation in favor of faith. After catching the criminals, Father Brown never turns them over to the police. Society exacts no vengeance, and the evildoers are let free to roam again, having confessed their sins in the Catholic manner. Some are redeemed; others continue in the life of crime. (Chesterton's contemporaries criticized him for relying too heavily on the deus ex machina.)

37. G. K. Chesterton, "A Defence of Detective Stories," 120.

38. Chesterton advocated this practice in many essays on everyday objects, as in "Lamp-Posts," which he described as "the fixed beacon of the branching thoroughfares, the terrestrial star of the terrestrial traveller." See *The Uses of Diversity*, 7.

39. Georg Lukács, "The Ideology of Modernism," 609.

40. Ibid., 610.

41. This somewhat oversimplified view accepts the workings of reason and logic as the basis for the detective story, whereas Borges's stories more accurately reflect the "abductive" method described by semioticians, wherein any set of anomalous conditions can be arbitrarily reduced to an orderly system.

42. Borges distorts popular speech as a way of parodying literary attempts to define "the Argentine" (lo argentino). As we know from his unsympathetic portrayal of Carlos Argentino Daneri in "El Aleph," Borges disliked literary constructions of nationhood, which he recognized as just as much a "pastiche of the art of rhetoric" as "the soft-spoken, literary Chinese of old literary convention." Borges and Adolfo Bioy Casares (H. Bustos Domecq), *Six Problems for Don Isidro Parodi*, 11.

43. "The Nights of Goliadkin" is an extended parody of Chesterton, as is evident in the following passage: "Beneath the lavish blessing of life-giving sunshine, the fence posts, the wires, the thistles wept with joy. The sky grew suddenly immense, and the plain glowed in the light. The heifers seemed to be dressed in new clothes." *Six Problems for Don Isidro Parodi*, 48. An extended subtext on sacred bulls dominates the volume, a pseudocabalistic reference to the Argentine worship of beef and hence to the founding text of the Argentine short story genre, Esteban Echeverría's "El matadero."

44. Chesterton, "A Defence of Detective Stories," 123.

45. Fredric Jameson, "On Raymond Chandler," 15.

46. No está escrita (interview). Monsiváis has been consistently critical of the Mexican detective novel, notwithstanding his friendship with Paco Ignacio Taibo II and his regard for Antonio Helú, creator of the cynical detective Máximo Roldán. Monsiváis wrote the prologue for a new edition of Helú's *Obligación de asesinar*.

47. La novela policiaca pertenece a esa clase de expresiones culturales que constantemente han de estar pidiendo perdón por haber nacido. In Colmeiro, *La novela policiaca española*, 9.

48. La novela policiaca es, de todos los géneros realizables en letra impresa, el más despreciado por los espíritus graves. Alejo Carpentier, "Apología de la novela policiaca," 462. Though the French taste for noir fiction spread to Spain early on, so did a contempt for the classic mystery. As Thomas Narcejac explains: "In France the detective novel has never been taken seriously. Claudel considered the genre a dungheap. Academics, critics, intellectuals, everyone agrees in ranking it at the level of the *folletín*. The detective novel is the victim of a kind of racial segregation: it's a 'negro' and literature is a nice neighborhood he's not allowed to live in." (En Francia nunca se ha tomado en serio la novela policial. Claudel la consideraba un 'género estercolario.' Académicos, críticos, hombres de letras, coinciden todos en situarla al nivel de folletín. La novela policial es víctima de una especie de segregación racial; es un 'negro' y la literatura es un barrio elegante donde no tiene derecho a instalarse.) See Thomas Narcejac, "De Poe al thriller policial," 204.

49. Dichotomies like "highbrow/lowbrow," which Laurence Levine famously scrutinized, emphasize the separation of culture into elite and popular phenomena. During the nineteenth century the refinements of class distinction encouraged the "sacralization" of art in which the elevation of certain genres was accomplished at least in part by the denigration of others. The wealthy and fashionable looked to the dictates of an intellectual elite in affirming the worth of their leisure-time pursuits. By the turn of the twentieth century in the United States (as, for instance, in Argentina), writing for the masses had begun to signify writing for a diverse, and therefore implicitly inferior, ethnic and racial audience. As Levine recognizes, today's high culture is often yesterday's popular culture. Discussions of the split between elite and popular culture can be found in Pierre Bourdieu, *Distinction: A Social Critique of the Judgment of Taste*; Terry Eagleton, *Criticism and Ideology*; and Lawrence Levine, *Highbrow / Lowbrow: The Emergence of Cultural Hierarchy in America* and *The Opening of the American Mind*. For discussions of mass-market fiction, detective literature, and popular culture, see John G. Cawelti and Bruce A. Rosenberg, *The Spy Story*; Bob Ashley, *The Study of Popular Fiction*; John Ball et al., *The Mystery Story*; Jacques Barzun, ed., *The Delights of Detection*; 9–23; Bernard Benstock, ed., *Art in Crime Writing: Essays on Detective Fiction*; Arthur Asa Berger, *Popular Culture Genres: Theories and Texts*; Ray Browne, *Heroes and Humanities: Detective Fiction and Culture*, and *Modern Mystery, Fantasy, and Science Fiction Writers*; John G. Cawelti, *Adventure, Mystery and Romance*; Howard Haycraft, *Murder for Pleasure*; Knight, *Form and Ideology in Crime Fiction*; Daniel Link, ed., *El juego de los cautos*; David Skene Melvin and Ann Skene Melvin, *Crime, Detective, Espionage, Mystery, and Thriller Fiction and Film*; Glenn W. Most and William W. Stowe, eds., *The Poetics of Murder: Detective Fiction and Literary Theory*; Martin Priestman, *Detective Fiction and Literature: The Figure on the Carpet*; Robin W. Winks, ed., *Detective Fiction: A Collection of Critical Essays*; and Thomas J. Roberts, *An Aesthetics of Junk Fiction*.

50. Edgar Allan Poe's epigraph to "The Purloined Letter" was "Nil sapientiae odiosius acumine nimio,"—"Nothing is more hateful to wisdom than too much cleverness" *(Tales of Terror and Detection)*. Raymond Chandler believed that attempts to categorize or define the detective novel destroyed its spontaneity. (Chandler called academics "the trained seals of the critical fraternity.") Chandler, "The Simple Art of Murder." Jacques Barzun also warned against the dangers of overinterpreting the detective story, in "Detection and the Literary Art." Roger B. Rollin argues in "Against Evaluation" that applying any literary-critical approach falsely elevates popular literature, thus denying its legitimacy independent of traditional literary criticism.

51. Reyes, "Sobre la novela policial," 342. In Hispanic letters, to speak of an author writing "for the market" labels his or her production as subliterary. Reyes tried to disassociate abundant output from inferior quality by pointing out that many great writers of the previous century, including Galdós, Dickens, and Balzac, were at least as prolific as contemporary detective writers. He observed that the Golden Age dramatist Lope de Vega was one of the great formula writers of all time.

52. Manuel Vázquez Montalbán wrote that "genre literature is unidimensional and closed. Literature must be pluridimensional and open." (La literatura de género es unidimensional y cerrada. La literatura tiene que ser pluridimensional y abierta.) (Vázquez Montalbán even claimed to have written his early works without ever having read a genre detective novel, with the sole inspiration of American film noir: unlikely, given the popularity of detective literature in Spain.) See Valles Calatrava, *La novela criminal española*, 8, 110 (Valles Calatrava highlights the relativity of concepts such as "quality" and "high literature"); Juan Madrid, *Cuadernos del asfalto*, 15. Gaya Nuno, in a similar vein, distinguishes detective novels from the "novela-novela" or "novela sin adjetivos" (Elogio y vejamen de la novela policiaca," 118). José F. Colmeiro, even as he questions the dichotomy between "arte culto" and "arte bajo," asks "¿Es la novela policiaca parte de la literatura sin adjetivos?" *(La novela policiaca española*, 17). Mexican critic Ilán Stavans also evaluates Latin American detective novels based on their subversion of, rather than conformance to, generic norms.

53. In "Postmodernism and Consumer Society" Fredric Jameson associates postmodernism with the specific economic and historical context of post-industrial, post–World War II America and Western Europe.

54. As George Yúdice comments on the exclusion of certain groups from representations of the "people": "The national-popular requires generalization across differences in religion, politics, and race" (in Néstor García Canclini, *Consumers and Citizens: Globalization and Multicultural Conflicts*, trans. George Yúdice, 164 n. 2). Because realism was so often the vehicle for inculcating hegemonic notions of the autochthonous, postmodernist criticism began to turn away from representational literature as falsely totalizing mode of expression.

55. As Neil Larsen remarks in "Postmodernism and Imperialism," "all roads to postmodernism do not lead through French poststructuralism" (124). From

the perspective of Latin Americanist critics such as Martín Hopenhayn, European postmodernism is a potentially fascist position, because it has been coopted by neoliberal agendas in favor of unbridled capitalism, anarchical deregulation, and the deauthorization of coherent political and economic ideologies such as Marxism. (Hopenhayn, "Postmodernism and Neoliberalism in Latin America," 99). The debate on ethical postmodernity and postcolonial discourse in the Latin American arena has been considerably enriched by the work of Julio Ramos, Carlos Alonso, Néstor García Canclini, Roger Bartra, Enrique Dussel, Carlos Monsiváis, and many others. Carlos Alonso's meditations on the role of the modernity myth in Latin America are particularly useful here: "The spatial arrangement of center and periphery was buttressed by a collection of narratives that sought to naturalize the hierarchy created by economics. . . . Spanish American reality was always at the risk of becoming the negative object of modern Western knowledge . . . wielded by Spanish American writers and intellectuals." See Alonso, "The Burden of Modernity," 95–96.

56. See Bakhtin, *The Dialogic Imagination*.

57. Mexican American critic Ilán Stavans argues in his study of the Mexican detective novel that "in the end, the creation of a detective text in Spanish is always a labor of imitation" (al fin y al cabo, la creación de un texto policial en español es siempre una tarea imitativa); "From Yates to Monsiváis, seldom has the motive force behind this genre's analysis removed it from the category of 'parody'; the truth is that no other classification has been sufficiently convincing." Stavans, *Antihéroes*, 12; 15. José Colmeiro suggests that because the detective novel both as a genre and as a modern phenomenon is innately "Other" to Spanish letters, Spanish writers must either create perfect imitations in camouflage or must approach it through postmodern techniques of pastiche and parody that burlesque both the model and the imitator. Colmeiro goes so far as to suggest that the detective novel would be unpalatable to Spanish audiences if it were not parodic: "The continuous play and experimentation with the rules of the genre with respect to the complicity of the reader, and the multiple metafictional references to the crime genre itself from within the text, [are] factors that have tended to favor the adaptation and acceptance of the genre on the part of the Spanish public." (El continuo juego y experimentación con los cánones del género a partir de la complicidad del lector así como las múltiples referencias metaficcionales sobre el propio género policiaco desde el mismo texto, [son] factores todos ellos que han tendido a favorecer la adaptación y aceptación del género por part del público español.) Colmeiro, *La novela policiaca española*, 265. Leonardo Padura praises the Cuban novel *El cuarto círculo* (by Luis Rogelio Nogueras and Guillermo Rodríguez Rivera) precisely for the element of parody that gives it the sense of an intellectual game. See "Novela policial y novela de revolución," 75. Elzbieta Sklodowska similarly posits that all Latin American detective narrative is parodic. Sklodowska follows Todorov's definition of parody, not as a denigrating joke but rather as a "creative transgression of the model." She rationalizes Borges's use of the (otherwise vacuous) detective genre on the basis that

his stories parody and transgress structural and narrative generic conventions ("Transgresión paródica de la formula policial en la novela hispanoamericana," 175). According to this theory, reworking any genre is necessarily an act of transgression: "Obviamente, en Borges, Nabokov y Robbe-Grillet se trata de una reelaboración del modo detectivesco y, en consecuencia, de su transgresión" (173). Sklodowska asserts that "la literatura de fórmulas—novelas de aventuras, la novela rosa, la narrativa detectivesca—no defamiliariza, sino reafirma, en vez de perturbar las emociones, trata de evitar todas las dificultades en la ejecución y en la recepción del texto. Según acierta en observar Michael Holquist, este tipo de literatura 'no causa dolor, sino suministra apaciguantes, no ofrece preguntas profundas, sino respuestas fáciles' (ibid., 174). Quoted in Holquist, "Whodunit and Other Questions," 137.

58. Ernest Bramah's blind detective Max Carrados, for example, is just as much a parodic adaptation of Poe's Dupin as Borges's Don Isidro Parodi; while Carrados takes Dupin's visual inertia to its logical extreme, the incarcerated Parodi does the same with his physical inertia.

59. Elzbieta Sklodowska praised Borges for the difficulty of his detective stories: "'Death and the Compass' frustrates the reader's expectations and at the same time forces him to abandon his passivity towards the literary game." ("La muerte y la brújula" burla las expectativas del lector y al mismo tiempo lo fuerza a abandonar una actitud pasiva frente al juego literario.) See "Transgresión paródica de la fórmula policial en la novela hispanoamericana." This kind of criticism denies the essentially dialogic machinery of the detective narrative, which Borges describes as a quest for meaning in which the reader must confront each detail given in the text "with incredulity, with a special perspicacity" (con incredulidad, con una suspicacia especial). Jorge Hernández Martín, *Readers and Labyrinths*, 57, 83. While formulaic elements assure a familiar, preestablished plot paradigm, the hermeneutic exercise balances this predictability. The puzzle story, if it fails to engage the reader's hermeneutic skills, fails as well on a generic level. See Victoria Ocampo, ed. and trans., *Roger Caillois y la Cruz del Sur en la Academia Francesa*, 50.

60. Holquist, "Whodunit and Other Questions," 135.

61. As Ángel Rama, David William Foster, Nicolas Shumway, and others have argued, the construct of "lo propiamente americano" is itself an exclusionary concept, and one whose terms vary according to the objectives of a particular nation-building endeavor. The Cuban socialist detective novel, which was conceived as an autochthonous literary project and a tool of political repression at the same time, is an example.

62. Alonso, "The Burden of Modernity," 96–97.

63. See Yúdice's introduction to García Canclini, *Consumers and Citizens*, xiv.

64. In *Adiós Madrid* Taibo names his main character after the Cuban writer Justo Vasco; Cuban Leonardo Padura appears as a friend of a friend in "Argen-Mex" writer Myriam Laurini's *Morena en rojo*; Padura, in turn, bases *Máscaras* on the life and vicissitudes of Virgilio Piñera.

65. Como si la oscuridad fuera su destino. Padura Fuentes, *Modernidad*, 157.

66. El detective es al delincuente lo que el crítico de arte es al artista; el delincuente *inventa*, el detective *explica*. Carpentier, "Apología de la novela policiaca," 464.

2. A Revolutionary Aesthetic

1. Lo mágico, lo 'real maravilloso' es aquí la visión caduca y pintoresca, mítica, que va quedando atrás, sobrepasada sin violencia por la nueva conciencia socialista, científica, revolucionaria. José Antonio Portuondo, "Una novela revolucionaria," 106.

2. Julie Marie Bunck, *Fidel Castro and the Quest for a Revolutionary Culture in Cuba*, 13.

3. In many cultures, visible homosexuality has been associated with literacy and cultural sophistication. José Quiroga views the character of Diego in *Fresa y chocolate*, Tomás Gutiérrez Alea's adaptation of Senel Paz's story "El lobo, el bosque y el hombre nuevo," as a sort of allegorically housetrained homosexual: one whose sexuality is subordinate to his role as a guardian and transmitter of the suppressed, soon-to-be-recovered greatness of Cuban literary culture represented by the prerevolutionary literary journals *Ciclón* and *Orígenes*. See Quiroga, "Homosexualities in the Tropic of Revolution," 137.

4. Cited in José Miguel Oviedo, "The Modern Essay in Spanish America," 399.

5. "Calibán," 75.

6. Los hombres de verdad no leen libros. La literatura es mariconería y pura maricón, yo. Quoted in Guillermo Cabrera Infante, "Vidas para leerlas," 5.

7. Eagleton, *Criticism and Ideology*, 2.

8. Portuondo, *Teoría y crítica de la literatura*, 219. Portuondo's usage here apparently does not denote Russian formalism.

9. Aberraciones típicas de la cultura burguesa. Quoted in Seymour Menton, *Prose Fiction of the Cuban Revolution*, 148.

10. The Unidades Militares de Ayuda a la Producción, or Military Units to Aid Production, were prison camps for homosexuals and other nonconformists. They ran from 1965 until 1967, when they were closed partly due to pressure by the Unión de Escritores y Artistas de Cuba. (UMAPs were paralleled in Spain during the 1960s by "homosexual centers" or penal camps.)

11. Dentro de la Revolución, todo; contra la Revolución, nada. Quoted in Salvador Arias, "Literatura cubana (1959–1978)," 18.

12. The Casa de las Américas awarded its 1962 prize to a novel titled *Maestra voluntaria*: the same year Alejo Carpentier's *Siglo de las luces* was published. A similar lack of official editorial support greeted Lezama Lima's *Paradiso* in 1966, Carpentier's *Concierto barroco* in 1973 and his *La consagración de la primavera* in 1978 (that year the UNEAC prize went to Luis Rogelio Noguera's spy novel *Y si muero mañana*) and *El arpa y la sombra* in 1979. MININT and MINFAR prizes were usually reserved for detective novels.

13. The Padilla affair had been brewing since the publication of Heberto Padilla's critically acclaimed book of poetry *Fuera del juego* in 1967 but came to a head with his controversial review of the exiled Cabrera Infante's book *Tres tristes tigres* and Lisandro Otero's *Pasión de Urbino*, which led to his imprisonment and public "confession" in 1971. For a lively account of the story, see Cabrera Infante, *Mea Cuba*. See also Rogelio Rodríguez Coronel, *La novela de la revolución cubana*, and Menton, *Prose Fiction of the Cuban Revolution*. Rodríguez Coronel describes Menton's book as "francamente malintencionado" (13).

14. Roque Dalton et al., *El intelectual y la sociedad*, 9.

15. Ibid., 13.

16. Yo creo que, para empezar, debemos reconocer que muchos de nosotros hemos sido responsable de haber creado una ilusión, la ilusión de que en Cuba existía una libertad absoluta para expresarse libremente, sin reconocer las exigencias de una sociedad en revolución. Ibid., 26.

17. Ibid., 45, 53, 55.

18. Ibid., 129, 148.

19. See, among others, Salvador Arias, *La cultura en Cuba socialista*; Rodríguez Coronel, *La novela de la revolución cubana*; José Antonio Portuondo, *Teoría y crítica de la literatura*; Dalton et al., *El intelectual y la sociedad*.

20. Dalton et al., *El intelectual y la sociedad*, 41.

21. Critics of Russian ideological realism included Portuondo, Edmundo Desnoes, José Rodríguez Feo, and even Che Guevara himself. At the same time, Che also decried "la angustia sin sentido y el pasatiempo vulgar" (the senseless anguish and vulgar pursuits) in literature and stressed its responsibility to educate the people. Among the nominally revolutionary writers of the present were many who suffered from the "original sin" of bourgeois values and these were in constant danger of "perverting" the new generation. See Ernesto Guevara, "El socialismo y el hombre en Cuba," 268.

22. As Michael Holquist notes, some American and British critics of the 1930s were also nostalgic for more populist literary tendencies: "what the structural and philosophical presuppositions of myth and depth psychology were to modernism (Mann, Joyce, Woolf, and so forth), the detective story is to postmodernism." See "Whodunit and Other Questions," 150.

23. El carácter crudo, desigual y decadente de los Estados Unidos, y la existencia, en ellos continua, de todas las violencias, discordias, inmoralidades y desórdenes. Roberto Fernández Retamar, "Calibán," 55.

24. Ibid., 11.

25. Definido como el conjunto de disposiciones neuróticas inconscientes que diseñan a la vez 'la figura del paternalismo colonial' y 'el retrato del racista cuya hija ha sido objeto de una tentativa de violación (imaginaria) por parte de un ser inferior.' Ibid., 28.

26. Influential contemporary texts included those by the German cultural critic Max Nordau, whose attacks on Whitman and Verlaine were widely read in Latin America. Oscar Montero has traced the fin de siècle linkage of the homosexual

body with the body politic and its cultural production; see "Julián del Casal and the Queers of Havana." In this context, homosexuality is not only synonymous with decadence, deviance, and criminality but also with tergiversation and subterfuge, given that a homosexual might pass for a heterosexual in order to infiltrate cultural discourse. Montero also describes "the erasure of homosexuality" by the *modernista* movement, Rodó and Rubén Darío in particular. Montero asserts: "Artistic and literary productions become decadent, and thus threatening to the integrity of the American republics, when they favor 'external adornment,' [Nordau's term] in short, when they do not signify clearly." See Oscar Montero, "*Modernismo* and Homophobia," 103.

27. No se trata sino de otra versión del impresionismo. . . . Pero este '*tipo* de creación' (me refiero al género y no a la especie) ya fue característico de otro tiempo: el de Walter Pater y Oscar Wilde: esta es la 'critica creadora,' la de 'el crítico como artista.' Roberto Fernández Retamar, "A propósito del Círculo de Praga y del estudio de nuestra literatura," 24. (Also in 1972, Casa de las Américas published a series of translations of prorealist, antimodernist criticism by Russian theorists.) The *modernista* poets conceived of the artist as "thinker": a solitary, morally (because aesthetically) superior being, tormented by the increasing materialism of bourgeois society. This position had definite ethical overtones; as Julio Ramos explains, art was defined as a nostalgic realm of endeavor that sought beauty and authenticity "in opposition to the massified experience of capitalist daily existence." As Ramos and others have pointed out, the modern intellectual subject sought to delineate a discursive space from outside society in order to legitimize his critique of it. This point of articulation is inseparable from an inherently modern conception of objectivity. Julio Ramos, *Divergent Modernities*, 225.

28. The use of the body metaphor to signify the political nation has characterized Latin American "diagnostic" literature since Independence. It was exercised to great effect in the nineteenth century by Esteban Echeverría in *El matadero*, Domingo F. Sarmiento in *Civilización y barbarie*, and Agustín Álvarez in *Manual de la patología política*; in the early twentieth century in César Zumeta's *El continente enfermo*, Manuel Ugarte's *Enfermedades sociales*, Alcides Arguedas's *Pueblo enfermo*, José Ingenieros's *Psicología genética*, and Carlos Octavio Bunge's *Nuestra América*; in the 1920s and 1930s in the regionalist novel *(La vorágine, Doña Bárbara, Don Segundo Sombra)*, Ezequiel Martínez Estrada's *Radiografía de la pampa*, and so on.

29. El crimen es un asunto de las clases altas—este tipo de crimen: exquisito, difícil, ingenioso—y corresponde a ellas cometerlo y resolverlo. Estamos, en fin, ante el dandyismo policial." Luis Rogelio Nogueras, *Por la novela policial*, 11, 24.

30. El concurso está dirigido al desarrollo de este género en nuestro país, por lo que las obras que se presenten serán de temática policial y tendrán un carácter didáctico, sirviendo asimismo como estímulo a la prevención y la vigilancia de todas las actividades antisociales y contra el poder del pueblo. Quoted in Enrique Sacerio-Garí, "Detectives North and South."

31. Los medios culturales no pueden servir de marco a la proliferación de falsos intelectuales que pretenden convertir el esnobismo, la extravagancia, el

homosexualismo y demás aberraciones sociales en expresiones del arte revolucionario, alejados de las masas y del espíritu de nuestra revolución. Quoted in
Arias, "Literatura cubana (1959–1978)," 28.

32. Cabrera Infante, "Vidas para leerlas," 16.

33. La novela policial cubana, sin desdeñar su función de entretener—no la
desdeñaba Brecht para su exigente concepción del teatre—se propone asimi-
simo una función educativa: ahondar en las causas de la criminalidad, social y
sicológicamente. Nogueras, *Por la novela policial,* 28.

34. José Ortega y Gasset's fundamental 1925 essay, *La deshumanización del
arte,* described how the hermetic, nonrepresentational art of the avant-gardes
revealed the true division of society into the elite and the masses. In Latin
America, the polarization of literary cliques into social(ist) realists and proponents of the modernizing avant-garde was evident in the famous *Boedo/Florida*
rivalry in Buenos Aires; the Mexican *Contemporáneos,* who were reviled for their
pro-European tastes and their rejection of burgeoning nationalist literatures;
and the Cuban editorial group *Orígenes,* whose sophisticated oeuvre and ties to
existentialism led to their ostracism in periods of cultural retrenchment after the
Revolution. In contrast, identity-centered literary movements of the first half
of the twentieth century, like *regionalismo, indigenismo,* and *negrismo,* united art
with overriding ethical and political concerns. Spanish American constructions
of literary history were often intensely nationalistic and focused on *lo autóctono:*
the recuperation of an often mythical home-grown tradition.

35. Theodor W. Adorno, "The Culture Industry Reconsidered." Adorno rejected the label "mass culture" because it implied that the artifacts of popular culture were spontaneous products of the masses. See also Walter Benjamin, "The
Work of Art in the Age of Mechanical Reproduction," and Antonio Gramsci,
"Sobre la novela policial."

36. Sirvieron y sirven para embrutecer a las masas y para alejarlas de los
verdaderos problemas sociales y políticos de nuestro tiempo. Nogueras, *Por la
novela policial,* 9. However, Gramsci described the detective novel as the outcome of a "process of schematization of intrigue as such, robbed of any element
of democratic, petit-bourgeois ideology" (proceso de la esquematización de la
intriga como tal, privada de todo elemento de ideología democrática y pequeño-
burguesa). In essence, Gramsci wondered whether the genre had the potential
to subvert the status quo. The alienated aficionado and the glorified criminal of
late-nineteenth-century detective literature, for Nogueras the very essence of a
perverse, perverting "individualism," seemed to Gramsci a possible vehicle for
questioning authority. Quoted in Acosta, *Novela policial y medios masivos,* 23.

37. Lukács criticized Heidegger for insinuating (as would Ortega y Gasset) that
the historical worldview was vulgar. See Lukács, "The Ideology of Modernism."

38. Una ideología de la seguridad, de la exaltación, de la omnisciencia de los
que vigilan la tranquilidad de la vida burguesa. Quoted in Giussepe Petronio,
Jorge B. Rivera, and Luigi Volta, eds. *Los héroes "difíciles,"* 37.

39. Colmeiro, *La novela policiaca española,* 60.

40. Una estable concepción del mundo en que apoyar las tablas de valores. Portuondo, *Teoría y crítica de la literatura*, 20.

41. Una reproducción de la vida, en la cual los hombres se reciben a sí mismos y a sus destinos interpretados con mayor amplitud y profundidad y con una claridad mucho más orientadora que la que suele darles la vida misma. Lisandro Otero, "Cuba: literatura y revolución," v.

42. José Antonio Portuondo defined the *teque* as "the apologistic exposition of revolutionary ideology, crude and elementary propaganda, noisy tributes to revolutionary proceedings," (la exposición apologética de la ideología revolucionaria, la propaganda elemental y primaria, el elogio desembozado de los procedimientos revolucionarios). *Astrolabio*, 131.

43. Jameson, *The Political Unconscious*.

44. These figures refer only to the novel. In the period of its first successes (1971–79), of the 59 novels of all types published on the Island, 14, or 25 percent, were detective novels (Rodríguez Coronel, *La novela de la revolución cubana*). From 1978 to 1983, 28 of 74 (38 percent) published novels were detective and spy stories (Padura, "Novela policial y novela de revolución," 84). From 1984 to 1986 the number of detective novels dropped sharply, to six. Combined, these last figures amounted to approximately 21 percent of the total number of novels published from 1980 to 1986 (Fernández Pequeño, "La novela policial cubana ante sí misma," 211, 214). While precise sales figures are difficult to substantiate, Nogueras notes that Ignacio Cárdenas Acuña's *Enigma para un domingo*, acknowledged to be the first example of the genre, sold 60,000 copies after it was published in 1971; his own *El cuarto círculo* (written with Guillermo Rodríguez Rivera) sold 40,000 copies (*Novela policial* 39, 41).

45. Cuba had been exposed to Enlightenment and positivist thought during the previous century and a half through the work of such figures as José Antonio Saco, Father Félix Varela, and Benjamín Céspedes in the nineteenth century, and of Enrique José Varona and the criminologist Israel Castellanos in the early part of the twentieth century. However, as Foucault points out, a certain clinical approach to social phenomena presupposes the existence of a flourishing bourgeois class, a development that was delayed by the anomalous late colonial status of Cuba. Revolutionary efforts to promote sex education were punctuated by reflections on the enormity of the task.

46. In recent years there has been evidence of a liberalization of attitudes toward alternative sexualities: the decriminalization of homosexuality, the opening of formerly mandatory HIV *sanatorias*, the release of Tomás Gutiérrez Alea's *Fresa y chocolate*, and the rehabilitation of homosexual writers in literary studies.

47. José Angel Bustamante, *Raíces psicológicas del cubano*, 2d ed., 8.

48. Ibid., 27.

49. Desiderio Navarro, "La novela policial y la literatura artística," 142.

50. En la novela detectivesca la célebre divisa *cherchez la femme* es sustituida por el prosaico "búsquese el heredero." Ivailo Znepolski, "Sociología de la novela detectivesca clásica," 277.

51. Justo Vasco Colás, "El reflejo de lo socialmente negativo en la literatura policial. Su valor educativo." Vasco emigrated to Spain in 1995.

52. El criminal anda perdido en la jungla de la ciudad, confundido su rostro entre los rostros borrosos de siete o diez millones de hombres y mujeres, y el detective es un profesional que cobra por su trabajo y para quien un crimen irresuelto es, no un insulto a su inteligencia, sino un mal negocio. Nada más. Nogueras, *Por la novela policial*, 25.

53. However, there is evidence of a general awareness that the ideological origins of the spy novel in late Victorian England were quite conservative and tended to support the notion of empire. See Juan Antonio Blas, "Novela de espías y espías de novela."

54. Alentar el odio contra el comunismo y el de apartar a las masas del movimiento revolucionario para convertirlas en 'mayorías silenciosas.' Nogueras, *Novela policial*, 60.

55. Cawelti and Rosenberg, *The Spy Story*, 13.

56. Thomas Narcejac, "De Poe al thriller policial," 205.

57. No tiene mucha integración. Luis Rogelio Nogueras and Guillermo Rodríguez Rivera, *El cuarto círculo*, 25.

3. Masking, Unmasking, and the Return to Signification

1. See David William Foster and Roberto Reis, eds., *Bodies and Biases: Sexualities in Hispanic Cultures and Literatures*, and Daniel Balderston and Donna J. Guy, eds., *Sex and Sexuality in Latin America*.

2. This opinion was not limited to Cubans. In critic George Grella's opinion, Spillane's Mike Hammer is an example of the deformation of the hard-boiled form "in the hands of the inept and the unthinking." See George Grella, "The Hard-Boiled Detective Novel," 106.

3. Su empecinada soltería, su afición a los chismes con damas de la aristocracia, su impecable toilette, su gusto por los perfumes y las exquisiteces culinarias, [y] sus hábitos de casamentero. Acosta, *Novela policial y medios masivos*, 86–89.

4. David William Foster has discerned a similar ideology, which he terms (following Adrienne Rich) "compulsory heterosexuality," under the Peronist regime in Argentina.

5. Carlos Alberto Montaner, *Fidel Castro and the Cuban Revolution*, 69.

6. Fidel y la masa comienzan a vibrar en un diálogo de intensidad creciente hasta alcanzar el clímax en un final abrupto, coronado por nuestro grito de lucha y de victoria. Ernesto "Che" Guevara, "El socialismo y el hombre en Cuba," 256.

7. La masa realiza con entusiasmo y disciplina sin iguales las tareas que el gobierno fija. Ibid., 255.

8. Ibid., 261. Notoriously, Che Guevara hated Virgilio Piñera's work, as demonstrated by his violent reaction to a copy of the *Teatro completo* (he threw it across a room in a 1964 encounter with Juan Goytisolo, yelling that it was the work of a "faggot").

9. Ian Lumsden, *Machos, Maricones, and Gays: Cuba and Homosexuality*, 217, n. 11.

10. Justo Vasco, "El reflejo de lo socialmente negativo en la literatura policial."

11. Un experto de nervios firmes hubiera concentrado el barraje primero en un hombro, luego en otro y después en el tercero, pero el turbinero no era un experto, carecía de miles de horas de paciente dedicación a la teoría y práctica del combate, estaba sobreexcitado, y la caótica emisión de proyectiles poseía escasa efectividad. Javier Morán (José Latour), "Choque de leyendas," 121.

12. Por lo general, nunca se dan cuenta de nada. Viven metidas en el micromundo de las colas, de lo que sacaron aquí o allá, sospechando de las llegadas tardes del marido, envidiando a los vecinos y repitiendo todos los días el mismo trabajo. Y no entienden nunca a sus hijos. Justo Vasco, *El Muro*, 60, 62.

13. Martin Leiner, *Sexual Politics in Cuba: Machismo, Homosexuality and AIDS*, 69, 74.

14. Cited in Leiner, *Sexual Politics in Cuba*, 45. Early sex-education literature was mostly imported from East Germany, revised to Cuban standards, and translated. Schnabl's book was the first to become available, in 1979, and sold out on its first day on the market. While the official attitudes toward women and homosexuals as expressed by the GNTES have become more progressive over the years, the policy of obligatory quarantine for all HIV-positive Cubans (recently discontinued) reveals a persistent prejudice against homosexuals among the decision-making elite.

15. Cubans also participated in these activities, as Guillermo Cabrera Infante describes with a slightly malicious virtuosity in an article on Piñera and Lezama Lima, "Vidas para leerlas."

16. Lourdes Argüelles and Ruby Rich, "Homosexuality, Homophobia, and Revolution: Notes toward an Understanding of the Cuban Lesbian and Gay Male Experience, Part I," 686.

17. Ibid., 99.

18. The massive exodus from the port of Mariel began in April 1980 after a handful of Cuban dissidents ran a stolen bus into the Peruvian embassy, requesting asylum. After a guard was killed, the embassy refused to return them to Cuban authorities, an action that incited thousands to enter the embassy. Fidel Castro opened the port of Mariel, and in the following months approximately 120,000 Cubans emigrated to the United States and other countries. During this period, many homosexuals were advised that they were eligible to apply for exit forms. Some heterosexual Cubans professed to be homosexual in order to secure permission to leave the island. See Allen Young, *Gays under the Cuban Revolution*. A New Left supporter of the Cuban Revolution, Young nevertheless criticizes its mistreatment of gays. His analysis is an important one, written shortly after the Mariel boatlift, in which thousands of homosexuals left Cuba, exhausted by historic and daily persecutions (and strongly encouraged by the government). Prior to the Revolution, he asserts, "homosexuality was not politicized, because the *locas*, like the women, knew their place" (5).

19. For specifically Latin Americanist perspectives, see Doris Sommer, Nicolas Shumway, Oscar Montero, David William Foster, Jorge Salessi, Daniel Balderston and Donna Guy, and Emilie Bergmann and Paul Julian Smith.

20. Michel Foucault, *The History of Sexuality. Vol. I: An Introduction*, 12.

21. My use of the term "pathologization" is intended to emphasize the growing focus on nonreproductive or deviant sexual activities as a type of disease that could be treated with varying degrees of success by therapeutic or educational means, as opposed to simple legal punishment. Pathologization has four components, which Foucault identifies as hysterization of women; pedagogization of children; socialization of heterosexual couples; and psychiatrization of deviants (*History of Sexuality*, 105).

22. Ante todo, las condiciones sociológicas: en primer lugar, se da el "hecho insólito"; es decir, el crimen misterioso tal como lo cuenta el periódico, el drama convertido en espectáculo . . . . En segundo lugar, las condiciones científicas. Análisis de huellas, de rastros, fisonomía o arte de averiguar el carácter de un individuo según los rasgos de su cara. En tercer lugar, una "materia" pintoresca, el caso policiaco, articulado en una "forma" rigurosa, la investigación policial, y por último, como nexo de unión, el policía, medio aventurero y medio sabio. Thomas Narcejac, "De Poe al thriller policial," 206–07.

23. Amelia S. Simpson, "From Private to Public Eye: Detective Fiction in Cuba," 109.

24. Asumir constantemente un posición de desenmascaramiento de toda coyuntura social o individual que permita la comisión de un delito común o un acto contra la Seguridad del Estado proletario. Vasco, "El reflejo de lo socialmente negativo en la literatura policial," 12.

25. Es obvio que cada uno de estos personajes requiere un tratamiento diferente, tanto en la vida como en la literatura. Pero todos requieren la misma atención, la misma vigilancia por parte de la sociedad. Ibid., 1.

26. José Fernández Pequeño, "Teoría y practica de la novela policial revolucionaria," 96.

27. According to a 1968 article in *Granma*, the crime rate was cut in half between 1959 and 1969. Luis Salas, *Social Control and Deviance in Cuba*, 7.

28. As Martín Hopenhayn observes, "In the decade of the sixties, the analytical exercise of sociology was, in good measure, determined by the idea of a 'militant science' that was identified with a model of the state and social organization that projected an extreme normativism in questions of the styles of development." "Postmodernism and Neoliberalism," 105.

29. See Lumsden, *Machos, Maricones, and Gays,* and Foster and Reis, eds., *Bodies and Biases.* A note on terminology: as David William Foster asserts, *gay* is "an index of foreign ideologies," specifically those of a privileged middle class (5). It connotes a lifestyle and a perception of male sexuality that are not directly transferable to Ibero-American contexts. However, it retains a certain utility in the context of the Havana literary scene prior to the Revolution.

30. Quoted in Young, *Gays under the Cuban Revolution*, 8.

31. Lombroso's impact was by no means limited to Cuba. In his 1946 sociological study *Crimen y criminal en la novela policiaca*, Peninsular critic Juan del Rosal concentrated his analysis on the works of Agatha Christie, focusing on the detective methods of Hercule Poirot. He associated crime, or specific crimes, with specific character types, which, reacting to a particular set of circumstances, produce a criminal act. Poirot, he believed, pursues the question of motive (external factors) to the exclusion of factors such as personality of the criminal (internal or "biological" factors). After Césare Lombroso's widely read 1876 study of the "Delinquent Man," the study of criminology became increasingly taken up with biological and evolutionary factors in criminal behavior. By the 1940s, del Rosal points out, criminology had gone beyond this anthropological approach and considered extraevolutionary factors such as environment to be much more important. See Juan del Rosal, *Crimen y criminal en la novela policiaca*, 341.

32. Su rutina gimnástica diaria era fuerte: veinticinco minutos de suiza, cuarenta tracciones de bíceps en suspensión de barra, cien cuclillas, cien abdominales con dos kilogramos de contrapeso en la nuca, cuarenta planchas, todo ello precedido de cinco minutos de calentamiento y seguido de cinco minutos de distensión. No era nada del otro mundo, pero le bastaba gozar de una magnífica forma física. Daniel Chavarría, *Joy*, 47. *Joy* was the winner of the 1976 MININT prize.

33. un tipo rarísimo, rubio, alto, de brazos larguísimos, con los ojos botados como un sapo. Siempre andan juntos en el carro. Tanto . . . que llama la atención! Edmundo Mas and Isabel Ramírez, *La voz de las huellas*, 140.

34. Se acercó un perrazo gris, al que el Coronel acarició con un gesto infantil, estúpidamente tierno. Chavarría, *Joy*, 31.

35. Ellos tienen un amigo de esa época que se llama Luisito . . . muy delicado él, usted me entiende?, que usa una ropita. . . . Y un día por la tarde que viene un mulato a verlo. Me preguntó por él, un mulato fuerte, que parecía gente de trabajo, pero no sé, muy arreglado. Armando Cristóbal Pérez, *La ronda de los rubíes*, 16, 62. (Just as homophobia is not unique to Latin American culture, the depiction of atavistic, deformed, and sexually perverse or indeterminate characters is not unique to the Cuban detective novel. In fact, it was widely practiced in North American pulp fiction of the 1920s and 1930s, including that of Raymond Chandler, and is a salient feature of Mickey Spillane's stories. Villains were quite often depicted as homosexual during the Cold War.)

36. Cada vez que preguntaba por él, le costaba trabajo describirlo sin ponerse en una situación embarazosa. Ibid., 60.

37. Cited in Young, *Gays under the Cuban Revolution*, 16.

38. Although homosexuality was decriminalized in 1979, an aspect of homosexual behavior that is still pursued and prosecuted (not only in Cuba) is public sexual activity. Theaters, parks, and other public gathering places are frequently subject to police raids, and gay couples are harassed, while heterosexual couples may often be left alone. Whereas public homosexual behavior had gone relatively unnoticed by the authorities under Batista, the socialist sex education agenda

prioritized the monogamous conjugal relationship, reinforcing the private nature of sexual activity and labeling public displays as indecent. Strong prejudices persist against other visible manifestations of sexuality such as the *jineteras*, young female prostitutes who seek out tourists in exchange for dollars, clothing, or even a meal. It is widely believed that the *jineteras'* behavior is not driven by necessity but rather by covetousness or the frivolous desire to have nice clothes.

39. *Y si muero mañana* sold 100,000 copies in the first two printings. It is one of the best-known novels of the genre. See Emilio Bejel, *Escribir en Cuba: Entrevistas con escritores cubanos, 1979–1989*, 278.

40. The fictional Delta 99 of *Y si muero mañana* alludes to the historic counterrevolutionary group Alpha 66. The paramilitary organization, which is still active, was formed in 1961 "with the intention of making commando type attacks on Cuba to maintain the fighting spirit of the Cuban people after the failure of the Bay of Pigs invasion" (Alpha 66 official Web site, http://www.alpha66.org/english/our%20history.htm). The idealization of revolutionary forces therefore corresponded to a palpable menace with which all Cubans were familiar.

41. Anti-Semitism is an unfortunate subtext to many Cuban detective novels. David Jaime, the criminal mastermind in Pablo Bergues's *Propietario del alba*, has an apparently Jewish name and also bears the descriptive nickname "El Cojo." The CIA agent in Arnaldo Correa's short story "Un caso difícil" is called Stein.

42. En los ojos cansados del viejo, en su obstinada cara judía, asomaba una expresión de incertidumbre." Nogueras, *Y si muero mañana*, 16.

43. La Infantería de Marina lo había endurecido, pero más aún lo había endurecido su trabajo en el centro secreto de pruebas de armas químicas, biológicas y sicológicas en Dugway, Utah. Allí, como adjunto de la CIA, había visto de frente el rostro de la guerra moderna, una guerra para la cual hombres como Duke (e incluso Kaplan) no estaban preparados: aerosoles capaces de producir alucinaciones y la muerte, ultrasonidos enloquecedores, microbios a los que una mutación genética convertía en asesinos. La guerra invisible, total. Ibid., 25.

44. The rather high number of CIA agents named Dick is of uncertain significance.

45. El único personaje que no está descrito es el investigador principal, Héctor Román (sólo se sabe su edad: unos 35 años en 1973). Sherlock Holmes es flaco, de nariz ganchuda y con grandes entradas; Poirot usa laca en el pelo, lleva bigotillos de manubrio y tiene, en conjunto, el aspecto de un sapo endomingado; Maigret es canoso, algo cargado de hombros y más bien alto. Pero Héctor Román . . . es como cada quien lo quiera ver. Nogueras, *Por la novela policial*, 36.

46. Nogueras, *Y si muero mañana*, 26, 41, 48.

47. El almuerzo en la casa del gordo y fofo León Ortiz se prolongó un poco por la presencia de un sujeto llamado Arnaldo Rodiles, gusano que había emigrado a París después de haber publicado en Cuba una novela de relativo éxito. Ibid., 29. The name Arnaldo Rodiles alludes to Reinaldo Arenas, who was still in Cuba at this time (and possibly to the position "de rodillas," on one's knees). Severo Sarduy had emigrated to Paris.

48. Con pulóver sin ajustadores, como para mostrar que tenía los pezones muy grandes. Ibid., 30. Women who dress provocatively are usually undesirables, like La Baby and Martica in Justo Vasco's *El muro*.

49. Tenía tanto miedo que se rindió dócilmente a la aguja. Su cuerpo de toro temblaba como si fuera gelatina." Ibid., 36, 39, 40, 42.

50. ¡Avemaría . . . qué cu . . . ba! Ibid., 39. The comment combines salacious objectification ("what an ass!") with a perverted reference to the home island. Bad language and slangy speech are usually reserved for villains.

51. Bustamante, *Raíces psicológicas del cubano*, 2d ed., 56.

52. This technique was also used by Daniel Chavarría in *Joy*. The text is full of references to bourbon, marketing phrases such as *champion salesman* and *star promoter*, and French gambling terms.

53. Recordó que en Cuba siempre andaba con objetos de los más picúos y a veces hasta un poco amariconados, como una pitillera de oro labrado, con cajita de música, o aquella boquilla larga de marfil que había usado la noche de la fiesta en casa de la querida de Papo Batista. Chavarría, *Joy*, 32.

54. Nogueras, *Y si muero mañana*, 55, 28, 56.

55. Se confunden el traidor con el chulo, la antigua niña bien con la puta de Colón, el doctor sin reválida con el pepillo de treinta años, el batistiano con el auténtico, el cantante mediocre con el politicastro, el vago con el soldado de fortuna . . . el católico con dientes para afuera con el gánster. Ibid., 56.

56. In "The Narrative Structure in Fleming" (151) Umberto Eco demonstrates how Fleming's villains are constructed as composite beings made up of all that was antithetical to British hegemonic values during the Cold War: "As a rule he is of mixed blood and his origins are complex and obscure; he is asexual or homosexual, or at any rate not sexually normal . . . there are gathered the negative values which we have distinguished in some pairs of opposites, the Soviet Union and countries which are not Anglo-Saxon (the racial convention blames particularly the Jews, the Germans, the Slavs and the Italians always depicted as half-breeds), Cupidity elevated to the dignity of paranoia, Planning as technological methodology, satrapic luxury, physical and psychical Excess, physical and moral Perversion, radical Disloyalty."

57. La novela policiaca cubana del los setenta era una literatura apologética, esquemática, permeada por concepciones de un realismo socialista que tenía mucho de socialista pero poco de realismo. Padura Fuentes, *Modernidad, postmodernidad y novela policial*, 153.

58. Padura Fuentes, "Novela policial y novela de revolución," 71.

59. Havana Prensa Latina, 25 June 1989; FBIS-LAT, 27 June 1989, pp. 4–6ª, quoted in José F. Alonso, "The Ochoa Affair: A Majority Faction in the Revolutionary Armed Forces?" Radio Martí - Cuban Situation Reports (May–August 1989, no.2, vol. 5).

60. Juan Armando Epple, "Entrevista: Leonardo Padura Fuentes," 56.

61. Lukács, "The Ideology of Modernism," 598.

62. Una novela de homosexuales, de máscaras, centrada en ese fenómeno de

trasvestismo moral que se ha vivido en Cuba en este tiempo." Epple, "Entrevista," 58.

63. homosexuales activos, ocultos tras una apariencia impenetrable de hombre-hombre—vulgo, bugarrón. Padura Fuentes, *Máscaras*, 73.

64. Homosexual de vasta experiencia depredadora, apático político y desviado ideológico, ser conflictivo y provocador, extranjerizante, hermético, culterano, posible consumidor de marihuana y otras drogas, protector de maricones descarriados, hombre de dudosa filiación filosófica, lleno de prejuicios pequeñoburgueses y clasistas. Ibid., 41.

65. Even if Padura doesn't fall into the same schematism as his predecessors, his methods of identification in many cases are still Lombrosian, as in this description of a pair of delinquents: "One was an enormous blond, over six feet tall and with extra-long arms, with a face covered with as many craters as the surface of the moon; the other, smaller and with skin so black it looked blue, he must have been the direct grandson and universal heir of Cro-Magnon Man himself: Darwin's theory of evolution was reflected in his exaggerated prognathism and in that narrow forehead from which gleamed the yellow lights of the eyes of a savage animal." (Uno era un rubio enorme, de más de seis pies y brazos larguísimos, con una cara poblada de tantos cráteres como la superficie lunar; el otro, más pequeño y de piel tan negra que parecía azul, debía de ser nieto directo y heredero universal del mismísimo hombre de Cromagnon: la teoría darwinista de la evolución se le reflejaba en su prognatismo exagerado y en aquella frente angosta donde brillaban las luces amarillas de unos ojos de animal selvático.) (*Máscaras*, 22) Despite revolutionary aspirations and real advances towards racial equality, a tacit racial bias persists in the detective story. This goes back to prerevolutionary social theory: African influence is associated not only with atavism and exaggerated sexuality but also with a gradual weakening of patriarchal family structure and a change toward a more matriarchal one—and therefore represents a threat to *machista* values. See for example José Ángel Bustamante's *Raíces psicológicas del cubano*.

66. Pues la verdad-verdad es que este maricón que se caga de miedo si le dan un grito, tiene unos cojones que le llegan a los tobillos. Aguantó como un hombre y se quedó aquí. Ibid., 64.

67. El problema . . . no era ser, sino parecer; no era el acto, sino la representación. Ibid., 73.

68. Quizá se besaron, se acariciaron tal vez, y Alexis se arrodilló, como un penitente, seguramente con la intención de satisfacer con su orificio más próximo la urgencia de su acompañante. Ibid., 35.

69. Mariconcitos de la vertiente lánguida, que parecían lamentar su inmaculada heterosexualidad. Ibid., 140.

70. Nelly Richard, "Cultural Peripheries: Latin America and Post-Modernist De-Centering," 8, 221.

71. El travestismo era algo más esencial y biológico que el simple acto mariconeril y exhibicionista de salir a la calle vestido de mujer. *Máscaras*, 73.

134 | NOTES TO CHAPTER 4

72. Larson, "Postmodernism and Imperialism," 123.

73. G. K. Chesterton, "On Detective Novels."

74. Esa máscara moral con que ha vivido mucha gente en algún momento de la existencia: homosexuales que aparentan no serlo, resentidos que sonríen al mal tiempo, brujeros con manuales de marxismo bajo el brazo, oportunistas feroces vestidos de mansos corderos, apáticos ideológicos con un utilísimo carnet en el bolsillo. *Máscaras*, 166.

4. Contesting "la mexicanidad"

1. Enrique Dussel, "Eurocentrism and Modernity," 75.

2. ¿A quién se le ocurre la parodia en un país barroco? Carlos Monsiváis, *Carlos Monsiváis*, 38.

3. La caracterización de la policía como una fuerza del caos, del sistema bárbaro, dispuesta a ahogar en violencia a los ciudadanos. Paco Ignacio Taibo II, "La 'otra' novela policiaca," 38.

4. Los ideólogos de la derecha mexicana y casi todos los viajeros edifican ese 'México,' y lo pueblan de prejuicios que se convertirán en juicios, de anotaciones fantasiosas sobre la psicología nacional que devendrán actitudes y formas de conducta. Carlos Monsiváis, "Los viajeros y la Invención de México," 205.

5. El uso de términos clave: misterio, primitivismo, barbarie, inocencia, paraíso perdido, atavismo, sensualidad, crueldad. . . . La impresión de una belleza irrecuperable expresada en monumentos coloniales, ruinas prehispánicas, aquello que ya no tiene continuidad ni descendientes a la altura de su grandeza. Ibid., 211.

6. La perfección de la técnica moderna y la popularidad de la 'murder story' no son sino frutos (como los campos de concentración y el empleo de sistemas de exterminación colectiva) de una concepción optimista y unilateral de la existencia. Octavio Paz, *El laberinto de la soledad*, 2d ed., 54. Translation from *The Labyrinth of Solitude*, trans. Lysander Kemp, Yara Milos, and Rachel Phillips Belash, 60.

7. Lo pintoresco, lo denso y oscuramente simbólico. Carlos Monsiváis, "De las relaciones literarias entre 'alta cultura' y 'cultura popular,'" 48–49.

8. Carlos Monsiváis, "Notas sobre la cultura mexicana en el siglo XX," 1501.

9. Ilán Stavans, *Antiheroes*, 28.

10. Las únicas defensas son la rabia y la pasión. Maricruz Jiménez Flores, "Tabaco para el puma, una denuncia de Juan Hernández Luna escrita con humor cáustico."

11. Antonio Helú, *La obligación de asesinar*, 19.

12. otra cuarenta y cinco especial . . . (.¡Demonio!)¿ Acaso son ustedes diputados? Ibid., 200.

13. Vicente Francisco Torres, *La otra literatura mexicana*, 41.

14. Y los policías del otro lado [the United States] presumen mucho del respeto a la Ley y yo digo que la Ley es una de esas cosas que está allí para los pendejos.

Tal vez los gringos son pendejos. Porque la Ley no se va a ninguna parte. Rafael Bernal, *El complot mongol*, 1.

15. Saben judo, karate y estrangular con cordones de seda . . . a nosotros en México no nos enseñan todos esos primores. A nosotros sólo nos enseñan a matar. Y tal vez ni eso. Nos contratan porque ya sabemos matar. No somos expertos sino aficionados. Ibid., 174.

16. Somos medio pendejos y matamos a la clientela. Ibid., 187.

17. La cara oscura era inexpresiva, la boca casi siempre inmóvil, hasta cuando hablaba. Sólo había vida en sus grandes ojos verdes, almendrados. Cuando niño, en Yurécuaro, le decían El Gato, y una mujer en Tampico le decía Mi Tigre Manso. (¡Pinche tigre manso!) Pero aunque los ojos se prestaban a un apodo así, el resto de la cara, sobre todo el rictus de la boca, no animaba a la gente a usar apodos con él. Ibid., 9.

18. Torres, *La otra novela mexicana*, 21.

19. Cuando hago examen de mi vida pasada me pasa lo contrario de lo que a Poirot: veo en la penumbra del pasado un bosque de casos sin resolver. Jorge Ibargüengoitia, *Autopsias rápidas*, 267.

20. "In 1964 in Guanajuato they discover the cadavers of some prostitutes, ordered killed and buried by the madames Chuy, Delfa and Eva, the *Poquianchis*. The trial, which the tabloid press parlays into big business, is mixed up with two stories that start in 1951: in living color the tale of the prostitutes' suffering, like the sisters Adelina and María, daughters of the peasant Rosario, bought from him by the *Poquianchis* under the pretext of finding them work, and their little sister Amparo, afterwards kidnapped; their castigation through confinements and beatings, their diet of beans when they close up the brothels, the murder by beating of Adelina by her own sister, maddened by seeing her defecate and other atrocities, as well as the life of the madames and Tepo, one of their sons, also involved in the white slave trade and smuggling, who dies in an altercation with some men and causes the desolation of his mother. In black and white, the life of Rosario and other peasants despoiled of their land, some assassinated and others jailed for protesting. The judge has to close the case quickly by orders from above. After serving her sentence one of the prostitutes opens another clandestine brothel." (En 1964 se descubren en Guanajuato cadáveres de prostitutas mandadas asesinar y enterrar por las lenonas Chuy, Delfa y Eva, *Las poquianchis*. El juicio, con el que hace un gran negocio la prensa amarillista, se mezcla con dos historias que comienzan en 1951: en color los sufrimientos de las prostitutas, como las hermanas Adelina y María, hijas del campesino Rosario, compradas a él por *Las poquianchis* con el pretexto de darles trabajo, y su hermana menor Amparo, raptada después; sus castigos de encierro y golpes, su dieta de frijoles cuando cierran los tugurios, el asesinato a palos de Adelina por su propia hermana enloquecida al verla defecar y otras atrocidades, así como la vida de las lenonas y Tepo, hijo de una de ellas, también dedicado a la trata de blancas y el contrabando, que muere en un enfrentamiento con unos tipos y causa el decaimiento de su madre. En blanco y negro la vida de Rosario y otros campesinos despojados

de sus tierras, unos asesinados y otros encarcelados por protestar. El juez debe cerrar pronto el proceso por orden superior. Tras purgar su condena una de las prostitutas abre otro prostíbulo clandestino.) Synopsis of the film *Las poquianchis* (Felipe Cazals, 1976. Screenplay by José Revueltas and José Agustín).

21. Puede funcionar a la vez como 'la historia' y 'la escritura legal' de una cultura fundada en la creencia de la verdad de la confesión y en las subjetividades palpables. Josefina Ludmer, *El cuerpo del delito*, 465.

22. Doris Sommer, "No Secrets," 10.

23. Truman Capote . . . los entrevistó por horas y días enteros y luego reconstruyó sus vidas. Yo hice lo contrario. . . . Inventé los personajes porque si llego a entrevistar a las Poquianchis me mandan a la chingada. Margarita García Flores, *Cartas marcadas*, 203.

24. Es posible imaginarlos: los cuatro llevan anteojos negros, el Escalera maneja encorvado sobre el volante, a su lado está el Valiente Nicolás leyendo Islas Marías, en el asiento trasero, la mujer mira por la ventanilla y el capitán Bedoya dormita cabeceando. Jorge Ibargüengoitia, *Las muertas*, 9. Translation from *The Dead Girls*, trans. Asa Zatz, 9.

25. Conviene notar que los motivos que tuvo el Inspector Cueto . . . son tan oscuros; El papel que desempeña el Inspector Cueto en la aprehensión de las hermanas Baladro es una de las partes oscuras de esta historia. Puede explicarse tentativamente así. *Las muertas*, 134, 137. Translation from *The Dead Girls*, 135, 137.

26. Según me dijeron se llamaba Ernestina, Helda o Elena. Ibid., 23. Translation from *The Dead Girls*, 23.

27. El tono de este documento es definitivo. El que lo lee ignorando la historia podría suponer que allí terminó la pesquisa. Ibid., 133; translation from *The Dead Girls*, 134.

28. Que ella vio a las hermanas Serafina y Arcángela Baladro empujar a dos mujeres que se cayeron de un balcón el día 14 de septiembre. Ibid., 143. Translation from *The Dead Girls*, 144.

29. Sklodowska's terminology describes Poniatowska's autorial/editorial project in *La noche de Tlatelolco*. See Elzbieta Sklodowska, *Testimonio hispanoamericano: Historia, teoría, poética*, 161.

30. See George Yúdice's introduction to Néstor García Canclini, *Consumers and Citizens: Globalization and Multicultural Conflicts*, xxi.

31. Somos imperturbables, enterotes, indios todos . . . [que] sufrimos en silencio la opresión de la clase media, nos levantaremos en armas y a la larga triunfaremos—nacionalizaremos el petróleo y la tierra será del que la trabaje—. El corolario implícito de esta visión es que la vida que llevamos es la Edad de Oro: fruto maduro de la semilla que sembraron Cuauhtémoc, el cura Hidalgo, Juárez, Madero y Zapata. Ibargüengoitia, *Autopsias rápidas*, 142.

32. James Bond llega a Munich y sabe dónde se puede comer el mejor *liverwürst* de la ciudad. A cierta hora dice "se me anteoja un *schnapps*." Es decir, es un señor que siempre sabe lo que quiere, siempre sabe dónde conseguirlo, y siempre tiene con qué pagarlo. . . . es el mejor tirador del Servicio Secreto . . . bebe como

cuba y nunca se emborracha. . . .Yo lo que digo es, por qué los mexicanos no hacemos algo así? Ibid., 35.

33. Carlos Fuentes's *Cabeza de la hidra* echoes this sentiment a little less subtly: "Yes, Félix Maldonado was a bad agent, an underveloped James Bond. But my intelligence service had to be organized with what the Mexican people offered: Félix, Emiliano, Rosita. Ashenden and Richard Hannay had Shakespeare behind them; my pathetic agents had Cantinflas in *The Unknown Policeman*." (Sí, Félix Maldonado era un mal agente, un James Bond del subdesarrollo. Pero mi servicio de inteligencia tenía que organizarse con lo que la mexicanidad me ofrecía: Félix, Emiliano, Rosita. Ashenden y Richard Hannay tenían detrás de ellos a Shakespeare; mis pobres agentes, a Cantinflas en *El gendarme desconocido*). Carlos Fuentes, *La cabeza de la hidra*, 243.

5. The Dismembered City

1. Mucha pseudodemocracia bárbara. Taibo, "La 'otra' novela policiaca," 38.

2. See Homi K. Bhabha, *The Location of Culture*, 2.

3. See Ángel Rama, *La ciudad letrada*.

4. See Michel de Certeau, "Walking the City," in *The Practice of Everyday Life*, 91–110.

5. See Octavio Paz, *Posdata*. Paz was obviously not the first to remark on the persistence of the Aztec past in the Mexican present, but he is perhaps the most famous. His *Crítica de la pirámide*, written the year after the massacre of student protesters at the Plaza de Tres Culturas in 1968, establishes the connection between Aztec sacrificial space and the contemporary event. Mexico itself, Paz wrote, is shaped like a giant pyramid whose apex, the sacrificial platform-altar, is the Plaza de Tres Culturas in the capital of the republic.

6. See García Canclini, *Consumers and Citizens*, 51.

7. Se desborda y se multiplica en ficciones individuales y colectivas. Néstor García Canclini, *Imaginarios urbanos*, 109.

8. Lo excepcional, lo desusado, no es que un latinoamericano resulte víctima, sino que pueda dejar de serlo. Monsiváis, "Ustedes que jamás han sido asesinados," 3.

9. See José Rabasa, *Inventing America: Spanish Historiography and the Formation of Eurocentrism*; Carlos Monsiváis, *Los rituales del caos*; and Roger Bartra, *La jaula de la melancolía*. Bartra traces the origins of the "signo de la melancolía" that supposedly afflicts the Mexican to classical and modern Western European culture. Melancholy, he observes, is common among identity theorists and can be found in many sociological analyses outside Mexico.

10. "No Happy Endings," interview with Paco Ignacio Taibo II by John F. Baker. Taibo's literary production is virtually ignored by the Mexican cultural elite. Taibo says of his critical reception: "I was a kind of nonexistent writer. My first book got three reviews in Mexico. Three very, very bad reviews. One of them was by a famous Mexican critic who reviews one book daily, and reads one

book a year, something like that. He'd read the flaps only. The second book got two reviews, also very bad. And I said well, the third one will get one review, and by the fourth I will disappear. But I disappeared even faster than that: the third one got no reviews at all. Only, it made the bestseller list in Mexico City."

11. "No Happy Endings."

12. Glen Close, "Taibo II Plots the Megalopolis." Close's perceptive analysis describes Belascoarán's mapping of the city according to Taibo's socialist ideology as an attempt to reimpose a sense of community on the dismembered landscape. "Using frequent topographical references to precise landmarks, streets and neighborhoods, Taibo plots points on an urban field which no individual imagination can any longer encompass. . . . His detectives strive to reclaim lost territories, to plot history, to suture urban fragments or "micropaisajes" and thus rearticulate a disintegrated D.F."

13. Bruno Bosteels, "The Usual Suspects: Paco Ignacio Taibo II's Narrative History of the Left in Mexico City."

14. Manuel Vázquez Montalbán, Salvador Vázquez de Parga, Juan Madrid, José F. Colmeiro, and Taibo are a few of the writers who have cited Himes as an important influence.

15. Su temática no era equiparable a la de la novela negra estadounidense, aunque estaba muy influida por los exponentes más radicales del género (curiosamente también los tardíos) Himes y Thompson, que pesaban más que los clásicos del género. La irracionalidad de la violencia, mostrada como una presencia en las ciudades que describían, que se desataba a la menor provocación, el nerviosismo de sus descripciones ambientales, el coloquialismo de los diálogos, habían pasado de Himes y Thompson a los autores mencionados. Taibo, "La 'otra' novela policiaca," 37. Taibo called the Himes/Thompson style *"ugly-dirty-fucking-realism."* Taibo, *Primavera pospuesta*, 22.

16. Chester Himes, *A Rage in Harlem*, 49.

17. Voy a averiguar tanto como pueda y chingarlos tanto como pueda. Taibo, *No habrá final feliz*, 101. Translation from *No Happy Ending*, trans. William I. Neuman, 139.

18. Chester Himes, *The Big Gold Dream*, 56.

19. No existe ciencia ninguna que pueda aproximar a un mexicano a descubrir la verdad. Juan Carlos Ramírez, "Paco Ignacio Taibo II: La lógica de la terquedad o la variante mexicana de una locura," 43.

20. Todo había parecido muy claro en los primeros instantes: sacar pistola, patear puerta, entrar cuarto. De acuerdo al guión escrito había que: o sacarle la caca al gordito a patadas, para que dijera el nombre del hotel de la calzada Zaragoza, o envolverlo en una conversación en la que soltara la papa. Héctor se sentía incapaz de ambas cosas. Taibo, *Cosa fácil*, 109. Translation from *An Easy Thing*, trans. William I. Neuman, 124–25.

21. Porque los finales felices no se hicieron para este país. . . . Héctor fue empujado por esas y otras oscuras razones hacia el desenlace." Ibid., 190. Translation from *An Easy Thing*, 222.

22. Ningún modelo operaba. Era una jodida broma, pero cuando en seis meses había logrado que lo intentaran matar seis veces, cuando la piel tenía las huellas de cada uno de los atentados . . . cuando había logrado sobrevivir aquellos meses . . . entonces, y sólo entonces, la broma dejaba de ser un fenómeno particular y se integraba en el país. Taibo, *Cosa fácil*, 15. Translation from *An Easy Thing*, 11.

23. Gilbert H. Muller, *Chester Himes*, 2. Himes was enormously bitter toward the American literary establishment for not recognizing his merit and intensely jealous of other black expatriate writers: "Every other American black living abroad was at least recognized if not helped. But as far as Americans were concerned, I was dead" (Himes, *My Life of Absurdity*, 144).

24. Himes, *A Rage in Harlem*, 20.

25. See Michael Denning, "Topographies of Violence: Chester Himes' Harlem Domestic Novels," for a thorough analysis of this topography.

26. Himes, *A Rage in Harlem*, 93.

27. Ibid., 148.

28. Himes, *The Real Cool Killers*, 8. This type of scene was inspired by Himes's compulsive rereading of William Faulkner's *Sanctuary* (cf. the opening scene) during the period in which he wrote the first Harlem stories.

29. The victims in Harlem are always the darkest-skinned, the honest, the pious, and the poor. Those who prey on them are usually light-skinned, especially the women. See Robert E. Skinner's analysis of skin color and character in *Two Guns From Harlem: The Detective Fiction of Chester Himes*, 50–67.

30. Chester Himes, *The Heat's On*, 146.

31. Ed and Digger are also able to get away with violent tactics that, during the 1960s, were becoming politically difficult for white police in black communities.

32. Usted me atraganta señor Cuesta . . . —dijo Héctor y poniéndose en pie le asestó un tremendo bastonazo en la mandíbula. Oyó el nítido crac del maxilar al quebrarse. Taibo, *Cosa fácil*, 189. Translation from *An Easy Thing*, 222.

33. Chandler was educated in England and, as he put it, he "had to learn American like a foreign language." See Most and Stowe, eds., *The Poetics of Murder*, 134.

34. Himes's knowledge of Harlem was sketchy and he admitted that he was out of touch with real Harlem slang. See Himes, *My Life of Absurdity*, 241.

35. Himes, *The Heat's On*, 44.

36. Himes, *A Rage in Harlem*, 27.

37. Taibo, *Adios Madrid*, 24.

38. "Every black person in America knows how to fight racism, whether he will do it or not, whether he will admit to this knowledge or not. Whether he is willing to risk his life for equality or not. Deep in the heart of every American black person is the knowledge that the only way to fight racism is with a gun." *My Life of Absurdity*, 27.

39. As a well-known theorist of genre fiction has noted, the maimed detective is a tradition that dates back to the pulp stories of the 1930s and 1940s: "one

would lose his sight just when it was needed most, one was an amnesiac, one had to crawl on the floor because of his deformed body; but they always got their criminals." See Ray Browne, Gary Hoppenstand, and Garyn G. Roberts, *More Tales of the Defective Detective in the Pulps*, 33.

40. The "double alienation" of the police and detective protagonists, who are set apart from their fellow beings by their scars as well as their chosen profession, is to some extent a function of the foreignness (both literal and critical) of Himes and Taibo to the environments they describe. Nora Alter uses this term to describe the Harlem detectives' final inability to belong in either the black or white world ("Chester Himes," 16).

41. See García Canclini, *Consumers and Citizens*. García Canclini's coinage identifies two different modes of social interaction: the physical and the virtual. He describes the horizontal and vertical growth of Mexico City in the second half of the twentieth century: "Territorial expansion and massification of the city, which reduced interneighborhood interaction, took place simultaneously with the reinvention of social and cultural bonds via radio and television. Today these media—with their vertical and anonymous logic—sketch out the new and invisible links of the city" (53). García Canclini comments specifically on the importance of certain activities as defining public interaction in late-twentieth-century Mexico City: shopping, neighborhood parties, "what youths learn while traversing the city on their way to work or to dance *danzón* or rock at night; the constant renewal of city life while waiting for the bus, buying tortillas" (54).

42. No tienen fidelidad a nadie . . . les gusta joder. No hay nada en el mundo que les guste más que el poder que ejercen cuando aterrorizan a alguien. Ángel Mercado, "Las pistas de PIT II." Web article, http://www.jornada.unam.mx/1996/jul96/960725/mercado.html.

43. Ramírez, "PIT II," 41.

44. La gente puede colaborar. No tienes idea de la cantidad de gente que escucha y lo ansiosa que está la gente de esta ciudad de colaborar en algo. Taibo, *Cosa fácil*, 102. Translation from *An Easy Thing*, 117.

45. Esta conciencia social adquirida por motivos emergidos de un humanismo elemental, primitivo, de una valoración de la situación eminentemente superficial, de una conciencia política construida desde el interior del mundo personal del detective, le permitía al menos concebir México desde una perspectiva acre, desde una posición crítica, desde afuera del poder y el privilegio. Ibid., 22. Omitted from translated edition.

46. Señora de las horas sin luz, protégenos, dama de la noche, cuídanos. Cuídanos, porque no somos de lo peor que le queda a esta ciudad, y sin embargo, no valemos gran cosa. No somos de aquí, ni renunciamos, ni siquiera sabemos irnos a otro lado para desde allí añorar las calles y el solecito, y los licuados de plátano con leche y los tacos de nana, y el Zócalo de 16 de Septiembre y el estadio de Cuauhtémoc y las posadas del Canal Cuatro, y en esta soledad culera que nos atenaza y nos persigue. Taibo, *No habrá final feliz*, 125. Translation from *No Happy Ending*, 174.

47. Himes, *My Life of Absurdity*, 111.

48. Muller, *Chester Himes*, 6.

49. ¿No era suya la misma impunidad que la de los otros? ¿No había podido tirar cartuchos de dinamita, balear pistoleros, volar camionetas sin que pasara nada? Casi estaba por aceptar la tesis del tapicero que repetía una y otra vez: "En este país no pasa nada, y aunque pase, tampoco." Taibo, *Cosa fácil*, 194. Translation from *An Easy Thing*, 227.

50. La defensa natural contra un enemigo que manejaba los medios de información, y que controlaba hasta los mitos. Ibid., 45. Translation from *An Easy Thing*, 48.

51. Una ante la tentación de las partes de la docena. Carmen Boullosa, *La Milagrosa* 12. Translation from *The Miracle-Worker*, trans. Amanda Hopkinson, 3.

52. Fredric Jameson, "On Raymond Chandler," 127.

53. No te vayas otra vez. Yo seguiré cosiendo tus ropas, te acompañaré en tus actos sin jamás verte. No volveré a escribirte. Tú estarás ahí para que yo te repita. Tus seguidores irán y vendrán para cumplir su labor de espejo. Ellos me dirán tu voluntad y me indicarán cómo imitarte. Yo obedeceré fiel como tu imagen. Y tú no escapes, sé que no quieres desvanecerte. Acordémoslo así. No es conveniente otra cosa. Boullosa, *La Milagrosa*, 111. Translation from *The Miracle-Worker*, 133–34.

54. Derrotada ante lo pujante e insaciable de los números plurales. Ibid., 100. Translation from *The Miracle-Worker*, 119.

55. Ibid., 113. Translation from *The Miracle-Worker*, 137.

56. Pertenezco a la 'Generación del Temblor,' esa que rompió con el mito de que era imposible actuar sin papá gobierno. . . . Yo me inserto en la tradición que narra el fin de siglo de nuestras ciudades. . . . El milenarismo, como tal, es muy interesante y pienso que el día de mañana, cuando este país sea mas libre, cuando todo esto pase y sean meras anécdotas lo que ahora vivimos, y mi hija revise los archivos y diga: "qué tiempos tan malos les tocaron vivir, en los años ochenta y noventa." Cuando ella me pregunta: "¿y tú qué hacías?" Mi respuesta será muy sencilla y congruente con estos tiempos: "escribía novelas policiacas, le diré." Maricruz Jiménez Flores, "Tabaco para el puma."

57. Crímenes insolubles que requieren delicadas investigaciones y tienen que llevarse con elemental discretion. Olivier Debroise, *Lo peor sucede al atardecer*, 19.

58. El mal está de moda. Pero ya no se trata de un asunto moral, sino de una manera de defenderse de la imbecilidad y la cursilería. De la angustia y el terror. . . . Encarar el mal, volverlo propio, proyectarlo, convertirlo en la estética de la época. Ibid., 117.

59. La noche que prendí fuego al Rata empezaron mis desgracias. Rolo Diez, *Luna de escarlata*, 17.

60. En esta nueva novela policiaca de habla española no se nacionalizaba un género, se construía un género nacional. Taibo, "La 'otra' novela mexicana," 38.

Epilogue

1. See Link, *El juego de las cautos*, 14. José Antonio Portuondo also noted the total lack of sentimentalism in the detective novel (*Astrolabio* 68). He attributed

the lack of development of the detective genre in Latin America to an excess of emotion in the literature of Spanish America: the result of a temperament (the "genio español e hispanoamericano") unsuited to the cold logic of the inductive detective plot.

2. Juan José Mira suggested that Dupin, Holmes, Philo Vance, Nero Wolfe, Poirot, and the rest of the solitary private detectives were effeminate, a point of view that would resurface in the socialist detective novel of Cuba: "It is no accident that the preeminent figures in the world of detective literature are solitary types, with no family obligations of any kind. For example, none of them, that I know of, talks about his parents. They don't exist. It's as if they entered the world by spontaneous generation. Another thing: the majority of them are confirmed bachelors." (No es por azar que las figuras más preeminentes de mundillo de la literatura policiaca, sean tipos solitarios, sin cargas familiares de ninguna clase. Que yo sepa, ningún detective habla por ejemplo de sus padres. No existen. Parece que han venido a este mundo por generación espontánea. Otra cosa: la mayoría de ellos son solteros contumaces.) See Mira, *Biografía de la novela policiaca*, 47.

3. Sólo hay esperanza en la acción. Taibo, *Cosa fácil*, 2d ed., 7.

4. Luis Adrián Betancourt, June 1997 interview.

5. Leonardo Padura Fuentes, June 1997 interview.

6. José Latour, *Outcast*, 19.

7. Ibid., 97.

8. Hay en ella una perversa condensación de la locura y el horror, aderezada con un montón de mitos. Es una ciudad francamente inestable, llena de vibras malignas y razones solidarias. La ronda la catástrofe y la alimenta la protesta de cada día. Ultimamente me trae jodido, porque se me escapa, no la acabo de pescar como hice otras veces. Taibo, *Primavera pospuesta*, 23.

9. July 1999 interview.

10. "No Happy Endings."

11. The term "impure" is García Canclini's. See *Culturas híbridas: Estrategias para entrar y salir de la modernidad*, 314.

12. See García Canclini, *Consumers and Citizens*.

13. See García Canclini, *Hybrid Cultures: Strategies for Entering and Leaving Modernity*. See also George Yúdice's introduction to this English translation of *Culturas híbridas*, in which he describes identity as a "coproduction" in which indigenous/historical and external/modern elements combine to restate identity both for the "popular" producers and the "elite" consumers (*Consumers and Citizens*, xxv). Yúdice points out the disparity between definitions of "popular" in the Unites States and Latin American contexts: "In Latin America . . . popular refers to the culture and practices of the peasantry and the working classes. . . . In the United States . . . it has become a synonym of mass culture." See p. 163, n. 2. Canclini's formulations in this book are not directed at literary production so much as at mass media and the festival-spectacle, and to apply them wholesale here would be unwise given the high rates of illiteracy in Mexico. Nonetheless,

the concept of the Latin American detective novel as evidence of coproductive activity among its producers provides a framework for situating the production, if not the consumption, of detective literature in a Latin American context.

14. García Canclini, *Consumers and Citizens*, 62.

15. Julio Ramos describes José Martí's "nostalgia for the great deed" as the poet's reaction to "the dissolution of the epic, collective dimensions that once defined literature." See Ramos, *Divergent Modernities*, xxxvii. Chandler alluded to Sir Thomas Malory's epic *Morte d'Arthur* in naming his detective Marlowe. Several scholars have investigated the chivalric antecedents of the hard-boiled genre.

16. La única novela legítima y ética de nuestro tiempo es la policiaca. César Güemes, "La poética del neocapitalismo viene a ser la novela policiaca."

17. La novela negra es un ojo crítico, condenatorio que desnuda hipocresías y que demuestra lo grotesco de la sociedad. Vanessa Calfán Oteo, "Género negro, una literatura de denuncia."

18. Nadie se asombra ya de que lo policiaco también *se hable* en español. Padura Fuentes, *Modernidad, posmodernidad, y novela policial*, 156.

Browne, Ray. *Heroes and Humanities: Detective Fiction and Culture.* Bowling Green: Bowling Green State University Press, 1986.

———, Gary Hoppenstand, and Garyn G. Roberts. *More Tales of the Defective Detective in the Pulps.* Bowling Green: Bowling Green State University Press, 1985.

Bruce-Novoa Valentin, David. "Violating the Image of Violence: Ibargüengoitia's *El atentado.*" *Latin American Theatre Review* 12, no. 2 (1979): 13–21.

Bueno, Eva P., and Terry Caesar, eds. *Imagination beyond Nation: Latin American Popular Culture.* Pittsburgh: University of Pittsburgh Press, 1998.

Buffington, Rob. "*Los Jotos*: Contested Visions of Homosexuality in Mexico." In *Sex and Sexuality in Latin America*, ed. Daniel Balderston and Donna Guy. New York: New York University Press, 1997. 118–32.

Bunck, Julie Marie. *Fidel Castro and the Quest for a Revolutionary Culture in Cuba.* University Park: Pennsylvania State University Press, 1994.

Bustamante, José Angel. *Raíces psicológicas del cubano.* 2d ed. Havana, 1960.

Cabrera Infante, Guillermo. "Vidas para leerlas." *Vuelta* 41 (April 1980): 4–16.

———. *Mea Cuba.* Barcelona: Plaza y Janés, 1992.

Caillois, Roger. *The Mystery Novel.* Translated by Roberto Yahni and A. W. Sadler. Bronxville, N.Y.: Laughing Buddha Press, 1982.

Calfán Oteo, Vanessa. "Género negro, una literatura de denuncia." *El Nacional,* 29 August 1997.

Calvino, Italo. "Why Read the Classics?" *The Uses of Literature.* Translated by Patrick Creagh. New York: Harcourt Brace Jovanovich, 1986. 125–134.

Campbell, Federico. "Ibargüengoitia: La sátira histórico-política." *Revista Iberoamericana* 55, nos. 148–149 (1989): 1047–055.

———. *Máscara negra: Crimen y poder.* Mexico City: Joaquín Mortiz, 1995.

Cancio Islas, Wilfredo. "'Máscaras', con la muerte en el alma." *El Nuevo Herald* (8 June 1997): 5c.

Cárdenas Acuña, Ignacio. *Enigma para un domingo.* Havana: Letras Cubanas (Dragón), 1971.

———. *Con el rostro en la sombra.* Havana: Letras Cubanas, 1981.

Cardi, Juan Ángel. *El American Way of Death.* Havana: Letras Cubanas, 1980.

———. *Una jugada extraordinaria.* Havana: Letras Cubanas, 1982.

———. *Dos casos de un detective.* Havana: Letras Cubanas, 1983.

Carpentier, Alejo. "Apología de la novela policiaca." 1931. *Crónicas* II. Havana: Arte y Literatura, 1976. 461–66.

Casal, Lourdes. "Cultural Policy and Writers in Cuba." In *The Cuba Reader: The Making of a Revolutionary Society,* ed. Philip Brenner et al. New York: Grove, 1989. 506–13.

Cassiday, Bruce, ed. *Roots of Detection: The Art of Deduction before Sherlock Holmes.* New York: Frederick Ungar, 1983.

———. *Modern Mystery, Fantasy, and Science Fiction Writers: A Library of Literary Criticism.* New York: Frederick Ungar, 1993.

Castellanos, Israel. *La delincuencia femenina en Cuba.* Havana: Dorrbecker, 1929.

———. *Medicina legal y criminologia afro-cubanas.* Havana: Molina y Cia., 1937.

———. *La talla de los delincuentes en Cuba.* Havana: Dorrbecker, 1927.

Cawelti, John G. *Adventure, Mystery, and Romance.* Chicago: University of Chicago Press, 1976.

———. "The Concept of Formula in the Study of Popular Literature." In *The Study of Popular Fiction: A Source Book*, ed. Bob Ashley. Philadelphia: University of Pennsylvania Press, 1989. 87–92.

———, and Bruce A. Rosenberg. *The Spy Story.* Chicago: University of Chicago Press, 1987.

Certeau, Michel de. *The Practice of Everyday Life.* Translated by Stephen Rendall. Berkeley: University of California Press, 1984.

Chace, William M. "Spies and God's Spies: Greene's Espionage Fiction." In *Graham Greene: A Revaluation. New Essays*, ed. Jeffrey Meyers. New York: St. Martin's, 1990. 156–80.

Chandler, Raymond. "The Simple Art of Murder." *Rex Stout Mystery Quarterly* 2 (1945): 94–97.

Chavarría, Daniel. *Joy.* 1977. Prol. Armando Cristóbal Pérez. Havana: Letras Cubanas, 1982.

———. "Con vocación de viajero y oficio de escritor." Interview. *Bohemia* 78, no. 38 (1986): 46–48.

———. *La sexta isla.* 2 vols. Madrid: Júcar, 1988.

———. *Allá ellos.* Mexico City: Joaquín Mortiz, 1992.

———. *Adiós muchachos.* New York: Akashic Books, 2001.

———. *The Eye of the Cybele.* New York: Akashic Books, 2001.

———. *Primero muerto.* Havana: Letras Cubanas, 1986.

———, and Justo Vasco. *Completo Camagüey.* Havana: Letras Cubanas, 1983.

Chesterton, Gilbert Keith. "On Detective Story Writers." *Come to Think of It . . .* New York: Dodd, Mead, 1931. 33–38.

———. "A Defence of Detective Stories." *The Defendant.* 4th ed. New York: Dodd, Mead, 1914. 118–23.

———. "The Ideal Detective Story." *Collected Works*, vol. 35. San Francisco: Ignatius Press, n.d. 399–403.

———. "On Detective Novels." *Generally Speaking.* New York: Dodd, Mead, 1929. 1–7.

———. "Sobre novelas policiales." *Charlas.* Buenos Aires: Espasa-Calpe, 1946. 9–14.

———. "The Domesticity of Detectives." *The Uses of Diversity.* New York: Dodd, Mead, 1921. 24–29.

———. *The Father Brown Omnibus.* New York: Dodd, Mead, 1951.

———. *The Man Who Was Thursday, a Nightmare.* New York: Capricorn Books, 1960.

———. *The Annotated Innocence of Father Brown.* Edited by Martin Gardner. Oxford: Oxford University Press, 1987.

———. *Heretics.* New York: John Lane, 1906.

———. *Lunacy and Letters.* Edited by Dorothy Collins. New York: Sheed and Ward, 1958.

Chiappini, Julio. *Borges y Chesterton*. Santa Fe: Zeus, 1994.

Chiunti Sánchez, Guadalupe. "¿Novela policiaca?" *La Palabra y el Hombre* 59–60 (1986): 51–52.

Clark, Stella T. "Testimonio, historia, y ficción: *Crónica de una muerte anunciada* y *Las muertas*." *Texto Crítico* 15, nos. 40–41 (1989): 21–29.

Close, Glen. "Taibo II Plots the Megalopolis." Forthcoming.

Coates, John. *Chesterton and the Edwardian Cultural Crisis*. Hull, England: Hull University Press, 1984.

Colmeiro, José F. *La novela policiaca española: Teoría e historia crítica*. Pról. Manuel Vázquez Montalbán. Barcelona: Ánthropos, 1994.

Coma, Javier. *La novela negra: historia de la aplicación del realismo crítico a la novela policiaca norteamericana*. Barcelona: Ediciones 2001, 1980.

———. *Diccionario de la novela negra norteamericana*. Barcelona: Anagrama, 1986.

Correa, Arnaldo. *Un caso difícil*. Havana: Capitán San Luis, 1991.

———. *Spy's Fate*. New York: Akashic Books, 2001.

Craig-Odders, Renée W. *The Detective Novel in Post-Franco Spain: Democracy, Disillusionment, and Beyond*. New Orleans: University Press of the South, 1999.

Cuentos policiacos cubanos. Montevideo: Signos y Amauta, 1989.

La cultura en Cuba socialista. Havana: Letras Cubanas, 1982.

Cunill, Felipe. "El factor Graham Greene." *Revolución y Cultura* 4 (1991): 17–19.

Dale, Alzina Stone. *The Outline of Sanity: A Biography of G. K. Chesterton*. Grand Rapids: Eerdmans, 1982.

Dalton, Roque, et al. *El intelectual y la sociedad*. Mexico City: Siglo Veintiuno, 1969.

Dean, Carolyn J. *The Self and Its Pleasures: Bataille, Lacan, and the History of the Decentered Subject*. Ithaca: Cornell University Press, 1992.

———. *Sexuality and Modern Western Culture*. New York: Twayne, 1996.

Debroise, Olivier. *Lo peor sucede al atardecer*. Mexico City: Cal y Arena, 1990.

de Man, Paul. "A Modern Master: Jorge Luis Borges." In de Man, *Critical Writings, 1953–1978*, ed. and with an introduction by Lindsay Waters. Minneapolis: University of Minnesota Press, 1989.

Denning, Michael. "Topographies of Violence: Chester Himes' Harlem Domestic Novels." *Critical Texts* 5, no. 1 (1988): 10–18.

De Quincey, Thomas. "On Murder, Considered as One of the Fine Arts." 1817. *Works*. Edinburgh: Adam and Charles Black, 1863.

De Vitis, A. A. *Graham Greene*. Rev. ed. Boston: Twayne, 1986.

Díaz, Désirée, and Arsenio Cicero Sancristóbal. "Leonardo Padura y Mario Conde: De semejanzas, persecuciones, y metáforas." Unpublished interview, n.d.

Diez, Rolo. *Luna de escarlata*. Mexico City: Roca, 1994.

———. *Paso del tigre*. Mexico City: Grupo Zeta, 1991.

Diez Borque, José María. *Literatura y cultura de masas: estudio de la novela subliteraria*. Madrid: Al-Borak, 1972.

Domínguez, Marta Susana. "El detective en el cuarto cerrado." In *Primeras Jornadas Internacionales de Literatura Argentina/Comparista Actas*, ed. Teresita Frugoni de Fritzsche. Buenos Aires: University of Buenos Aires, 1996. 381–86.

Dussel, Enrique. "Eurocentrism and Modernity (Introduction to the Frankfurt Lectures)." In *The Postmodernism Debate in Latin America*, ed. John Beverley et al. Durham: Duke University Press, 1995. 65–76.

Eagleton, Terry. *Criticism and Ideology*. London: New Left, 1976.

———. *Literary Theory: An Introduction*. Minneapolis: University of Minnesota Press, 1983.

East, Andy. *The Cold War File*. Metuchen, N.J.: Scarecrow, 1983.

Eco, Umberto. "The Narrative Structure in Fleming." Rpt. from Umberto Eco, *The Role of the Reader: Gender, Language, and Myth: Essays and Popular Narrative*. Edited by Glenwood Irons. Toronto: University of Toronto Press, 1992. 157–82.

———. "Innovation and Repetition: Between Modern and Post-Modern Aesthetics." In *Reading Eco: An Anthology*, ed. Rocco Capozzi Rocco. Foreword by Thomas Sebeok. Bloomington: Indiana University Press, 1997. 14–33.

———. *Apocalípticos e integrados ante la cultura de masas*. Barcelona: Lumen, 1968.

———, and Thomas A. Sebeok, eds. *The Sign of Three: Dupin, Holmes, Peirce*. Bloomington: Indiana University Press, 1983.

Epple, Juan Armando. "Entrevista: Leonardo Padura Fuentes." *Hispamérica* 24, no. 71 (1995): 49–66.

Evenson, Debra. *Revolution in the Balance: Law and Society in Contemporary Cuba*. Boulder: Westview, 1994.

Ferman, Claudia. "México en la postmodernidad: Textualización de la cultura popular urbana." *Nuevo Texto Crítico* 4, no. 7 (1991): 157–67.

Fernández Pequeño, José M. "La novela policial cubana ante sí misma (1979–1986)." *La Palabra y el Hombre* 70 (1989): 205–16.

———. "Teoría y practica de la novela policial revolucionaria." *La Palabra y el Hombre* 66 (1988): 93–101.

———. "El cuento policial revolucionario entre el poder y el deber (1973–1987)." *Revista de Literatura Cubana* 9, no. 17 (1991): 86–103.

Fernández Retamar, Roberto. "Hacia una nueva intelectualidad revolucionaria en Cuba." *Casa de las Américas* 40 (1967): 10–11.

———. "A propósito del Círculo de Praga y del estudio de nuestra literatura." *Casa de las Américas* 74 (1972): 20–26.

———. "Calibán." *Calibán y otros ensayos*. Havana: Arte y Literatura, 1979.

———. *Idea de la estilística*. Havana: Pueblo y Educación, 1983.

———. *Para el perfil definitivo del hombre*. Havana: Letras Cubanas, 1985.

Ferrari, Osvaldo, and Jorge Luis Borges. *Borges en diálogo*. Buenos Aires: Grijalbo, 1985.

Fielder, Leslie. "Towards a Definition of Popular Literature." In *The Study of Popular Fiction: A Source Book*, ed. Bob Ashley. Philadelphia: University of Pennsylvania Press, 1989. 11–16.

Fornet, Ambrosio. *Antología del cuento cubano contemporáneo*. Mexico City: Era, 1967.

Fosca, François. *Histoire et technique du roman policier*. Paris: Nouvelle Revue Critique, 1937.

Foster, David William. *Cultural Diversity in Latin American Literature.* Albuquerque: University of New Mexico Press, 1994.

———, and Roberto Reis, eds. *Bodies and Biases: Sexualities in Hispanic Cultures and Literatures.* Minneapolis: University of Minnesota Press, 1996.

Foster, Hal, ed. *The Anti-Aesthetic: Essays on Postmodern Culture.* Port Townsend, Wa.: Bay Press, 1983.

———. *The Return of the Real: The Avant-Garde at the End of the Century.* Cambridge: MIT Press, 1996.

Foucault, Michel. *The History of Sexuality. Vol. I: An Introduction.* 1976. New York: Vintage, 1990.

———. *The Order of Things: An Archaeology of the Human Sciences.* New York: Vintage, 1973.

———. "What Is an Author?" In *The Critical Tradition: Classic Texts and Contemporary Trends,* ed. David Richter. New York: St. Martin's, 1989. 978–87.

Franco, Jean. *Modern Culture of Latin America.* London: Pall Mall Press, 1967.

Freeman, R. Austin. "The Art of the Detective Story." *Nineteenth Century and After.* (May 1924): n.p.

Frye, Northrop. *The Anatomy of Criticism.* 3rd ed. Princeton: Princeton University Press, 1971.

Fuentes, Carlos. *La cabeza de la hidra.* Barcelona: Librería Argos, 1978.

Gans, Herbert. *Popular Culture and High Culture.* New York: Basic Books, 1975.

García Canclini, Néstor. *Consumers and Citizens: Globalization and Multicultural Conflicts.* Translated by George Yúdice. Minneapolis: University of Minnesota Press, 2001.

———. *Culturas híbridas: estrategias para entrar y salir de la modernidad.* Mexico City: Grijalbo, 1990.

———. *Imaginarios urbanos.* Buenos Aires: Editorial Universitaria de Buenos Aires, 1997.

———. *Hybrid Cultures: Strategies for Entering and Leaving Modernity.* Translated by Christopher L. Chiappari and Silvia L. López. Minneapolis: University of Minnesota Press, 1995.

García Chichester, Ana. "Codifying Homosexuality as Grotesque: The Writings of Virgilio Piñera." In *Bodies and Biases: Sexualities in Hispanic Cultures and Literatures,* ed. David William Foster and Roberto Reis. Minneapolis: University of Minnesota Press, 1996. 294–315.

García Flores, Margarita. *Cartas marcadas.* Mexico City: UNAM, 1979.

García Núñez, Fernando. "La imposibilidad del libre albedrío en *La cabeza de la hidra,* de Carlos Fuentes." *Cuadernos Americanos* 1, no. 252 (1984): 227–34.

Gaya Nuño, J. A. "Elogio y vejamen de la novela policiaca." *Cuadernos Hispano-americanos* 256 (1971): 113–21.

Giardinelli, Mempo. *El género negro.* Mexico City: UNAM, 1984.

Gide, André. *Reportajes imaginarios.* Translated by Margarita Abella Caprille and Marta Acosta van Praet. Buenos Aires: Emecé, 1944.

González Morales, Antonio. "La novela policiaca." *Arbor* 108, no. 423 (1981): 107–13.

Gramsci, Antonio. "Sobre la novela policial." *Literatura y vida nacional.* Buenos Aires: Lautaro, 1961. In *El juego de los cautos: la literatura policial: de Poe al Caso Giubileo,* ed. Daniel Link. Buenos Aires: La Marca Editora, 1992. 23–25.

Greene, Graham. *Graham Greene's Classic Tales of Espionage and Suspense.* New York: Galahad, 1987.

———. *Our Man in Havana, an Entertainment.* New York: Viking, 1958.

———. *The Lawless Roads.* 1939. New York: Penguin, 1982.

Grella, George. "The Hard-Boiled Detective Novel." In *Detective Fiction: A Collection of Critical Essays,* ed. Robin Winks. Englewood Cliffs: Prentice-Hall, 1980. 103–20.

Grossvogel, David. *Mystery and its Fictions: From Oedipus to Agatha Christie.* Baltimore: Johns Hopkins University Press, 1979.

Güemes, César. "La poética del neocapitalismo viene a ser la novela policiaca." *La Jornada* (27 April 1999).

Guevara, Ernesto. "El socialismo y el hombre en Cuba." 1965. *Escritos y discursos* 8. Havana: Ciencias Sociales, 1985.

Gugelberger, Georg M., ed. *The Real Thing: Testimonial Discourse and Latin America.* Durham: Duke University Press, 1996.

Gutiérrez Carbajo, Francisco. "Caracterización del personaje en la novela policiaca." *Cuadernos Hispanoamericanos* 371 (1981): 320–37.

Gyurko, Lanin A. "Individual and National Identity in Fuentes' *La cabeza de la hidra.*" In *Latin American Fiction Today: A Symposium Sponsored by the Department of Spanish and Italian, School of Humanities, Latin America Area Studies Program,* ed. Rose S. Minc. Takoma Park, Md.: Hispamerica, 1981. 33–47.

———. "Fuentes, Guzmán, and the Mexican Political Novel." *Ibero-Amerikanisches Archiv* 16, no. 4 (1990): 545–610.

Halperin, Maurice. *Return to Havana: The Decline of Cuban Society under Castro.* Nashville: Vanderbilt University Press, 1994.

Hart, Patricia. *The Spanish Sleuth.* Rutherford, N.J.: Fairleigh Dickinson University Press, 1987.

Hayes, Aden W., and Khachig Tololyan. "The Cross and the Compass: Patterns of Order in Chesterton and Borges." *Hispanic Review* 49, no. 4 (autumn 1981): 395–405.

Haycraft, Howard. *Murder for Pleasure.* New York: Appleton-Century, 1941.

———, ed. *The Art of the Mystery Story.* New York: Simon and Schuster, 1946.

Helú, Antonio. *La obligación de asesinar.* Prol. Carlos Monsiváis. Mexico City: Miguel Ángel Porrúa, 1997.

Herald, Diana Tixier. *Genreflecting: A Guide to Reading Interests in Genre Fiction.* 4th ed. Englewood, Col.: Libraries Unlimited, 1995.

Hernández Castellón, Raúl. *La revolución demográfica en Cuba.* Havana: Ciencias Sociales, 1988.

Hernández Luna, Juan. *Quizás otros labios.* Mexico City: Roca, 1994.

———. *Tabaco para el puma*. Mexico City: Roca, 1996.

Hernández Martín, Jorge. *Readers and Labyrinths: Detective Fiction in Borges, Bustos Domecq, and Eco*. New York: Garland, 1995.

———. "On the Case." *Américas* 47, no. 2 (1995): 16–21.

Himes, Chester. *My Life of Absurdity*. 1976. New York: Paragon House, 1990.

———. *A Rage in Harlem*. [*For Love of Imabelle* 1957.] New York: Vintage, 1985.

———. *The Real Cool Killers*. 1959. New York: Vintage, 1988.

———. *All Shot Up*. 1960. Chatham, N.J.: Chatham Bookseller, 1973.

———. *The Big Gold Dream*. 1960. London: W. H. Allen, 1988.

———. *The Heat's On*. 1966. Chatham, N.J.: Chatham Bookseller, 1975.

———. *Plan B*. Edited by Michel Fabre and Robert E. Skinner. Jackson: University Press of Mississippi, 1993.

Holden, Jonathan. "The Case for Raymond Chandler's Fiction as Romance." *Kansas Quarterly* 10 (1978): 41–46.

Holquist, Michael. "Whodunit and Other Questions: Metaphysical Detective Stories in Postwar Fiction." In *The Poetics of Murder: Detective Fiction and Literary Theory*, ed. Glenn W. Most and William W. Stowe. San Diego: Harcourt, 1983. 149–74.

Hopenhayn, Martín. "Postmodernism and Neoliberalism." In *The Postmodernism Debate in Latin America*, ed. John Beverley et al. Durham: Duke University Press, 1995. 93–109.

Hoskins, Robert. *Graham Greene: A Character Index and Guide*. New York: Garland, 1991.

Hoveyda, Fereydoun (René Ballet). *Historia de la novela policial*. Madrid: Alianza, 1967.

Huertas, Begoña. *Ensayo de un cambio: la narrativa cubana de los '80*. Havana: Casa de las Américas, 1993.

Hühn, Peter. "The Detective as Reader: Narrativity and Reading Concepts in Detective Fiction." *Modern Fiction Studies* 33, no. 3 (1987): 451–66.

Ibargüengoitia, Jorge. *Las muertas*. 1977. Barcelona: Argos Vergara, 1983.

———. *The Dead Girls*. Translated by Asa Zatz. New York: Avon, 1983.

———. *Dos crímenes*. Mexico City: Joaquín Mortiz, 1979.

———. *Autopsias rápidas*. Mexico City: Vuelta, 1988.

———. *La casa de usted y otros viajes*. Mexico City: J. Mortiz, 1991.

———. *Viajes en la América ignota*. Mexico City: J. Mortiz, 1988.

Irving, Clifford, and Herbert Burkholz. *Spy: The Story of Modern Espionage*. New York: Macmillan, 1969.

Irwin, John. *The Mystery to a Solution: Poe, Borges, and the Analytic Detective Story*. Baltimore: Johns Hopkins University Press, 1994.

Jameson, Fredric R. *The Political Unconscious: Narrative as a Socially Symbolic Act*. Ithaca: Cornell University Press, 1981.

———. "On Raymond Chandler." In *The Poetics of Murder*, ed. Glen W. Most and William W. Stowe. New York: Harcourt, Brace, 1983.

———. "Postmodernism and Consumer Society." In *The Anti-Aesthetic: Essays* on *Postmodern Culture*, ed. Hal Foster. Port Townsend, Wa.: Bay Press, 1983. 111–25.

Jiménez, Onilda. "Un nuevo fenomeno de la literatura cubana: La novela policial." *Círculo* 9 (1980): 93–100.

Jiménez Flores, Maricruz. "Tabaco para el puma, una denuncia de Juan Hernández Luna escrita con humor cáustico." *Crónica* (17 July 1997).

Jrade, Cathy L. *Modernismo, Modernity, and the Development of Spanish American Literature*. Austin: University of Texas Press, 1998.

Kafalenos, Emma. "The Grace and Disgrace of Literature: Carlos Fuentes' *The Hydra Head*." *Latin American Literary Review* 15, no. 29 (1987): 141–58.

Knight, Stephen. *Form and Ideology in Crime Fiction*. Bloomington: Indiana University Press, 1980.

Koldewyn, Phillip. "*La cabeza de la hidra*: Residuos del colonialismo." *Mester* 11, no. 1 (1982): 47–56.

"Kuhn, Franz Felix Adalbert." *Encyclopaedia Britannica*. 13th ed. 1926. 941–42.

Lacan, Jacques. "Seminar on 'The Purloined Letter.'" Translated by Jeffrey Mehlman. In *The Purloined Poe*, ed. John P. Muller and William J. Richardson. Baltimore: Johns Hopkins University Press, 1988.

Lamadrid Vega, José. *La justicia por su mano*. Havana: Arte y Literatura, 1973.

Landeira, Ricardo. *El género policiaco en la literatura del siglo XIX*. Alicante: Publicaciones Universidad de Alicante, 2001.

Larsen, Neil. "Postmodernism and Imperialism: Theory and Politics in Latin America." In *The Postmodernism Debate in Latin America*, ed. John Beverley et al. Durham: Duke University Press, 1995. 110–34.

Latour, José. *Outcast*. New York: William Morrow, 2001.

Laurini, Myriam. *Morena en rojo*. Mexico City: Joaquín Mortiz, 1994.

Laurini, Myriam, and Rolo Diez. *Nota roja 1970's: la crónica policiaca en la ciudad de México*. México: Diana, 1993.

———. *Nota roja 1980's: la crónica policiaca en la ciudad de México*. Mexico City: Diana, 1993.

Leiner, Martin. *Sexual Politics in Cuba: Machismo, Homosexuality, and AIDS*. Boulder: Westview, 1994.

Levine, Lawrence. *The Opening of the American Mind: Canons, Culture, History*. Boston: Beacon, 1996.

———. *Highbrow/Lowbrow: The Emergence of Cultural Hierarchy in America*. Cambridge: Harvard University Press, 1988.

Levine, Robert M. *Tropical Diaspora: The Jewish Experience in Cuba*. Gainesville: University Press of Florida, 1993.

Lindstrom, Naomi. *The Social Conscience of Latin American Writing*. Austin: University of Texas Press, 1998.

———. "The Argentine Reading of Chesterton." *The Chesterton Review: The Journal of the Chesterton Society* 6 (1980): 272–79.

Link, Daniel, ed. *El juego de los cautos: la literatura policial: de Poe al caso Giubileo*. Buenos Aires: La Marca Editora, 1992.

———, and Guillermo Rodríguez Rivera. *El cuarto círculo*. Havana: Letras Cubanas, 1979.

Novás Calvo, Lino. *8 narraciones policiacas*. Compilación y prólogo José Fernández Pequeño. Santiago de Cuba: Oriente, 1995.

O'Brien, Geoffrey. *Hardboiled America: Lurid Paperbacks and the Masters of Noir*. New York: Da Capo, 1997.

Ocampo, Victoria, ed. and trans. *Roger Caillois y la Cruz del Sur en la academia francesa*. Buenos Aires: Sur, 1972.

O'Prey, Paul. *A Reader's Guide to Graham Green*. London: Thames and Hudson, 1988.

Ortega y Gassett, José de. *The Dehumanization of Art*. 1925. Translated by Helen Weyl. Princeton: Princeton University Press, 1968.

———. *La rebelión de las masas*. 12th ed. Madrid: Alianza, 1995.

Otero, Lisandro. "Cuba: literatura y revolución." Supplement to *Siempre!* 226 (15 June 1966): iii–v.

Oviedo, José Miguel. "The Modern Essay in Spanish America." In *The Cambridge History of Latin American Literature. Vol. 2: The Twentieth Century*, ed. Roberto González Echevarría and Enrique Pupo-Walker. New York: Cambridge University Press, 1996. 365–424.

Padura Fuentes, Leonardo. *Máscaras*. 1995. Barcelona, Tusquets, 1997.

———. *Vientos de cuaresma*. 1993. Havana: UNEAC, 1994.

———. *Pasado perfecto*. 1991. Havana: Unión, 1995.

———. "Paisaje del otoño." Barcelona: Tusquets, 1998. [unpublished ms.]

———. *Modernidad, posmodernidad, y novela policial*. Havana: Unión, 2000.

———. "Novela policial y novela de revolución." *Letras Cubanas* 10 (1988): 55–89.

Paterson, Thomas G. *Contesting Castro: The United States and the Triumph of the Cuban Revolution*. New York: Oxford University Press, 1994.

Paz, Octavio. *Corriente alterna*. Mexico City: Siglo Veintiuno, 1967.

———. *El laberinto de la soledad*. 2d ed. Mexico City: Fondo de Cultura Económica, 1959.

———. *The Labyrinth of Solitude and Other Writings*. Translated by Lysander Kemp et al. New York: Grove, 1985.

———. *Posdata*. Mexico City: Siglo Veintiuno, 1970.

———. "Vuelta a *El laberinto de la soledad* (Conversación con Claude Fell)." *El ogro filantrópico*. Madrid: Seix Barral, 1979. 17–37.

Pereira, Armando. *Novela de la revolución cubana*. Mexico City: UNAM, 1995.

Pérez, Louis A. *Cuba: Between Reform and Revolution*. New York: Oxford University Press, 1995.

———. *Essays on Cuban History: Historiography and Research*. Gainesville: University Press of Florida, 1995.

Pérez, Armando Cristóbal. "El género policiaco y la lucha de clases, un reto para escritores revolucionarios." *Bohemia* 40 (1973).

———. *La ronda de los rubíes*. Havana: Arte y Literatura, 1973.

————, and Ernesto Morales Alpízar. *Siete variaciones policiales.* Havana: Arte y Literatura, 1975.

Pérez Valero, Rodolfo. *El misterio de las cuevas del pirata.* Havana: Gente Nueva, 1980.

————. *No es tiempo de ceremonias.* Havana: Arte y Literatura, 1974.

————. *Para vivir más de una vida.* Havana: Arte y Literatura, 1976.

————. "El autor y la utilidad profiláctica de su obra. Un ejemplo: la vigilancia." Unpublished paper presented at Cuban Detective Writers' Round Table, 28 December 1983.

————, and Juan Carlos Reloba. *Confrontación.* Havana: Letras Cubanas, 1985.

Petronio, Giuseppe, Jorge B. Rivera, and Luigi Volta, eds. *Los héroes "difíciles": literatura policial en la Argentina y en Italia.* Buenos Aires: Corregidor, 1991.

Petronio, Giuseppe. "La literatura policial, hoy." In *Los héroes difíciles,* ed. Petronio et al. 29–56.

Piglia, Ricardo. Introducción. *Cuentos de la serie negra.* Buenos Aires: CEAL, 1979. In *El juego de los cautos: la literatura policial: de Poe al caso Giubileo,* ed. Daniel Link. Buenos Aires: La Marca Editorial, 1992. 55–59.

Plans, J. J. "Historia de la novela policiaca." *Cuadernos Hispanoamericanos* 236 (1969): 421–43; 675–99; 127–45.

Plasencia, Azucena. "Padura y el falso policiaco." *Bohemia* (1997): B12–13.

Poe, Edgar Allan. *Tales of Terror and Detection.* New York: Dover, 1995.

Porter, Dennis. "Detection and Ethics: The Case of P. D. James." In *The Sleuth and the Scholar,* ed. Barbara A. Rader and Howard G. Zettler. New York: Greenwood, 1988. 11–18.

Portuondo, José Antonio. *Astrolabio.* Havana: Arte y Literatura, 1973.

————. "Una novela revolucionaria." *Casa de las Américas* 71 (1972): 105.

————. *Teoría y crítica de la literatura.* Prol. Roberto Fernández Retamar. Mexico City: Nueva Imagen, 1984.

Prada Oropeza, Renato. "Estructura y significación en *Y si muero mañana.*" *Texto Crítico* 13, nos. 36–37 (1987): 68–78.

Priestman, Martin. *Detective Fiction and Literature: The Figure on the Carpet.* London: Macmillan, 1990.

Pronzini, Bill, and Jack Adrian. "On Hard-Boiled Crime Fiction." *Para-doxa* 1, no. 2 (1995): 145–60.

Pronzini, Bill, and Martin H. Greenberg, eds. *The Ethnic Detectives: Masterpieces of Mystery Fiction.* New York: Dodd, Mead, 1985.

Quijano, Aníbal. "Modernity, Identity, and Utopia in Latin America. In *The Postmodernism Debate in Latin America,* ed. John Beverley et al. Durham: Duke University Press, 1998. 201–16.

Quiroga, José. "Homosexualities in the Tropic of Revolution." In *Sex and Sexuality in Latin America,* ed. Daniel Balderston and Donna J. Guy. New York: New York University Press, 1997. 133–54.

Rabasa, José. *Inventing America: Spanish Historiography and the Formation of Eurocentrism.* Norman: University of Oklahoma Press, 1993.

Rabonowitz, Peter J. "Chandler Comes to Harlem: Racial Politics in the Thrillers of Chester Himes." In *The Sleuth and the Scholar: Origins, Evolution, and Current Trends in Detective Fiction*, ed. Barbara A. Radar and Howard G. Zettler. New York: Greenwood, 1988.

Rainov, Nikolai Bogomil. *La novela negra*. Havana: Arte y Literatura, 1975.

Rama, Ángel. *La ciudad letrada*. Hanover, N.H.: Ediciones del Norte, 1984.

Ramírez Heredia, Rafael. "La novela policial en México." *La Palabra y el Hombre* 53–54 (1985): 29–31.

Ramírez Pimienta, Juan Carlos. "Paco Ignacio Taibo II: La lógica de la terquedad o la variante mexicana de una locura." *Mester* 21, no. 1 (1992): 41–50.

———. "Antihéroes: México y su novela policiaca." Review. *Revista de Literatura Mexicana Contemporánea* 1, no. 1 (1995): 22–25.

Ramos, Julio. *Desencuentros de la modernidad en América Latina*. Mexico City: Fondo de Cultura Económica, 1989.

———. *Divergent Modernities: Culture and Politics in Nineteenth-Century Latin America*. Translated by John D. Blanco. Durham: Duke University Press, 2001.

Ramos, Samuel. *Profile of Man and Culture in Mexico*. Translated by Peter G. Earle. Austin: University of Texas Press, 1975.

Recio Tenorio, Berta. *Una vez más*. Havana: Letras Cubanas, 1980.

Rehder, Ernest. "Jorge Ibargüengoitia on Conspiracy and Espionage and His Adventures with the CIA." *SECOLAS Annals* 23 (1992): 81–88.

———. *Ibargüengoitia en Excelsior, 1968–1976: una bibliografía anotada con introducción crítica y citas memorables del autor*. New York: Peter Lang, 1993.

Reloba, Juan Carlos. *La única posibilidad*. Havana: Letras Cubanas, 1984.

Revueltas, Eugenia. "La novela policiaca en México y en Cuba." *Cuadernos Americanos* 1, no. 1 (1987): 102–20.

Reyes, Alfonso. "Sobre la novela policial." 1945. *Ensayos*. Edited by Roberto Fernández Retamar. Havana: Casa de las Américas, 1968. 339–44.

———, trans. and prologue. *El hombre que fue jueves*. Buenos Aires: Losada, 1938.

Richter, David H., ed. *The Critical Tradition: Classic Texts and Contemporary Trends*. New York: St. Martin's, 1989.

Rix, Rob, ed. *Leeds Papers on Thrillers in the Transition: "Novela negra" and Political Change in Spain*. Sheffield, England: Trinity and All Saints College, 1992.

Rivera, Jorge, ed. *El relato policial en la Argentina*. Buenos Aires, EUDEBA, 1986.

———, and Jorge Lafforgue. *Asesinos de papel: Ensayos sobre la novela policial*. Buenos Aires: Colihue, 1996.

Roberts, Thomas J. *An Aesthetics of Junk Fiction*. Athens: University of Georgia Press, 1990.

Rodó, José Enrique. *Ariel*. Prol. Antonio Lago Carballo. Madrid: Espasa-Calpe, 1991.

Rodríguez Coronel, Rogelio. *La novela de la revolución cubana*. Havana: Letras Cubanas, 1986.

Rodríguez Manzanera, Luis. *Criminología*. Mexico City: Porrúa, 1979.

Rodríguez Monegal, Emir. *Borges por él mismo*. Caracas: Monte Ávila, 1980.

———. *Jorge Luis Borges: A Literary Biography.* New York: Dutton, 1978.

Rojas Requeña, Iliana, and Jorge Hernández. *Balance crítico de la sociología latino-americana actual.* Havana: Ciencias Sociales, 1987.

Rollin, Roger B. "Against Evaluation: The Role of the Critic of Popular Culture." In *The Study of Popular Fiction: A Source Book,* ed. Bob Ashley. Philadelphia: University of Pennsylvania Press, 1989. 16–22.

Rosal, Juan del. *Crimen y criminal en la novela policiaca.* Madrid: Instituto Editorial Reus, 1947.

Sacerio-Garí, Enrique. "Detectives North and South." *Proceedings of the Xth Congress of the International Comparative Literature Association.* New York, 1982. New York: Garland, 1985.

Salas, Luis. *Social Control and Deviance in Cuba.* New York: Praeger, 1979.

Salessi, Jorge. *Médicos maleantes y maricas: higiene, criminología, y homosexualidad en la construcción de la nación Argentina. (Buenos Aires, 1871–1914).* Rosario [Argentina]: B. Viterbo, 1995.

Sandoval, Alejandro. "Narrativa policial cubana." *Plural: Revista Cultural de Excelsior* 11, no. 128 (May 1982): 57–64.

Sayers, Dorothy, ed. *The Omnibus of Crime.* New York: Payson and Clarke, 1929.

Schenkel, Elmer. "Circling the Cross, Crossing the Circle: On Borges and Chesterton." In *Jorge Luis Borges: Thought and Knowledge in the Twentieth Century,* ed. Alfonso de Toro and Fernando de Toro. Frankfurt: Vervuert-Iberoamericana, 1999. 289–306.

Schwarz, Mauricio-José. *La música de los perros.* Mexico City: Roca, 1996.

———. "La Semana Negra." http://spin.com.mx/~mschwarz/snes.html.

———. Interview. 19 July 1998. Gijón, Spain.

Segura, Gerardo. *Todos somos culpables: entrevistas con escritores policiacos mexicanos.* [Saltillo, Coahuila, Mexico]: Fondo Estatal para la Cultura y las Artes de Coahuila, 1996.

Sherman, Scott. "Democratic Detective." *Boston Review* 21, no. 2 (1996): n.p.

Shumway, Nicolas. *The Invention of Argentina.* Berkeley: University of California Press, 1991.

Simons, Geoff L. *Cuba: From Conquistador to Castro.* New York: St. Martin's, 1996.

Simpson, Amelia S. "From Private to Public Eye: Detective Fiction in Cuba." *Studies in Latin American Popular Culture* 8 (1989): 107–28.

———, ed. *Detective Fiction from Latin America.* Rutherford, N.J.: Fairleigh Dickinson University Press, 1990.

———. *New Tales of Mystery and Crime from Latin America.* Rutherford, N.J.: Fairleigh Dickinson University Press, 1992.

Skinner, Robert E. *Two Guns from Harlem: The Detective Fiction of Chester Himes.* Bowling Green: Bowling Green State University Press, 1989.

Sklodowska, Elzbieta. "Transgresión paródica de la formula policial en la novela hispanoamericana." *Hispánica Posnaniensia* 1 (1990): 171–83.

———. *Testimonio hispanoamericano: historia, teoría, poética.* New York: Peter Lang, 1992.

Smith, Paul Julian. *The Body Hispanic: Gender and Sexuality in Spanish American Literature.* Oxford: Clarendon, 1989.

Smorkaloff, Pamela. Web article "Cuban Literary Culture at a Crossroads." www.soc.9c.edu/cuba/cubanlit.html.

Sommer, Doris. *Foundational Fictions: The National Romances of Latin America.* Berkeley: University of California Press, 1991.

———. "No Secrets." In *The Real Thing: Testimonial Discourse and Latin America,* ed. Georg M. Gugelberger. Durham: Duke University Press, 1996. 134.

———, ed. *The Places of History: Regionalism Revisited in Latin America.* Durham: Duke University Press, 1999.

Sontag, Susan. "Against Interpretation." In *The Critical Tradition: Classic Texts and Contemporary Trends,* ed. David H. Richter. New York: St. Martin's, 1989. 545–50.

———. "One Culture and the New Sensibility." *New York Times* (31 December 1987).

Stavans, Ilán. *Antihéroes: México y su novela policial.* Benito Juárez, D.F.: J. Mortiz, 1993.

———. *Antiheroes.* Translated by Jesse H. Lytle and Jennifer A. Mattson. Rutherford, N. J.: Fairleigh Dickinson University Press, 1997.

———. "An Appointment with Hector Belascoarān Shayne, Mexican Private Eye: A Profile of Paco Ignacio Taibo II." *Review* 42 (1990): 5–9.

Symons, Julian. *Bloody Murder: From the Detective Novel to the Crime Story: A History.* London: Faber and Faber, 1972.

Taibo II, Paco Ignacio. *Adios Madrid.* Mexico City: Promexa, 1993.

———. *Algunas nubes.* 1985. 5th ed. Madrid: Júcar, 1987.

———. *Amorosos fantasmas.* Mexico City: Promexa, 1990.

———. *La bicicleta de Leonardo.* Mexico City: Joaquín Mortiz, 1993.

———. *Calling all Heroes: A Manual for Taking Power.* Preface by Jorge Castañeda. Translated by John Mitchell and Ruth Mitchell de Aguilar. Kaneohe, Hawaii: Plover, 1990.

———. *Cosa fácil.* 1977. 2d ed. Mexico City: Promexa, 1992.

———. *Cuatro manos.* Vitoria: Ikusager, 1994.

———. *Desvanecidos difuntos.* Mexico City: Promexa, 1991.

———. *Días de combate.* Barcelona: Grijalbo, 1976.

———. *An Easy Thing.* Translated by William I. Neuman. New York: Viking, 1990.

———. *No habrá final feliz.* Mexico City: Planeta, 1989.

———. *No Happy Endings.* Translated by William I. Neuman. New York: Mysterious Press, 1993.

———. "No Happy Endings." Interview with Paco Ignacio Taibo II. By John F. Baker. *Boston Review* (February–March 2001).

———. "La 'otra' novela policiaca." *Los Cuadernos del Norte* 8, no. 41 (1987): 36–41.

———. *Primavera pospuesta.* Mexico City: Joaquín Mortiz, 1999.

————. *Regreso a la misma ciudad y bajo la lluvia.* 1989. Trans. *Return to the Same City.* New York: Mysterious Press, 1996.

————. *Sintiendo que en el campo de batalla.* Mexico City: Júcar, 1989.

————. *Sombra de la sombra.* Mexico City: Fascículos Planeta, 1986.

————. *Sueños de frontera.* Mexico City: Promexa, 1990.

————. *La vida misma.* Mexico City: Planeta, 1990.

Todorov, Tzvetan. *The Poetics of Prose.* Ithaca: Cornell University Press, 1977.

Torres, Vicente Francisco. *La otra literatura mexicana.* México: UAM, 1994.

————. "La novela policiaca mexicana." *La Palabra y el Hombre* 53–54 (1985): 37–42.

————, ed. *El cuento policial mexicano.* Mexico City: Diógenes, 1982.

Trujillo Muñoz, Gabriel. *Mezquite Road.* Mexico City: Planeta, 1995.

————. *Testigos de cargo.* México: CONACULTA/CECUT, 2000.

Usigli, Rodolfo. *Ensayo de un crimen.* Mexico City: Océano, 1987.

Valencia Castillo, Francisco. "Cultura popular en México." *Plural: Revista Cultural de Excelsior* 11, no. 128 (May 1982): 69–73.

Valles Calatrava, José R. *La novela criminal española.* Introduction by Manuel Vázquez Montalbán. Granada: University of Granada Press, 1991.

Vasco Colás, Justo. "El reflejo de lo socialmente negativo en la literatura policial. Su valor educativo." Unpublished paper presented at Cuban Detective Writers' Roundtable, 28 December 1983.

————. *El Muro.* 1986. Havana: Letras Cubanas/Radar, 1990.

————. *Mirando espero.* Barcelona: Tempore, 1998.

————. Interview. 18 July 1998. Gijón, Spain.

Vázquez Montalbán, Manuel. Introduction to *La novela criminal española,* by José R. Valles Calatrava. Granada: University of Granada Press, 1991.

————, pról. *La novela policiaca española,* by José F. Colmeiro. Barcelona: Anthropos, 1994.

————. "Contra la novela policiaca." *Ínsula* 512–13 (1989): 9.

Vázquez de Parga, Salvador. *La novela policiaca en España.* Barcelona: Ronsel, 1993.

Vega, Jesús. "Cuando se habla de máscaras." *Éxito* (4 June 1997): 54–55.

Veloso, Antonio, and Rodolfo Pérez Valero. *Crimen en noche de máscaras.* Havana: Letras Cubanas, 1986.

Waugh, Hillary. "The Mystery Versus the Novel." In *The Mystery Story,* ed. John Ball. San Diego: University of California Press, 1976. 61–82.

Wilkinson, Stephen. "The Cuban Detective Novel." Presented for an MA in Hispanic studies, Birbeck College, London, 1993.

Wilson, Edmund. "Who Cares Who Killed Roger Ackroyd?" In *Detective Fiction: A Collection of Critial Essays,* ed. Robin Winks. Englewood Cliffs: Prentice-Hall, 1980. 35–40.

————. "The Historical Interpretation of Literature." In *The Critical Tradition: Classic Texts and Contemporary Trends,* ed. David H. Richter. New York: St. Martin's, 1989. 588–96.

Winks, Robin W., ed. *Detective Fiction: A Collection of Critical Essays.* Englewood Cliffs: Prentice-Hall, 1980.

Woeller, Waltraud, and Bruce Cassiday. *The Literature of Crime and Detection: An Illustrated History from Antiquity to the Present.* Translated by Ruth Michaelis-Jena and Willy Merson. New York: Ungar, 1988.

Yates, Donald. *Latin Blood: The Best Crime and Detective Stories of South America.* New York: Herder and Herder, 1972.

Yndurain, Francisco. "Sociología y literatura." *De lector a lector.* Madrid: Estudios Escelicer, 1973.

Young, Allen. *Gays under the Cuban Revolution.* San Francisco: Grey Fox, 1981.

Znepolski, Ivailo. "Sociología de la novela detectivesca clásica." In Nogueras, *Novela policial 2,* 245–97.

Index

Persephone Braham is assistant professor of Spanish at the University of Delaware.